THE BALLOT
AND THE BIBLE

"What a gift Kaitlyn Schiess is to the church. Somehow, Kaitlyn serves up rigorous academic research with illuminating insight and theologically rich wisdom, all perfectly peppered with wit. And in these pages, she is operating at the height of her powers. *The Ballot and the Bible* is brilliant and fascinating and about so much more than politics. This book should be required reading for hermeneutics classes, as well as anyone who teaches the Bible."

—Sharon Hodde Miller, author of *The Cost of Control: Why We Crave It, the Anxiety It Gives Us, and the Real Power God Promises*

"It's not often that a book both challenges your fundamental beliefs and elevates them at the same time. *The Ballot and the Bible* is such a book. Schiess addresses foundational questions about the nature of our political life together and establishes the urgency of reevaluating our civic norms. This is a book about faith, politics, and the Bible that our churches and our democracy need."

—Jemar Tisby, *New York Times* bestselling author of *The Color of Compromise* and *How to Fight Racism*; professor, Simmons College of Kentucky

"This clever, judicious, and remarkably persuasive book challenges us to rethink how we apply Scripture to politics. It reminds us that while a 'plain and literal' interpretation of the Bible is not actually possible, a humble and faithful interpretation is. I'm so grateful for the wisdom Kaitlyn Schiess brings to this conversation. I pray that we listen to her."

—Beth Allison Barr, bestselling author of *The Making of Biblical Womanhood: How the Subjugation of Women Became Gospel Truth*; professor, Baylor University

"A wonderfully illuminating history of how Americans have reached for the Bible—for better or worse—to shape our shared political life. From John Winthrop's 'city on a hill' to Eisenhower's Cold War Christianity to the peculiar marriage of evangelicals and Donald Trump, Schiess takes us on a journey that allows any Christian to see how the Bible can shape our political engagement, or, if we aren't careful, our politics can shape our Bible. Highly recommended!"

—Phil Vischer, VeggieTales creator; cohost of the *Holy Post* podcast

"We are formed in community, and, as Kaitlyn Schiess shows in her remarkably deft historical account and analysis, that community shapes not only how we view politics but also how we read and apply the Bible to our politics. Whether you lean left or lean right, whether you come from a red state, blue state, or a purple one, if you are a Christian who seeks to apply biblical principles to your political thinking, you will find something instructive, challenging, and enlightening in this book."

—**Karen Swallow Prior**, author of *The Evangelical Imagination: How Stories, Images, and Metaphors Created a Culture in Crisis*

"*The Ballot and the Bible* offers keen, level-headed, and perceptive insights into the use of Scripture in our political life that will empower readers without leaving them either complacently cynical or myopically gullible. Spend time with Kaitlyn Schiess by reading this book, and you'll gain confidence in your own ability to navigate political issues. Kaitlyn's combination of pastoral care with real pastoral wisdom is rarer than it ought to be, and it's part of what makes me confident in Kaitlyn's leadership, and our need for it, for years to come. *The Ballot and the Bible* is a wonderful contribution, and I highly recommend it."

—**Michael Wear**, president and CEO, Center for Christianity and Public Life; author of *The Spirit of Our Politics*

"History does not repeat itself, but it does rhyme. That maxim is certainly on display in Schiess's compelling book about the use—and misuse—of the Bible in the political arena throughout US history. With accessible scholarship and wisdom, she reveals how the use of Scripture in today's polarized political environment echoes its use in previous eras. But Schiess is also careful to highlight and honor the unique contours of each generation's engagement with the Bible. This book is a must-read for every Christian who cares about the role of faith in the public square."

—**Skye Jethani**, author of *What If Jesus Was Serious?*; cohost of the *Holy Post* podcast

THE BALLOT
AND THE BIBLE

HOW SCRIPTURE HAS BEEN USED AND
ABUSED IN AMERICAN POLITICS
AND WHERE WE GO FROM HERE

KAITLYN SCHIESS

BrazosPress
a division of Baker Publishing Group
Grand Rapids, Michigan

© 2023 by Kaitlyn Schiess

Published by Brazos Press
a division of Baker Publishing Group
Grand Rapids, Michigan
www.brazospress.com

Printed in the United States of America

Library of Congress Cataloging-in-Publication Control Number: 2023008746
ISBN: 978-1-58743-596-6 (paper)

The author is represented by the literary agency of The Gates Group, www.the-gates-group.com.

Baker Publishing Group publications use paper produced from sustainable forestry practices and post-consumer waste whenever possible.

23   24   25   26   27   28   29   7   6   5   4   3   2   1

To the people who picked me up and put me
back together when people I trusted abused the Bible:

Kelsey and Joshua Hankins

Barry Jones

Sandra Glahn

Cindy Rawles

Momma and Daddy

CONTENTS

Introduction

Is That Your Bible?

In June 2020, during nationwide protests over the killing of George Floyd, President Donald Trump posed with a Bible outside St. John's Episcopal Church in Washington, DC. Police used riot-control tactics to clear protesters from Lafayette Square to prepare for the photo op. Trump bounced the Bible in his hands for a few moments before holding it up for reporters to photograph. When asked, "Is that your Bible?" President Trump responded, "It's *a* Bible."

For many Americans, the scene epitomized the relationship between Scripture and politics: the Bible is a prop, a tool for leaders to exploit for their purposes. For many American Christians, that question Trump received is important. We consider ourselves "Bible people," and we put great stock in *personal* faith. Owning and reading our *own* Bibles, spending daily "quiet time" reading them, taking them to church so that we can read along on our own—much of American Protestantism is shaped by Bible ownership.

But it's also an important question for American Christians in another sense. We live in a Bible-haunted nation. Our history is full of politicians invoking biblical images. Much of our shared language comes from the Old and New Testaments. Our national story has been shaped by biblical accounts of wandering, exile, and redemption. So, for American Christians living in a nation deeply shaped by the Bible, it might be worth asking the same question the reporter asked Trump: Is that *your* Bible? Do you feel as if your team has scored some points when national leaders quote it? Do you feel responsible to correct when it is misused? Does it more strongly shape your politics than how loosely and conveniently it seems to shape national politics?

While I was writing this book, the US Supreme Court overturned the 1973 *Roe v. Wade* decision that federally protected abortion access. In the final weeks of writing this book, President Biden announced a plan to forgive federal student loan debt, restructure repayment plans, and allow people paying their reduced minimum monthly payment to not accrue interest. In both of these important moments, Scripture played a crucial role.

The abortion debate batted Psalm 139 and Numbers 5 back and forth. The student loan debate pitted the Old Testament law's description of Jubilee against proverbs such as the beginning of Psalm 37:21: "The wicked borrow and do not repay." While much could be said about the interpretation and applicability of these verses, something more foundational is going on. People on both the right and the left constantly claimed that the other side was hypocritical for caring about what the Bible taught in one case but ignoring it in another. This raises an important question at the heart of this book: *How* should Scripture inform our political beliefs?

For all our familiarity with the Bible, we are woefully ignorant about *how* or *why* we are using the Bible in politics. How can we apply passages written thousands of years ago to political issues today? How can we dialogue with people who interpret passages differently than we do? How can we respond to social-media posts with cherry-picked verses?

To be clear, this book will not give you a list of interpretation methods or rules, nor will it give the definitive interpretations of the passages that are typically referenced in political conversations.

Instead, it poses the question "Is that your Bible?" to the complicated and contentious history of American politics. It notes moments of proper application and examples of deep misuse. It describes examples of biblical argumentation from pastors, politicians, pundits, and ordinary people.

There are many interesting examples in American history that this book does not cover: we could spend entire chapters on the perennial fights about the faith of the Founding Fathers, the biblical passages about war and peace cited during the Vietnam War, or Jimmy Carter's religious background. This book focuses less on how the Bible has influenced specific policies, though we'll have plenty of reason to note that occasionally. The real goal is to examine how the Bible has shaped more general, foundational political theology questions: What is government? What is the relationship between theology and politics? How should Christians think about their political participation? These questions typically get lost in our conversations. We jump into the juicy fight of the moment, whip out our favorite Bible verses, and completely forget to ask if we even agree on the nature of human government or the relationship between the church and earthly governments.

In focusing on American history, this book has two goals: (1) to mine history for examples of biblical interpretation distanced enough from our own context that we might be able to see things clouding our judgment in the heat of our own debates, and (2) to gain a rough sketch of some of the political biblical-interpretation trends and traditions that have shaped America.

All of us have inherited theological traditions, reading habits, and political biases that shape how we read Scripture. Many of us are more shaped by our political hermeneutics than our theological traditions. These reading habits cross denominations and party affiliations, making up the wider hermeneutical context of American political thought.

If we want to understand Scripture better and apply it more faithfully—as well as to converse with compassion and conviction on topics where we are in disagreement with others—we will need to know our Bible *and* our history. We will need to examine not only our stated principles of biblical interpretation but also the habits of our hearts. We will need to see passages of Scripture in new light, look at them through old conflicts, and ask fresh questions about our politics and our faith.

This book is motivated by the conviction that, for Christians, the answer to the question "Is that your Bible?" is an emphatic *yes*. The Bible is not a free-floating book of ageless wisdom, an interesting historical document, or a weapon that can be put in the service of any political goal. The Bible is a gift from God to the church, given for a particular purpose: to shape that community into the kind of people who can fulfill their commission to make disciples of all nations and steward God's good creation, anticipating its final redemption.[1]

As such, the Bible should be read as the book of the church, in the church. Our reading of Scripture should be informed both by the global historic church (receiving the theology handed down to us, learning from Christians throughout history and around the world) and by the church in a particular time and place. We will be more faithful readers and doers of the Word of God if we learn how the church has received and read the Bible in the time and place nearest us. What habits—good and bad—are we prone to? What insights are unique gifts of our time and place, and what are our unique mistakes?

Learning our own history will not magically solve our problems. We will remain often confounded about how—or if—the Bible addresses the pressing political questions of our day. But my hope is that these chapters will give us examples to wrestle with and a history to reflect on. Most of all, I hope these chapters deepen our desire to be shaped by Scripture—to allow the language, images, and grand story of this marvelous book to impact every area of our lives, including the few but important moments we spend in a voting booth.

A City on a Hill

An American Legacy of Puritan Biblical Interpretation

For we must consider that we shall be as a city upon a hill. The eyes of all people are upon us.

—John Winthrop, "A Model of Christian Charity," 1630

A city on a hill. These words have captivated Americans for generations. They encapsulate our sense of collective destiny, divine mission, and moral strength. They pack into one little phrase a larger tale about a band of religiously persecuted patriots who crossed a dangerous ocean, discovered a new land, and built the United States of America.

These words have come to have such deep political significance for Americans that we might forget they come from Jesus's Sermon on the Mount:

You are the light of the world. A town built on a hill cannot be hidden. Neither do people light a lamp and put it under a bowl.

Instead they put it on its stand, and it gives light to everyone in the house. In the same way, let your light shine before others, that they may see your good deeds and glorify your Father in heaven. (Matt. 5:14–16)

John Winthrop, the governor of the Massachusetts Bay Colony, reached for these words (among many others) in his 1630 message "A Model of Christian Charity." History textbooks often style Winthrop as the "puritan Moses,"[1] delivering a speech at the dawn of America's founding that would shape the ethos of the following centuries.

The history is more complicated than that: Winthrop's speech was not a missive on American exceptionalism, and it did not become influential in American identity until the late twentieth century. Even more complicated are the questions of whether Winthrop's use of Matthew 5 exemplified good hermeneutics, whether the resulting history resembles anything like faithful biblical interpretation, and how Christians should approach applying biblical commands and promises to our political communities. What is the city on a hill? *Who* is it? And do Jesus's words mean anything for our political life together?

How the "City" Became Co-opted

Winthrop's speech has been called the "most famous lay sermon in American history" even though it probably wasn't a sermon.[2] It has been cited as the source of America's supposed strengths *and* ills even though it went practically unnoticed by American politicians and historians for over three hundred years. It has been called the "book of Genesis in America's political Bible" even though its original author was neither American nor could have imagined the founding of the country over a hundred years later.[3]

It is not clear exactly when Winthrop wrote "A Model of Christian Charity" or where (or even if) he delivered it, though the common story is that he gave it aboard the ship *Arbella* as it journeyed across the Atlantic.[4] The bulk of the text covers Winthrop's understanding of Christian charity. God has ordained a hierarchal social order, Winthrop says, in which the rich should not abuse their wealth but provide for the poor, and the poor should not rebel against their station but receive God's gifts through the rich.[5]

Winthrop goes on to describe Christian obligations of charity in surprisingly radical ways. Everyone should care for the poor, lend generously to siblings in Christ, and forgive freely if their debtors cannot pay back their loans. Winthrop describes the love that must bind together the fellow Christians journeying into a new colony: "We must bear one another's burdens. We must not look only on our own things, but also on the things of our brethren." He quotes Isaiah 58:6–7 when describing giving to the poor: "Is not this the fast I have chosen, . . . to let the oppressed go free and to break every yoke, to deal thy bread to the hungry and to bring the poor that wander into thy house . . . ?"[6] Winthrop's words express something all Christians can support: a desire for our communities to be ordered by God's vision for his creatures' flourishing.[7]

Winthrop's words are also full of much more apprehension than later storytelling would lead us to believe. While he does use strong language to describe the commission of this group of Christians, the biblical references to Israel's covenant with God and Jesus's famous sermon are used to inspire caution and reverence more than self-importance. The people are asking God for "favor and blessing," but they also know that if they disobey his commands, "the Lord will surely break out in wrath against us."[8] It is not exactly surprising that later politicians would favor the more triumphant-sounding language.

It is easy to understand why someone might read "A Model of Christian Charity," or even just the phrase "a city upon a hill," and hear undertones of a familiar story about a nation blessed by God. The speech makes perfect sense as the potent beginning to a narrative many Americans today know well. But Winthrop's words went largely unnoticed for hundreds of years, in part because using the biblical language of the covenant to describe the colonies was commonplace at the time.[9] Even historians who did reference "A Model of Christian Charity" focused more on the charity part than on a city on a hill.[10] The history of our associations of a city on a hill with American exceptionalism and the Christian founding of our country begins not in 1630 but in 1961.

By the time John F. Kennedy spoke to the Massachusetts State Legislature a few weeks before his inauguration, the Puritans had increasingly become a part of the story that America told of its founding.[11] They were exemplars of the American dream, the root of America's Christian past, and, for the president-elect from Massachusetts, an important connection to trailblazing forebears. "For we are setting out upon a voyage in 1961 no less hazardous than that undertaken by the *Arabella* in 1630," Kennedy said, using a characteristic mispronunciation of the ship's name.[12] The world was watching, the task was daunting, and the language of "a city upon a hill" was ripe for appropriating.

Ronald Reagan would transform the little phrase into "one of the most familiar lines in the liturgy of the American civil religion."[13] He referenced the phrase in various speeches throughout his career, but he gave the most detailed explanation of his city on a hill in his 1989 farewell speech:

> I've spoken of the shining city all my political life, but I don't know if I ever quite communicated what I saw when I said it. But in my mind, it was a tall proud city built on rocks stronger than oceans, wind swept, God blessed, and teeming with people of all kinds living in harmony and peace—a city with free ports that hummed with commerce and creativity, and if there had to be city walls, the walls had doors, and the doors were open to anyone with the will and the heart to get here.[14]

For Reagan, the city on a hill powerfully revved up American pride. He used it to describe a standard of moral goodness, commercial power, or military strength from which America was close to falling. He used it to imbue any political message with the urgency and significance of divine mandate.[15]

Historian Richard Gamble says Reagan "invented" the "city on a hill" as Americans know it today. What was once primarily a metaphor that Jesus used to describe the identity of his followers was now a political slogan.[16] With the backing of a conservative political lobby, Newt Gingrich released a film in 2011 called *A City on a Hill: The Spirit of American Exceptionalism*. Glenn Beck made a short film about "A Model of Christian Charity" in 2014.[17] During the 2016 election, Hillary Clinton included in her list of affirmations of America: "We're still Reagan's shining city on a hill."[18] Now the shining city was not Jesus's but Reagan's.

What began as a religious call for right living in 1630 became a defense of American exceptionalism in the Cold War era. It became a signature of Reagan's presidency, and afterward "virtually no serious political figure could escape the obligation to quote it."[19] Wrapped up in this one little phrase is a host of moral, political, and religious ideas of great importance to many Americans. Yet the history of the phrase is not the history of a biblical truth piloting the grand trajectory of a nation. Rather, it's the history of how America seized a metaphor and shaped it into a story to tell about ourselves.

It's a story both common and complicated, a story of taking biblical language and employing it in service of unfamiliar goals. As such, it's an important starting place for us to begin thinking about how to faithfully interpret Scripture politically.

The "city upon a hill" image exemplifies a common problem: we pluck promises of provision or judgment that were given to Israel or the church and apply them wholesale to America. We misapply promises because we misunderstand *who* is being addressed. We are often narcissistic and nationalistic readers, seeing our own nation as the subject of every promise or command. This problem might be the besetting sin of American political theology.

And yet we all recognize that Scripture has much to say not only about how Israel was to organize itself as a community or how the church should build a life together but about a host of other issues relevant to our political lives. It tells us about what kind of creatures humans are, what it looks like for us to live together in peace, what appropriate authority looks like, and how to structure a flourishing community. But before we rush into pulling passages from Scripture and applying them to our own political context, we need to have a hermeneutic that can prevent us from misapplication and misunderstanding. The Sermon on the Mount *should* inform our political theology, just maybe not in the way it has in the past.

Israel, the Church, and America

Just after delivering the Beatitudes—blessed are the poor in spirit, the meek, the peacemakers—Jesus launches into his famous metaphors of salt, light, and a city on a hill. We're so familiar with these words that we might not even pause to ask who Jesus is addressing. Who is the "you" that Jesus calls "the salt of the earth" (Matt. 5:13) and "the light of the world" (5:14) and compares to "a town built on a hill" (5:14)?

One thing we know for sure is that the "you" is plural. English does not have a distinct second-person plural pronoun like many other languages, so when we say "you," it's not clear apart from context if we're addressing one person or many. But in Greek it is clear. Jesus basically says, "Y'all are the salt of the earth" and "Y'all are the light of the world."[20] Jesus is addressing a group, but what group? The crowd listening to the sermon, the Jewish people, the not-yet-existing institutional church? There is a long history of interpretation here that follows larger disagreements about how to define and understand the church, but Jesus is clearly *not* describing an earthly political arrangement.

Of course, America isn't the first nation to use cosmic language to understand its significance. A century before Jesus's sermon, Cicero used the image of a city as a light to the world to describe Rome. Jesus takes this image and uses it to describe the good deeds of people that prompt praise to God (Matt. 5:16) rather than promoting military or economic strength.[21]

Jesus draws on language and images Scripture uses to describe the *people of God* in his sermon. The Old Testament uses light imagery to describe God (Gen. 1:3; Isa. 60:1–3) and speaks of the identity, orientation, and mission of the people of God as a light to the world, a blessing to the nations (Gen. 12:2; 22:18; Isa. 2:2–5; 42:6; 49:6).[22] God has always been concerned with the whole world, and even his particular blessings have a universal purpose.

10

If you go back and read the whole sermon, you'll see that this one little phrase is part of a larger point: God's people are blessed for *the sake of the world.* We are oriented not merely inward toward each other but also always outward toward the world. Our witness and our work are public, not hidden or private or separate.

A theologian in the early church, John Chrysostom, interprets the passage this way: "Jesus says in effect: 'You are not accountable only for your life but also for that of the entire world.'"[23] It is especially ironic that the phrase "city on a hill" has been twisted into elevating America above other nations when it was first used in a sermon urging God's people to live for the sake of the larger world. "America First" and "city on a hill" contradict each other.

Biblical scholars have also seen in Jesus's language a reference to Jerusalem on Mount Zion—not only drawing his listeners back to the identity and mission of the Jewish people but reminding them of their ultimate hope. Isaiah 2 is one place this image is beautifully painted for God's people:

In the last days

> the mountain of the LORD's temple will be established
> > as the highest of the mountains;
> it will be exalted above the hills,
> > and all nations will stream to it.

Many peoples will come and say,

> "Come, let us go up to the mountain of the LORD,
> > to the temple of the God of Jacob.
> He will teach us his ways,
> > so that we may walk in his paths."
> The law will go out from Zion,
> > the word of the LORD from Jerusalem.
> He will judge between the nations
> > and will settle disputes for many peoples.
> They will beat their swords into plowshares
> > and their spears into pruning hooks.
> Nation will not take up sword against nation,
> > nor will they train for war anymore. (vv. 2–4)

Jesus is using language familiar to his audience to connect the mission, identity, and hope of the people of God throughout all time.[24] God has always instructed his people to be oriented toward the world, and we have always awaited a city on a hill where the people of all nations will live in peace together by the power of our redeeming God.

Scripture is full of references to mountains and hills. There is a reason that the gospel writers take the time to say that Jesus was giving this sermon on a *mountainside* and why we continue to refer to this sermon as the Sermon on the Mount. In Israelite tradition, mountains were places of divine revelation. It is noteworthy that Jesus does not *receive* revelation on the mountain but *gives* it. This helps us know how to interpret his city on a hill. Jesus is describing a people who proclaim God's revelation to the world, who act as conduits of God's light in their own communities. Jesus is proclaiming a new era, a new people, a new program. Biblical scholar Jonathan Pennington calls the Sermon on the Mount the "founding document" for a vision of flourishing for the new community of the church.[25]

Covenants and Political Theology

When Winthrop uses this passage in "A Model of Christian Charity," he appropriates the language Jesus used to describe the new covenant. He never explicitly claims "chosen" status for his people, but over the course of the short speech, he claims the promises of biblical passages as if that were true. As he weaves passages from both Testaments into one depiction of the nascent community in America, he sometimes subtly alters references to the Mosaic law into commands for the church. Winthrop describes the colonists as entering a covenant with God, gaining a special commission, and being subject to blessing and judgment on the basis of their obedience.

Winthrop's approach is in keeping with a larger theological position common at the time, an approach that treated all earthly governments (especially one's own) as party to a covenant with

God. America was far from alone in this; during the period of the Revolution, many European communities were also looking to the Old Testament as they created new political structures.[26] The Puritans were following precedent from their previous communities in viewing all of society—their churches and civil governments—as covenanted with God.

In a universally Christian society, this idea makes a lot of sense. Government and church leaders alike are following God, and people in Scripture are often judged for communal sins, so it makes sense to think of one's community as facing consequences—good or bad—together. Puritan theologians extrapolated from the covenants described in Scripture the idea that all nations lived under an "implied covenant" with God. Nations could expect to be rewarded or punished on the basis of their adherence to Christian principles.[27]

This idea gave theological meaning to disasters, diseases, and wars, as well as to blessings such as harvests and military victories.[28] This is also why people like Winthrop conceived of church and political government as singular: the moral strength of the whole determined the blessings or curses. Rightly, this approach roots governmental authority in God's judgment rather than abstract political theories, and it describes both church and government leaders as subject to divine accountability. Winthrop was far from alone in thinking this way, and it's unlikely he thought of his own community as *uniquely* covenanted with God—the way later generations of Americans would. He thought of the Massachusetts Bay Colony as *a* city on a hill, not *the* city on a hill.[29]

This legacy—of using the language of biblical covenants to describe our nations—is a robust one in American history. You've probably heard or seen 2 Chronicles 7:14 referenced during election seasons: "If my people, who are called by my name, will humble themselves and pray and seek my face and turn from their wicked ways, then I will hear from heaven, and I will forgive their sin and will heal their land."

This instruction refers God's people back to the Abrahamic covenant. The promises—especially to heal their *land*—are rooted in a specific covenant that can't be applied to any and all nations. Yet we read our own nation back into the text and tend to replace the rewards of these promises with our own national ambitions. We don't need to add words to the verse to distort it; all it takes is visually associating this verse with American flags, military symbols, and other symbols of wealth, health, or strength. We misunderstand who "my people" is, and we imbue the words "heal their land" with our own understandings of healing. All people should be exhorted to humble themselves, pray, seek the face of God, and turn from wicked ways. But no earthly government is promised healing. We're awaiting a new city, with new bounds of citizenship.

When we come to biblical texts looking for political instruction, we are never coming as blank slates. We bring our cultural and political contexts, our theological systems, and our own questions, needs, and desires. This is not necessarily a bad thing, but it can be dangerous if left unexamined. Winthrop and Reagan brought their political theologies to the text, and we will bring our own. Thinking about how we can read Scripture faithfully in the political sphere is never just about a list of principles or universal rules. It is about allowing Scripture to shape our theology and, in turn, allowing good theology to shape our interpretation and application.

There are some unique challenges when it comes to thinking about covenants in political theology. We need to be careful about how we read God's covenants in relation to our own time and God's providence, where we place ourselves in God's story, and how we apply God's Word in our different contexts.

What Time Is It?

The Puritans didn't emphasize the nation's virtuous strength (as in Reagan's "shining city") but rather its coming judgment. It's an emphasis that has waxed and waned in American political rhetoric, and we owe some of that to the Puritans.

It did not take long for Puritans in the Massachusetts Bay Colony (and for other colonists in their own contexts) to bemoan the moral state of their communities. By the time Winthrop died in 1649, his community looked little like his grand vision of brotherly love, care for the poor, and faithful worship.

Across New England, Puritans disagreed about a range of issues, and their communities had lost much of their religious zeal.[30] The Puritans had conceived of a society where the church and civic community were synonymous, but twenty years later, more than half of the adults in Boston did not belong to a church.[31] This led to a rise in a form of preaching called the jeremiad, a sermon in the style of biblical laments and prophecies that would exercise great influence over American religion and politics.[32] The Puritans were already familiar with this sermonic form: many of them left England for fear of the judgments coming to the morally declining church.[33] Jeremiads describe moral decline, warn of coming judgment, and exhort listeners to urgent action.[34]

Winthrop's speech is not quite a jeremiad, but it illustrates the theological context that made jeremiads so popular. If the community was party to a special covenant with God, then the members could expect their obedience to be rewarded and their disobedience punished in ways similar to those found in biblical accounts. Winthrop (and generations of politicians and pastors after him) appropriates the terms of Old Testament covenants, warning listeners that material blessings or judgments will follow their actions. These accounts also often favor decline narratives (assurances of blessings do not pack the same punch), placing a community in a certain spot in history and narrating the past and the future with astonishing certainty.

There are two problems here. First, we tend to take promises of blessing and judgment from different covenants and apply them to our own communities. And second, we read Scripture as if we know with certainty where we stand in it. While we may know better than to take promises given to Israel and apply them to a specific nation today, our reading of Scripture often comes with an assumption about what "time" it is.

We operate out of either a decline or progress narrative in which history's trajectory is intelligible to us. To say that things are always moving in one direction (constantly improving or continually degenerating) is to say that history follows a certain course that we can accurately chart. We make political judgments as if we are standing high above history, knowing what has come before and what will come after us, and can judge the "direction" we are headed in. Christians can sometimes have theological reasons—for example, our beliefs about the end times—for holding to progression or declension narratives. But we are also often swayed by the general mood of our culture or context. When are the "good times"—in our wistfully remembered past or just around the bend of our next great improvement? Where do we find ourselves in the grand scheme of time? These questions will shape how we read Scripture, where we see ourselves in stories or instructions, and when and how we think certain verses are applicable.

The Missing Noachian Covenant

There's another pitfall when we misapply biblical covenants to our own nations: we miss the covenant for *all* nations that is actually in the Bible. We tend to think of Noah as a children's story about a cute little ark with its cute little animals and a cheery rainbow at the end. We miss the crucially important covenant described in that (much darker than advertised) story. In Genesis 9, after Noah and his family come out of the ark, God establishes a covenant with Noah, his family, and all living creatures. This covenant is important for thinking about what God demands of modern nations, because unlike the Mosaic covenant that Puritan writers referenced or the new covenant Jesus described, this covenant was made with *all* people. "I now establish my covenant with you and with your descendants after you and with every living creature that was with you—the birds, the livestock and all the wild animals, all those that came out of the ark with you—every living creature on earth" (Gen. 9:9–10).

God made a covenant with every living creature, and the rest of the Old Testament shows how nations are judged on the basis of that covenant. God was grieved with the ways of the world before the flood: the endless ways people can mistreat each other are well documented in just the first few chapters of Genesis. After the flood he makes clear both the obligation for all humans to treat each other well and the reason for this (they are made in his image).

There is a long tradition of Israel's prophets condemning the nations for their mistreatment of humans made in the image of God. These noncovenantal nations are not judged for disobeying the stipulations of the Mosaic covenant; rather, they are judged for the way they treat other humans. They are condemned for violence (Joel 3:2–3, 5–6; Amos 1:11–12; 2:1–3; Hab. 2:12–13; Jer. 49:16; 51:35, 49; Ezek. 25:15), oppressing the poor (Mal. 3:4; Isa. 10:20; 19:20), gloating in others' destruction (Ezek. 25:3), taking advantage of others (Ezek. 26:2), and slavery (Ezek. 29:7). This does not give us a comprehensive list of the policies any nation should adopt, but it does give us some general guidance about how God judges all nations.[35] The United States of America as a nation is not party to a special covenant, but it is party to the Noachian covenant, and it will be judged, like all nations, by those standards.

We miss this covenant when we appropriate covenants with Israel for our own countries—to our own peril. The demands of the Noachian covenant provide a foundational political ethic for Christians, whether political leaders or citizens participating in the larger political process. The image of God is not a doctrinal obscurity, something we read in Genesis and affirm as theologically correct with no other effects in our personal and political lives. Our appropriate discomfort with applying promises to Israel to our own nation does not leave us without biblical resources for political work. The Noachian covenant and the prophecies against the nations should shape the demands we as citizens make on our governments.

In addition, in Scripture, covenants are initiated by God: God begins the conversation, sets the terms, and graciously invites humans into special relationship with him (for some examples, see Gen. 12; 15; 17; Exod. 19–24; 2 Sam. 7; Jer. 31). By contrast, in Winthrop's "A Model of Christian Charity," *the humans* decide that they are in a covenant with God. This is akin to reverse engineering the covenant process, putting humans in God's role.[36]

Winthrop describes the collective action and posture of his people in just that way. They approach God ("We have hereupon besought him"), determine the terms of the covenant ("draw our own articles"), and describe how they will know if they have kept it. He even writes as if God has responded: "then hath he ratified this covenant." Winthrop ends the document with a quotation from Deuteronomy: "For I command you today to love the LORD your God, to walk in obedience to him, and to keep his commands, decrees and laws; then you will live and increase, and the LORD your God will bless you in the land you are entering to possess" (30:16).[37] Now the land that the colony is crossing an ocean to "possess" is a divine gift.

When *we* set the terms of our own covenants, we will claim promises that are not ours to claim, such as a divine right to a land God never gave.

Applying Biblical Standards Faithfully

It is easy, with hindsight, to see the problems in misapplying biblical promises. But we also know that making faithful political decisions in our world requires us to turn to Scripture, and we don't want to ignore huge chunks of it because it was delivered to the people of Israel or directed specifically to the church. No one really does this either: we are all in the business of picking and choosing which passages apply to our own contexts. Some Christians will find passages about Israel's sexual misconduct and subsequent judgment and apply them to their own nation; others will apply passages about caring for the poor and foreigners to their own nation's immigration or welfare policies. We are not without resources for judging between these different applications, but we need to be honest about whether we are picking and choosing— and, if we are, *why* we are doing so.

Winthrop wanted to apply biblical standards to his earthly community, and most Christians want to do the same. While there are examples of these Puritan communities that highlight the *danger* of this (making church membership a requirement for civil participation, excommunicating people from the church *and* the city), we can also see commendable examples. When merchant Robert Keayne took advantage of the scarcity of imported goods in the fledgling community, Boston courts fined him for price gouging—for not making "others' conditions our own" as Winthrop had described.[38] That sounds like Christian theology informing policy in a positive way. Winthrop was right to think that Christian commitments should inform how we approach the shape, purpose, and rules of civil government.

He was also right to think that ideas, stories, and concepts from God's dealings with Israel have relevance for us today. Christians see the Old Testament as prefiguring events in the New, and we agree with Winthrop that God's revelation informs our understanding of human nature, the purpose and structure of human communities, and the character and work of God in human history.

We want to share at least one thing with Winthrop—"thinking in biblical time."[39] We want to be so immersed in Scripture's language and story that it flows out of us in all we say and do.[40] We want to identify with the people of God described throughout all of Scripture, believe that God's Word is living and active, and expect ancient stories to speak to our lives today. But we also want to avoid plucking passages out of their context and avoid overconfidently applying them to specific political projects. Richard Bauckham says that our reading of Scripture for politics needs to be "both more disciplined and more imaginative" than current attempts.[41] This will require knowing our Bible and ourselves better, and it will require reliance on the Holy Spirit as much as reliance on Bible-study tools.

In his influential work of political theology *Desire of the Nations*, Oliver O'Donovan describes the "unique covenant" between God and Israel as "a point of disclosure from which the nature of all political authority comes into view."[42] He treads the line well between an overidentification of Israel's covenantal status with any other earthly nation and a strictly literal approach that allows us to appreciate the Old Testament only from afar. O'Donovan describes earthly political work as providing us with "partial indications of what God is doing in human history," while that political work must also be placed in the context of God's wider redemptive purpose.[43]

We need to be wary of pulling passages out of their context. But we also need to be wary of any approach to Scripture that does not place both the text and our own work in the larger context of God's redemptive story. We can find prophetic passages, stories of the rise and fall of rulers, and divine instructions in Scripture that *are* relevant and instructive for our time, but that does not mean that all biblical language is free-floating, ready to be affixed to any project or idea. First and foremost, the biblical text's rightful place is within the "economy of God's communicative grace."[44]

A Nation and a Sermon

Many Americans celebrate the fact that our nation's political history is full of biblical references, images, and allusions. In some ways, it is. We want ourselves saturated in Scripture, breathing in and out its life-giving message. But one of the problems with using biblical language in politics is the way that words and phrases can be plucked from their context, stripped of their content, and refilled with alternate meanings. Many Americans will think of Lincoln before Jesus when they hear the phrase "a house divided," or remember President Bush's speeches after 9/11 before they think of the beginning of John's Gospel when they hear "the light shines in the darkness and the darkness will not overcome it."

This is the power and peril of biblical language, and Jesus's words to his people that they would be like a city on a hill are an excellent example. The complicated history of this little phrase reminds us to interrogate the overly familiar language coursing through our political system. Richard Gamble said that the metaphor "vanishes into America's political rhetoric the way a repeated pattern disappears into busy wallpaper."[45] We need to have eyes to see those repeated patterns and hearts intent on seeking after God's truth above all else.

Submission and Revolution

Romans 13 and American Identity

Romans 13:1–7 is the quintessential political passage. "Let everyone be subject to the governing authorities, for there is no authority except that which God has established," it begins. It connects earthly rule with divine rule (v. 2), warns against rebelling against authority (vv. 2–3), describes rulers as bearing "the sword" as "God's servants" (v. 4), and exhorts Christians to pay taxes and respect rulers (vv. 6–7). You don't even need to exegete the passage or describe its details to use it in a political argument. In America, "Romans 13" is shorthand for "The Bible commands obedience to government authorities."

It was used against the 2016 Black Lives Matter protests, with pastor Robert Jeffress saying in an interview, "The New Testament says in Romans 13:4 that law enforcement officers are ministers of God sent by God to punish evildoers."[1] Former US attorney general Jeff Sessions said in defense of the Trump administration separating immigrant children from their parents at the US border, "I would cite you to the Apostle Paul and his clear and wise command in Romans 13 to obey the laws of the government."[2]

During the COVID-19 pandemic, Christians cited Romans 13 against churches that disobeyed local meeting restrictions or mask mandates. You probably felt differently about the meaning of this passage depending on which of these circumstances you were thinking about.

Romans 13 has always been key for Christians thinking about government—about the relationship between divine and human authority, Christians' civic obligations, and the purpose and meaning of human government. The passage took on unique importance, however, during a contentious, defining moment in American history: the Revolutionary War.

The Revolutionary War was flush with biblical justifications or condemnations. Loyalist priests invoked Romans 13 or 1 Peter 2:17 to quelch revolution, while revolutionaries invoked the Bible's language of freedom (Gal. 5:1; 2 Cor. 3:17) and highlighted unjust kings in Scripture, from Pharoah to Rehoboam, to justify it. These passages are important texts for political theology, but they are also a case study in selective application.

We tend to invoke passages like Romans 13 selectively, depending on the issue or politician. How can we know when to say, "Let everyone be subject to the governing authorities" (Rom. 13:1), and when to say, "We must obey God rather than human beings!" (Acts 5:29)? How can we guard ourselves against self-serving selectivity and recognize when the biblical witness goes against our political goals rather than supporting them? The warring pulpits during the American Revolution provide some insight for us today.

The Revolutionary Pulpit

The Revolutionary War was shaped by the Bible because the people of the colonies were shaped by the Bible. In particular, the Great Awakening in the 1730s and 1740s would greatly shape how the early nation read and interpreted the Bible. The Great Awakening engaged everyday people, encouraging them to make their faith personal. Religious authority was more diverse, with people looking to traveling preachers and their own reading of Scripture for guidance on theological questions. Many traveling preachers used a style of communication persuasive to average people: unlike the rhetorical conventions learned by the wealthy and well-educated, these preachers overcame the class divide by using familiar language and appealing directly to Scripture.[3] The Bible became a source of shared language, an accessible and authoritative text that the entire population was familiar with. This common language became ripe for use in political discourse.[4]

Biblical language was so ubiquitous that some people might not have even realized they were using it. Daniel Dreisbach identifies an incredibly long list of phrases George Washington used that are biblical in origin but were not necessarily cited directly (or applied correctly).[5] Thomas Jefferson and Benjamin Franklin each suggested similar biblical images for the official seal of the United States: Jefferson proposed an image of the Israelites following the cloud of smoke wandering in the desert; Franklin suggested an image of the Israelites watching Pharaoh and his army drown in the Red Sea.[6]

The Bible provided a shared language and meaning, and clergy had a large role in shaping national identity. One scholar has called this period the "age of the sermon," because the preacher was often the main educator in a community, the "chief counselor," and potentially the most educated person in town.[7] Sermons were especially important as the rebellious colonists moved toward all-out war. In a violent, chaotic, and uncertain time, people were hungry for communal identity and values. Sermons were—and remain—profound acts of community creation.[8]

The Loyalists

While much of what is popularly known about the Bible and the Revolution focuses on the Patriots, there is much to be learned by examining the biblical exegesis of the traitors—the Loyalists.

Our understanding of the Loyalists is tainted by our patriotism as well as how difficult it is to understand history from the loser's perspective, so to speak. They were not "sadly deluded, stubbornly obnoxious, and crassly self-serving lackeys of the British tyrants," says Mark Noll, despite how many historians have seen them this way.[9] Loyalist clergy genuinely believed that the English monarchy was a good system of government providing provision and protection and that the Bible gave a clear and universal command to obey and honor rulers.[10]

In 1780, in the heat of the Revolutionary War, Charles Inglis, rector of Trinity Church in New York, preached a sermon on 1 Peter 2:17 titled "The Duty of Honouring the King." Inglis pled with his congregation to obey God's law and honor the king. "Professing Christians, who really believe in a divine Revelation, and acknowledge its Authority," he exclaimed, "should make no Conscience of dishonouring their King, and rebelling against him—that they should knowingly trample on the Law of God, and act as if no such Law existed—that instead of obeying this Law, they should be Trumpeters of Sedition and Rebellion: This is astonishing indeed!"[11] Inglis gave a traditional Loyalist sermon against the Revolution. His central text was a favorite among Loyalist clergy, but he also referenced Romans 13, 1 Timothy 2:1–3, and Jesus's instruction to "Give unto Caesar what is Caesar's."

In addition, he referenced classic Loyalist themes. He emphasized that the early church was oppressed by Rome and still submitted, highlighting that Romans 13 taught submission to unjust rulers. He connected the duties owed to God and to earthly rulers with more biblical language: "Duties which God hath thus united and joined together, no Man should ever presume to put asunder" (borrowing Jesus's words about divorce). He described the chaos and violence of the rebellion as a form of God's judgment on their shared national sin. He reminded his congregation that Jesus's kingdom is "not of this world," which means that it "does not interfere with earthly kingdoms."

He also drew on less directly biblical ideas. He described the rebellion as the fruit of fearing "imaginary dangers," passions being inflamed by "artifice and zeal." He appealed to anti-Catholicism, reminding his people that the rebels were in league with the French, the "Popish, inveterate Enemies of our Nation, of our Religion and

Liberties." He praised the king, "whose Life is a shining Example of Religion and Virtue, and is a strong Incentive to the Practice of both by others."

The Patriot Answer

The Loyalists had Romans 13 and 1 Peter 2:17, but the Patriots had their own favorites: Micah 6:8 to describe the demands of public life, Proverbs 29:2 to describe the effects of a wicked ruler, and Galatians 5:1 to describe the freedom they were seeking. But more than specific verses with clearly applicable language, Patriot preachers drew analogies between the Israelites and themselves.[12]

The exodus loomed large for colonists who felt oppressed by a corrupt empire (not large enough to incite very many of them to apply this logic to slavery, but some of them saw the parallels).[13] The story of Deborah, Barak, and Jael in Judges 4–5 was significant, especially a passage little-known today that took on a life of its own in the Revolutionary era: the "curse of Meroz." In Deborah's song in Judges 5, she says that the angel of the Lord has cursed the city of Meroz "because they did not come to help the LORD" (v. 23). Patriots cited this curse against Loyalist or apathetic colonists who were not willing to fight for the revolution.[14]

The stories of corrupt kings like Ahab, who conspired to murder his subject Naboth, or Rehoboam, who unjustly taxed the people and split the kingdom of Israel, were great sources of passionate preaching for the Revolutionaries.[15] The story of Esther was also a favorite because it could be used to criticize an unjust government while focusing criticism away from the king and onto his policies or evil underlings.[16] Scripture was not merely historical fact or a theological resource but a "master narrative" that could illuminate contemporary conflicts. Revolutionaries and Patriots alike expected to see in biblical stories familiar dynamics and perennial human problems. For Patriot preachers, preaching on biblical commands or universal moral rules was far surpassed with "overwhelming application by analogy, models, parallels, exempla, and metaphors."[17] This was how many of them responded to the

Loyalist interpretation of Romans 13: the rest of Scripture, as well as Paul's own life and practice, qualifies what sounds like a harsh and universal statement in Romans 13.[18] Responding to "literal" interpretations of Romans 13 was nothing new for these preachers: they drew on Protestant justifications for resisting Catholic princes, including the tension between this command and the one in Acts 5:29.

They found, as many others before them had, that Romans 13 described how governing authorities should act: as ministers of God for good.[19] Just as the Loyalists had a deeply moral argument—it is wrong to rebel against lawful authority—the Patriots did as well. Drawing on stories of corrupt kings in Scripture and frequently citing 1 Samuel 8 (when Israel's request for a king is depicted as a refusal of God's rule), they taught that rebellion was righteous: "Rebellion to Tyrants is Obedience to God." This became such a frequent motto that Franklin wanted it to be on the seal of the new nation.[20]

Jonathan Mayhew, a Congregational minister from Massachusetts, wrote *A Discourse Concerning Unlimited Submission and Non-Resistance to the Higher Powers* in 1750, almost three decades before the war began. His work was frequently praised and referenced by Revolutionary leaders and thinkers.[21] The discourse is about Romans 13 directly. He begins by clarifying that while Christ's kingdom is "not of this world," God has still given us some instruction about government. Mayhew appeals in part to history: Paul was responding to early Christians who thought their faith exempted them from all kinds of human association, including paying their taxes. He argues that the text's description of earthly authorities implies that subjects have obligations, but rulers do too: "Rulers have no authority from God to do mischief."[22]

Mayhew further contends that the passage doesn't teach "absolute, unlimited obedience," just as biblical commands to children to obey their parents do not require submission to abuse. People are required to obey only those who "actually perform the duty of rulers, by exercising a reasonable and just authority, for the good of human society." The purpose of government given in the passage is important for the question of obedience: if you submit to the king for the good of the society but he "turns tyrant, and makes his subjects his prey to devour and destroy, instead of his charge to defend and cherish," you have obligation to "throw off . . . allegiance to him, and to resist, and that according to the tenor of the apostle's argument in this passage."[23]

Revolutionary Biblical Interpretation

Galatians 5:1 became its own battleground during the war, exemplifying an important difference between the Loyalists and the Patriots—one that still shapes our interpretive disputes. This verse has all the makings of a good Patriot rallying cry: it connects freedom and Jesus ("It is for freedom that Christ has set us free"), it encourages resistance to opposition ("stand firm"), and it contrasts freedom with the threat of slavery ("and do not let yourselves be burdened again by a yoke of slavery").

The word "liberty" was central to the political and religious rhetoric of the time, and Loyalist exegetes quickly noted that the political and theological meanings could not be mixed. One Loyalist sermon cautioned that it was important to understand Paul's context: he had Jewish law in mind, so the liberty he writes about is spiritual, not political.[24] Paul is referring to liberty from the ceremonial law and freedom from sin, said another Loyalist priest. "This passage cannot, without infinite perversion and torture, be made to refer to any other kind of liberty," he argues, concluding, "The word liberty, as meaning civil liberty, does not, I believe, occur in all the Scriptures."[25]

Generally speaking, the Patriots went to the Old Testament and the Loyalists went to the New Testament. When it came to preaching about the Revolution, the Loyalists were less likely to turn to stories of ancient Israel or dictates of Mosaic law and were more likely to appeal to direct commands in the New Testament or the example of Jesus.[26] While the Loyalists might have seemed to have direct biblical commands on their side, they faced the challenge of the "patriot monopoly" of the Bible. Increasingly in this period, new political ideas about liberty and representation were so intimately tied to biblical language that even if Loyalists could cite "Obey the governing authorities," the Bible had been "won" to the other side.[27]

This was not just a difference between Old and New Testament but a difference between relying on direct commands that had the benefit of clear moral direction ("The Bible says it; I believe it; that settles it") and relying on the affective power of drawing on Old Testament stories of corrupt kings, courageous fighters, and startling prophecies.

Finally, much of the polemical preaching from the Revolutionary era sounds startlingly familiar today. Some Loyalist preachers described the difference in interpretation as the difference between "feelings" and solid biblical truth. Others said that while the Patriots were preaching "the politics of the times," their Loyalist churches were growing because they preached nothing but the gospel. Even if the Bible's teaching seems "obsolete," one Loyalist wrote, it remains the word of the Lord—implying that the Patriots were discarding biblical truth that didn't fit contemporary attitudes.[28]

Christian Obligations and Romans 13

Before thinking more broadly about what this history can teach us about biblical interpretation today, let's think a little more about Romans 13:1–7. This short teaching on the Christian's relationship to human rulers has consistently puzzled interpreters.

Submission to human government seems like a strange topic for Paul—imprisoned and persecuted at various points in his life—and it comes at a strange place in the Letter to the Romans. Some scholars argue that in light of Paul's earlier teaching on the temporal nature of the world, he may want to prevent readers from thinking they can simply reject or opt out of temporal human affairs.[29] Yes, the world is dominated by sin and ruled by Satan, but God has not abandoned creation or human affairs. Others argue that these instructions are part of a larger set of instructions for dealing with outsiders (Rom. 12:14–21) and that Paul is articulating a strategy for this fledgling religious minority to present themselves well to the wider world.

While many details about the Epistle to the Romans are hotly debated, we do know that it was written during the first five or six years of Nero's reign, during a period of relative calm for Christians (in contrast to many interpretations that stress that Christians were persecuted in this period).[30]

Other historical details remain disputed. Some have seen the section as a warning against Jewish zealotism, taxation rebellion, or political subversiveness by an already vulnerable religious group.[31] Most of these interpretations rightfully take the historical context of the letter seriously, trying to understand why Paul would give such confusing commands. If we can find some historical context that makes his argument make more sense—if Jewish rebellion was threatening to rope Christians into greater persecution or if Paul was thinking about recent rebellions over taxes—his instructions can be narrowly applied to that situation rather than read by Christians today as instructive for them too.

While the historical situation is certainly relevant, many of these arguments should not be given *too* much weight: they often particularize the instructions to the point of meaninglessness for modern readers. They also make important biblical interpretations overly dependent on uncertain historical research. Revolutionary-era preachers should remind us that while historical context is important, if newly discovered historical data can drastically change our interpretations, we should be wary. Many of them gave great weight to the historical context as they understood it at the time (believing it was a time of increased persecution rather than the relative calm most historians now think was occurring at the time). Later scholarship that described a different context for the letter made their interpretation, that Paul was giving firm instructions in the face of oppressive persecution, flimsy. Historical data should inform our biblical interpretation because God revealed himself in particular times and places in human history, condescending to our cultural and political specifics, but if the Holy Spirit uses Scripture to instruct and convict believers throughout all of history, our interpretations cannot be ones that only recent historical data made possible. Historical data should inform our interpretations but not determine them. If an interpretation cannot stand without the historical details being correct, it's not a very good one.

Regardless of its historical context, we know that Romans 13:1–7 is not a comprehensive political theory or the whole of Christian teaching on politics. While it has ongoing relevance to us today, Paul was not writing a treatise on politics; he was instructing the people of God at a particular place and time. His words should be read in the context of the whole counsel of Scripture, not isolated as the singular Christian teaching on politics. Christians have misinterpreted these verses to support all sorts of oppression: from the German state church's acquiescence to Hitler's Third Reich, to Christian support of the apartheid regime in South Africa, to defenses of the Fugitive Slave Act in America.[32]

Romans 13:1–7 deals with a specific example of the kinds of obligations that a Christian has both within the church and outside it—obligations that prioritize the common good of others above individual rights.[33] Paul is concerned not only with articulating some of these obligations but also with "redrawing" the boundaries of the people of God. Since the people of God are no longer bound by ethnicity or nationality, they must consider what it means to live well in various political arrangements.[34]

Paul would obviously agree that when there is conflict between rulers' commands and God's commands, Christians obey God (Acts 4:19; 5:29). "Submitting" to earthly authorities cannot mean anything that would conflict with the full biblical witness. Romans must be read alongside, for example, Revelation's depiction of Christians refusing to comply with corrupt and abusive power. Additionally, the same word in Greek, *hypotassō*, "to submit," is used of Christians submitting to spiritual leaders (1 Cor. 16:16), all Christians submitting to each other (Eph. 5:21), prophets submitting to other prophets (1 Cor. 14:32), and wives submitting to husbands (Eph. 5:24). In none of these instances would most interpreters see total, unquestioning obedience. While "submission" is often used to describe human relationships, "obedience" is reserved for God.[35]

The justification for the command to submit—that earthly authority is instituted by God—both strengthens and nuances the command. On the one hand, the following verses will show that wrongful rebellion against human authorities is tantamount to rebellion against God. On the other hand, Paul is forcefully denying a central political claim of the Roman Empire. The true deity behind Roman authority is not Mars or Jupiter, or any of the many Greco-Roman deities, but the God of justice and mercy, incarnate in Christ, who was crucified for the sake of his creation.[36]

Paul thus denies Rome's central justifying claims—that its law is redemptive, that its rule produces peace, that its authority comes from the gods. Instead, he shows the real reason for its authority. While earthly rulers are in some sense elevated by this passage, in another sense they are seriously demoted.[37] As New Testament scholar Michael Gorman has put it, "Jesus and Caesar cannot both rule the universe."[38] The gospel leaves no room for nationalism or blanket approval of whoever wields the most power.

Even still, many readers are troubled that Paul seems to evaluate earthly governments as overwhelmingly good.[39] It's strange that Paul of all people would overlook that human rulers make poor or evil judgments. Some scholars reason that Paul's experiences with rulers had been positive, but that contradicts his actual personal history (Acts 16:22–24; 2 Cor. 11:25–29). Others reason that Paul is aware of unjust government and is speaking of the ideal government, but that doesn't seem to serve the pastoral goals of the letter; still others reason that Paul means that God uses all rulers, just and unjust, for good ends.[40] This last option captures the larger sense of the passage affirming God's sovereignty, and it aligns with other scriptural teachings about God using rulers for ends other than that which they intend.

Still, why would Paul promise that those who do "good" will receive reward? Some argue that the language used in Romans 13:3 and 1 Peter 2:14 should be understood not as a generic description of "doing good" and receiving rewards but as technical terminology that describes the public recognition citizens were given when they contributed to the common good.[41] In that case,

Paul is not saying that people will be universally rewarded for their good deeds (again, his life attests to the opposite). Rather, he's encouraging Christians to serve their larger community and receive the rewards given to public acts of service. Here we can recognize that Paul's instruction echoes that of Jeremiah 29:7, which tells a marginalized people to "seek the peace and prosperity of the city" even while facing hostility.

While believers are forbidden from acting on their own behalf, God has ordained an institution with legitimate power to punish evil. At best, rulers enact a "partial, anticipatory, provisional manifestation of God's wrath against sin."[42] While unbelievers have their own reasons for obeying (avoiding punishment, receiving honor), Christians have special motivation: God has ordained these leaders, so submitting to them fulfills a Christian obligation. Once again, Paul refuses to separate social and religious actions from civic and spiritual obligations.[43]

Romans 13:1–7 does not provide a clear application to all Christians in all times and places. Rather, it gives a general exhortation as to the posture Christians should have toward governing authorities. These seven verses, rather than offering a complete Christian theory of government, exhort believers to recognize their various obligations to others, including obligations that take distinctly political forms.

When it comes to applying teachings like this to our own contexts, we should, like the Revolutionary-era preachers, discern the moral logic of the passage and determine what that posture and way of thinking demand of us today.[44] As we read Scripture, we can ask not only *what* is allowed and what is forbidden but also *why*, *how*, and *when*. How are the biblical authors, inspired by the Spirit, approaching moral problems as complex as the ones we face? What story about faithfulness is told here, and how can we model it?

Romans and the Revolution

We can learn many things from how various preachers interpreted Romans 13 in the Revolutionary era, but these lessons might not be what you would expect. Rather than finding in our history one right and one wrong interpretation of Romans 13, the battling pulpits of the time help us think more carefully about our own context, the affective power of the biblical story and language, and our selective prioritizing of certain biblical texts.

Context and Bias

The most obvious thing to learn is that American Christians have always tried to claim to take Scripture more "seriously" or "literally" than their opponents. The language the Loyalists used to defend their own position and criticize the Patriots sounds eerily familiar to Americans in the twenty-first century: "I'm not doing any fancy interpretive moves. I'm just reading the Bible, and this is what it says." "*They* put politics in their preaching, while *we* stick to the Bible." "They let their feelings influence them, so they make the Bible say what they want it to say."

This history should also teach us that sometimes these accusations are true. But they rarely fall along the lines we expect or like. People citing Romans 13 to criticize social-justice protests, for example, have to ask whether their interpretation would allow the Revolutionary War, which created the country they feel they are defending. People who accuse the "other side" of letting politics drive their interpretation have to grapple with the fact that none of us come to the biblical text as a clean slate.

We all bring our political preferences, lived experiences, and theological frameworks to our Bible reading. Some of these biases are good (solid theological grounding that keeps us within the bounds of orthodox Christian faith), some are bad (political idolatry that requires us to ignore or distort uncomfortable passages), and some are neither or both (our personal history and communal context that can bring gifts *and* challenges). This history should teach us to hold a fine tension between embracing the good elements of these biases and questioning the biases that can lead our interpretations astray.

The Revolutionary era was a period that shaped the religious ethos of the new country. We wanted democracy in all things, including our biblical interpretation. We wanted to shrug off all authority, including the tradition and authority of the church. The Bible could be interpreted by anyone, and people did not need anything but their own reason to understand it well. This history should remind us that while we cannot free ourselves from biases and context, we can rely on the diverse witness of the church throughout time and around the world to help us understand Scripture more clearly. We actually do need more than a Bible and our own minds. We need each other.

The Power of Story

It's not fair to say that the Loyalists took the Bible more seriously than the Patriots. But it is fair to say that the Patriots focused on different areas of Scripture—not just the New Testament versus the Old, but direct moral teachings in epistles versus narratives and prophecies.[45] As we see throughout American history, there is power in using biblical language of all kinds, but there is a special kind of power that comes through storytelling. In this way, the Patriots could tell a dramatic, divine story and connect it with the pressing demands of the contemporary moment.

The Patriots could stir the emotions of their congregations, helping them imagine themselves as players in a divine story. While a Loyalist preacher could exert moral authority by saying that God inspired the apostle Paul to say, in essence, "Obey the king," a Patriot preacher could describe in great detail the courage of David fighting Goliath or Daniel being thrown in the lions' den or Jael piercing a man's skull with a tent peg. Patriots were, of course, influenced by political theory and their own immediate interests in the war, but they were also genuinely moved by biblical accounts that seemed to speak to their own context.[46]

This reality is both warning and exhortation for us. The warning is for both preachers and listeners to be aware of the way human hearts are easily captivated by stories, especially stories that promise an exciting and meaningful role for the listener. People who appeal to Scripture should feel the weight of that responsibility and fear the consequences if they misuse it. Christians in the pews (and on the couch watching cable news) should be aware of the ways they can be swept up into a drama and given a part to play. The exhortation is for all of us as well. It is not a weakness or defect of humans that we are captivated by stories. We were meant to be drawn into the true divine drama, honored and dignified by a God who made us in his image and gave us parts to play in his story. God wants us to love the true story of redemption and to participate in it. The best answer to the power of corrupted or false stories is not shutting ourselves away from all storytelling but learning to hear the words and to love the shape of the truest, most beautiful story on earth.

Cherry-Picking

Perhaps no lesson is more salient from this history than this: when it comes to interpreting the Bible in politics, we all cherry-pick verses. There is sometimes a good impulse at the heart of this mistake. A moral dilemma or a political problem presents itself, and Christians go to Scripture to find guidance. Maybe they use a concordance to look up verses that address the topic; maybe their situation reminds them of a biblical story; maybe they let the wind flip the pages of their Bible and point a finger at a verse, looking for guidance. There are also, of course, less honorable motives for cherry-picking verses. We want God's stamp of approval on what we were going to do anyway, and we want the rhetorical power of divine judgment against our enemies.

Whatever our motives, our political conversations will never go anywhere so long as we pit verse against verse, stacking up references like tally points against one another. We need to learn how to integrate biblical truths across the canon, think about how passages help interpret each other, and refuse to base an entire political position on select verses.

We need to practice reasoning well with each other (and with ourselves) by refusing to ease the inherent tension between "Let everyone be subject to the governing authorities" and "We must obey God rather than human beings." Different political circumstances—different times and places, with different histories and moral questions—will require different biblical emphases, and knowing what passage is fitting for any given moment will require wisdom, the guidance of the Holy Spirit, and the assistance of the whole communion of saints (both our neighbors now and the witness of Christians throughout global history).

The opposite of cherry-picking Bible verses is not separating theology from politics. Rather, it's *doing good political theology.* When we arrive at a pressing political concern with no prior work done, we are more likely to grab for easy verses that seem applicable (even if they aren't). When we've done the hard work of thinking about what God requires of human communities, rulers, and citizens—looking at the whole Bible for guidance, learning what Christians before us and beside us have done, incorporating the wisdom we can gain from sociology, history, and political theory—we will be more prepared to address the problem in front of us. Doing that work is not easy, but it doesn't require a PhD either. Christians have been hashing this out in their communities since the beginning of the church—just look at Romans 13.

"The Bible through Slave-Holding Spectacles"

The Bible in the Civil War

Biblical interpretation in the Civil War is a crucial illustration of the way Scripture has been conscripted into political use entirely foreign—even contrary—to its purposes. We tend to think that committing to biblical authority will safeguard us from wrong interpretation, yet abolitionists and slaveholders alike held the Bible in high regard. Abolitionists drew on passages about liberation and Paul's demolition of the divide between "slave and free." Defenders of slavery drew on the "curse of Ham" in Genesis 9:18–29 and on Old and New Testament depictions of slavery to paint their cause as biblically justified. Both sides used Philemon to support their position.

Civil War hermeneutics highlights many relevant issues for biblical interpretation and politics. It shows how our methods can be similar and yet we can come to different conclusions, how our biases play a significant role in our interpretation, and how our communities shape our political imaginations. This chapter focuses on cultural and political influences on our reading of Scripture and charts a way to learn from the most vulnerable and oppressed among us. We need to recognize our own biases and learn from the evil in our nation's history if we want our hermeneutics to be sound.

Civil War Biblical Swamp

The Civil War era was full of theological and political pressures: the moral calamity of slavery, fear over new methods of biblical interpretation, and what Mark Noll calls the "theological crisis" of the war itself.[1] Nearly a century after the founding of the nation, a "uniquely American way of interpreting the Scriptures" had been firmly cemented in the American culture. This approach combined Reformed *sola scriptura* and a "commonsense" democratic reading.[2] Americans claimed to rely on Scripture alone, interpreted it for themselves, and closely identified the Bible with American ideals and republican political theory.

Americans of the time believed they didn't need a priest or king to interpret the Bible for them. This meant that preachers had to be careful if they interpreted a text against the grain of community sensibilities. As two historians of the era described it, if a pastor preached in a disagreeable way, "a mere grumble from a few congregants would send others scurrying to check their Bibles."[3] America, deeply religious but averse to hierarchy or religious authority, would continually turn to the Bible for defining moral and political debates, grounding national identity, and understanding historical developments.[4]

The Civil War exemplifies America's strange relationship with the Bible.[5] Women sewed special pockets into soldiers' clothes for them to carry small Bibles with them into battle, and popular stories circulated about the miraculous protection they provided.[6] The Bible was described as a weapon of war, and stories spread about soldiers capturing Bibles from across battle lines as another form of offensive combat.[7]

The Civil War erupted at a time when America was awash in biblical language and references. But it was also a time when Americans were deeply divided over the Bible's meaning in public life. This context was ripe for a moral and political crisis. American Christians discovered that "the Bible they had relied upon for building up America's republican civilization" was not as unifying, clear, or easy to interpret as they thought.[8] For example, preachers and politicians referenced the same passage we looked at in the last chapter: Romans 13. Preachers in the North referenced Romans 13 often as a text that clearly condemned rebelling against earthly authorities. But the Confederates had a good response: What about the rebellion that began our nation?[9]

Before examining some of the hermeneutical lessons we can learn from this period, we need to quickly examine some of the most popular and persistent biblical interpretations and choices—not only from the proslavery and abolitionist camps but especially from the enslaved and free Black people who turned to Scripture to find strength and hope in a story of liberation.

The Proslavery Bible

For the first fifty years of America's history, there were hardly any biblical defenses of slavery. The cultural assumption of slavery was so strong that no one needed to defend an institution that seemed natural to most white Americans.[10] It is remarkable to note that an evil this great and pervasive in American society was initially met with little resistance. Once the system of slavery was finally questioned, often on biblical grounds, the movement to defend it theologically sprang up with a force.

Proslavery writers had some favorite verses. They noted Abraham's owning slaves (Gen. 17:12), legal stipulations about slaves (such as Deut. 20:10–11), and New Testament verses that seemed to sanction slavery (such as 1 Cor. 7:21; Col. 3:22; 4:1; 1 Tim. 6:1–2, and the book of Philemon).[11] Increasingly, they argued that the Bible did not just *allow* slavery but described a divine moral order that *required* slavery. Christians criticizing slavery were not just misunderstanding Scripture; they were an "affront to God's goodness and subversion of divine order."[12]

Slaveholding and proslavery Christian leaders wrote endlessly about the importance of the Bible to their position and the disregard their opponents had for Scripture. One striking example comes from Congregational preacher Leonard Bacon. After noting the Bible's positive depictions of slavery, he argues that abolitionist Christians have done "violence" to the text. He says that while he assumes they have "no lack of reverence toward the Word of God," they nevertheless "torture the Scriptures into saying that which the anti-slavery theory requires them to say."[13]

Curse of Ham

Proslavery writers and preachers also crafted an account of human history and society from a combination of biblical texts and scientific racism. Scientific racism is the pseudoscientific effort to "prove" the biological and mental inferiority of non-white people groups. Proslavery Christian leaders argued that all humanity descended from Adam and Eve and so were spiritually equal, but the story of Noah described an "ethnic theology" that explained the division of people into different groups, with different characteristics and destinies in the context of divine providence.[14] Proslavery leaders took contemporary theories of race that posited biological differences between groups of people as producing differences in intelligence, civility, and physical capabilities and melded these theories to the story of Noah and his children to produce the "curse of Ham" justification for slavery.

In Genesis 9:18–28, Noah's youngest son, Ham, sees his drunken father's nakedness and tells his two brothers about it. The two brothers cover their father with a garment, walking into his tent backward so as not to see his nakedness. When Noah wakes up, he curses Ham's son Canaan and praises his other sons, saying that Canaan will be their slave. Needless to stay, the story is bizarre and continues to confuse biblical interpreters. (What exactly was Ham's sin? Why is his son cursed instead of him? Why was this whole situation such a big deal to Noah?)

The curse of Ham took on a life of its own in the antebellum South. There were direct references to it, of course, but also countless allusions in sermons, Sunday school lessons, and political speeches. While many professional theologians did not engage with the text, the story "haunted" America for centuries.[15] The curse of Ham was attractive because it fit neatly into preexisting ideas that humanity could be divided into essential racial types, and it provided a theological justification for the conditions slaves were forced to live in.[16] It is an inescapable reality that slaveholding whites had economic incentives to find biblical justification for their exploitation of Africans. The story of Noah and Ham and Canaan "framed the ethos of the plantation within a sacred history," legitimizing the institution of slavery as well as the brutal and racialized nature of slavery in America.[17]

While the story has been interpreted in the context of various social arrangements throughout history, by the time of the Civil War it was hard for many Christians to see anything in the passage other than a justification for racial chattel slavery. Whereas past interpreters might have seen in the character of Ham a serf or a slave, by this time most white Americans envisioned him as an African.[18]

Spiritual Freedom and Earthly Order

Just as the curse of Ham fit neatly into Southern culture and racist ideology, other Bible verses fit into a theology that sharply divided spiritual freedom for all Christians and the kind of political liberty that was reserved for white men. Preachers regularly argued that when Scripture spoke of liberation and freedom, it was "spiritual," not physical or political.[19] Biblical freedom was about freedom from sin, and the Bible frequently described a hierarchal social order. This combination—spiritual freedom and earthly order—was how slaveholding ministers justified baptismal vows for slaves that required them to promise that their spiritual salvation would not result in their seeking physical liberation.[20]

The Abolitionist Argument

White abolitionists had their own favorite biblical passages. They cited Deuteronomy 23:15 ("If a slave has taken refuge with you, do not hand them over to their master"), Galatians 3:28 ("There is neither Jew nor Gentile, neither slave nor free, nor is there male and female, for you are all one in Christ Jesus"), Colossians 4:1 ("Masters, provide your slaves with what is right and fair, because you know that you also have a Master in heaven") in conjunction with the "golden rule" of Matthew 7:12 ("So in everything, do to others what you would have them do to you"), and 1 Timothy 1:10 (which condemns "slave traders and liars and perjurers"). They also referenced emancipatory texts like the biblical account of the exodus, the Jubilee in the Mosaic law, and Jesus's "Jubilee sermon" in Luke 4, as well as the condemnation of unjust religious practices in Isaiah 58:6.[21]

Moral arguments are never made in a vacuum. Just as these debates about the Bible and slavery were happening from particular contexts and perspectives (the biases of a slaveholding man, the comfort of a Northern white woman), they were also happening in a particular *theological* context. This was a period with significant changes in biblical studies and theology.

Historical criticism—which looks to the historical context of the Bible and tries to reconstruct its original meaning without reference to doctrinal commitments—became popular in this period. Theological trends followed: many interpreters aimed to cast off the cultural and historical "baggage" of Scripture in order to find universal principles underneath. In other words, they tried to discern "the kernel of universal truth lying beneath the superficial meaning of individual passages." This approach fit their needs: it disfavored interpreting isolated texts, gave room for moral intuition, and subordinated the question of particular verses to larger principles.[22]

Many of the abolitionist arguments were historical. They rejected the idea that African Americans were actual descendants of Ham and argued that slavery in ancient Israel or first-century Rome was better than chattel slavery. Some even denied that ancient Hebrews practiced any real kind of slavery, making complicated arguments about the meaning of "slave" in different biblical contexts.[23] Even if slavery was condoned in Scripture, many writers (including Abraham Lincoln) argued that the Roman system was not based in race but was "a slavery of whites" (the racial category they put all Romans in), a possibility they thought no white Christian could tolerate.[24] As we will see, these arguments leave much to be desired.

Other antislavery Christians avoided the technical questions about translation or history and pointed to biblical principles of love and justice.[25] There were better and worse forms of this argument—from describing the grand redemptive narrative of Scripture or working out a rich theology of human social life to generally waving at the Bible and proclaiming it opposed to slavery (as proslavery writers also did, in the opposite). Faithful antislavery advocates had to toe a careful line, however. Relying on historical criticism or new theological developments made their arguments unpersuasive to opponents. Some abolitionists jettisoned the Bible entirely—the radical abolitionist William Lloyd Garrison claimed slavery was simply "not a Bible question."[26]

Black Christians and the God of the Oppressed

Black Christians approached Scripture very differently from their white abolitionist counterparts. Many preachers and writers referenced the Bible without concern over slavery passages.[27] Instead, they went to passages about injustice and oppression, inhabiting biblical narratives of liberation and drawing on biblical language of condemnation of the wealthy and powerful for their own polemics. Figures like Nat Turner, who led a violent slave rebellion in 1831, saw in the Bible a righteous indignation against injustice that motivated revolt. When asked before his execution if he felt his actions were justified, he replied, "Was not Christ crucified?"[28]

Not all Black people accepted the Bible as authoritative, but their criticism largely focused on the people who used it against them.[29] For example, Frederick Douglass said, "It is no evidence that the Bible is a bad book, because those who profess to believe the Bible are bad. The slaveholders of the South, and many of their wicked allies at the North, claim the Bible for slavery; shall we, therefore, fling the Bible away as a pro-slavery book?" Douglass knew the power of Scripture did not lie exclusively in the hands of white slaveholders—his own master had refused to let him read the Bible because "if he learns to read the Bible, it will forever unfit him to be a slave."[30]

Black Americans in this period focused on verses that declared their dignity and humanity in the face of exploitation. Verses like Psalm 68:31 ("probably the most widely quoted verse in Afro-American religious history," one historian says) described African nations as significant, powerful, and oriented toward God.[31] Moses's father-in-law, Jethro, was referenced often as an example of God's people learning from African people.

Even more prominent, however, was the way that Black people drew on biblical narratives, prophecies, and accounts of judgment to apply to their own context. The exodus was a familiar and important biblical account—a dramatic story that conveyed the suffering, oppression, and redemption of God's people. While Christians have drawn on the exodus in creative ways throughout church history, "African Americans inhabited the exodus story of liberation like no other people before them."[32]

It was more than drawing on this one story, however. It was about seeing the whole of the Bible, the whole of Christian faith, as from the perspective of "slavery's children."[33] Enslaved people could look to the oppressed Israelites, to the oppressed within Israel (the widow, orphan, and foreigner), and to the "suffering servant" himself, Christ. They found in the Bible a story of God identifying with the oppressed and bringing victory to the unlikeliest people. As biblical scholar Allen Callahan has described it, "The Bible privileges those without privilege and honors those without honor."[34]

Many of the enslaved learned the Bible through storytelling, call-and-response in secret churches, and the singing of spirituals. They told biblical stories from memory, making it easier to blend elements of different stories and to draw on language from one story to tell another.[35] Some scholars describe the slavery debate among white people as the difference between the "plain reading" of the text that supported slavery and the "sophisticated interpretive practice" required for an antislavery position. Enslaved people proved that racism and love of money played more of a role in supporting slavery than a "plain reading" of the Bible.[36]

In the twentieth century, Black theologian James Cone noted that enslaved Africans' imaginations were deeply shaped by biblical language and emancipatory energy. The storyteller in a community rehearses God's action in history, God's presence and protection for his people, and relates those stories to the contemporary needs of God's people. "The past and present is joined dialectically, creating a black vision of the future."[37] This approach to Scripture identified the people of God across history and allowed an oppressed people to speak of their future liberation in covert ways. White slaveholders could overhear enslaved people singing about "crossing the river Jordan and entering the New Jerusalem" without knowing that they were singing about escaping and finding refuge north of the Mason-Dixon Line.[38] To white ears, those biblical references were historical or otherworldly. To enslaved people, God was leading people into the Promised Land in the present day.

Two crucial works from this period—David Walker's *Appeal to the Colored Citizens of the World* and Maria Stewart's *Religion and the Pure Principles of Morality*—are instructive for us today. David Walker was never enslaved, but his father had been, and he saw the abuse and oppression firsthand. An early abolitionist, Walker used the Bible as both the intellectual basis and the emotional power of his critique of chattel slavery.

In addition to numerous other biblical references, Walker's central argument in *Appeal* is close attention to the exodus.[39] He describes the way Joseph was treated in Egypt—by Africans, he emphasizes—where he was given political power, an Egyptian marriage, and economic inclusion. Walker argues that the Egyptians treated the Israelites better than Christian slaveholders treated their captive laborers, that African Americans suffered far more than those in the biblical story.

Walker writes in the preamble, "I will not here speak of the destructions which the Lord brought upon Egypt, in consequence of the oppression and consequent groans of the oppressed—of the hundreds and thousands of Egyptians whom God hurled into the Red Sea for afflicting his people in their land." Walker's tone is confident and firm: "Jesus Christ the King of heaven and of earth who is the God of justice and armies" goes before his people, and he will not stand for the idolatry of white slaveholders.[40]

Walker uses biblical language even when not directly citing Scripture. He appeals not only to the language of the Bible but also to the visual absurdity of slaveholding people appealing to Scripture. One of his favorite phrases to highlight this point is "the Bible in their hands": "Have not the Americans the Bible in their hands? Do they believe it? Surely they do not. See how they treat us in open violation of the Bible!"[41]

Walker's pupil Maria Stewart began speaking publicly after his death, becoming the first American woman to lecture to a mixed-gender audience. She was a free-born African American, abolitionist, women's rights activist, and evangelist. Where Walker focuses on the exodus, Stewart grounds her argument on a biblical anthropology from Genesis, apocalyptic judgment, and an appeal to Christian virtue.[42]

She blends biblical narrative with her own (a common approach to antislavery storytelling). For Stewart, there is no divide between personal piety ("From the moment I experienced the change, I felt a strong desire . . . to devote the remainder of my days to piety and virtue") and justice (the next sentence: "All the nations of the earth are crying out for Liberty and Equality"). Later she alludes to Psalm 68:31, that her heart's desire is for Ethiopia to "stretch forth her hands unto God." She yearns for both political freedom and spiritual piety.[43]

She grounds her claims for equality and justice in creation: "He hath formed and fashioned you in his own glorious image, and hath bestowed upon you reason and strong powers of intellect." She weaves back and forth, as Walker does, between these biblical claims and political ones based in America's broken promises

46

("He hath crowned you with glory and honor . . . and according to the Constitution of the United States, he hath made all men free and equal").[44]

Stewart ends *Religion and the Pure Principles of Morality* with eschatological judgment. She is so certain that her people will be vindicated that she can speak as if it has already happened: "O, ye great and mighty men of America, you rich and powerful ones, many of you will call for the rocks and mountains to fall upon you, and to hide you from the wrath of the Lamb, and from them that sitteth upon the throne; while many of the sable-skinned Africans you now despise, will shine in the kingdom of heaven as the stars forever and ever."[45]

She references two political favorites toward the end: Jeremiah 6:14 and 8:11 ("Peace, peace; when there is no peace" KJV) and Proverbs 14:34 ("Righteousness exalteth a nation, but sin is a reproach to any people" KJV). Blending biblical language with contemporary concerns, she says with prophetic power, "Oh America, America, foul and indelible is thy stain! Dark and dismal is the cloud that hangs over thee, for thy cruel wrongs and injuries to the fallen sons of Africa." Then, alluding to the second sin in the Bible: "The blood of her murdered ones cries to heaven for vengeance against thee."[46]

Civil War Hermeneutics

What can the Civil War period—especially the difference between the approaches to the biblical text described here—teach us about political hermeneutics today? Most important, while white people fought about German historical criticism, idealist and transcendentalist philosophy, and the genealogy of Noah's sons, Black people approached the relationship between ethics and Scripture in an entirely different way. What does that teach us?

Prooftexts versus Narrative

Many of the scholars writing about the Bible in this period will contrast the "literal" hermeneutic of the South with the increasingly "liberal" hermeneutic of the North.[47] But both white slaveholders and white abolitionists had their favorite verses, and both had narratives that made sense of those prooftexts. Each of those narratives was informed by other sources of knowledge and experience—the proslavery folks read the Bible with the "plantation ethic" of hierarchy, order, and racial subjugation in mind while the antislavery folks read the Bible with republican egalitarianism and American ideals of freedom in mind.[48]

The question is not *whether* we read Scripture within a narrative framework but *which framework* we use. We are storytelling creatures, constantly making connections and drawing lines between different ideas, looking for themes and similarities, and trying to tell the kind of story that we would want to play a part in. While some white abolitionists resorted to abstract moral principles drawn from cherry-picked verses, many of them were also just . . . doing theology. The proslavery proponents may have claimed they were taking the Bible "literally" when they quoted verses about slaves obeying their masters, but abolitionists could claim the same when they quoted verses about the image of God, commands to sacrifice for the weak and poor, and narratives of liberation. Both sides had to appeal to narratives that could make sense of both kinds of verses in Scripture.

Social Location

Many Black Americans, by contrast, appealed to the story of God's redemptive work in creation. They described themselves as participants in that narrative, finding themselves in the biblical stories in a very different position than white debaters. Slaveholders needed to appeal to "the security of specific, literal, written warrant" to justify actions that were deeply contrary to Christian faith, while enslaved and free Black people saw their own plight narrated in Scripture.[49] We should note that the most marginalized and oppressed people were the most able to grasp the meaning of the Bible—a text written by marginalized and oppressed people.[50] During a debate about slavery in Cincinnati in 1845, minister Jonathan Blanchard said of proslavery Christians, "They have seen the Bible through slave-holding spectacles; and have interpreted Hebrew words by European and American practices."[51]

While all humans are impacted by their cultural and political contexts, certain forces are more seductive than others—power and wealth among the most seductive. It is not that white people were inherently less able to read the Bible well and Black people were inherently more able to understand it. But one significant lesson from the Bible—its own composition and a constant theme of its narrative—is that the powerful are often deceived about their own sin and the powerless are prioritized by God.

Providence and Reading History

Americans have always sensed that God is on "our side." Everyone appealed to divine providence in this period, in a dizzying diversity of ways. The Civil War exemplifies the difficulties with understanding our earthly causes as part of a divine purpose—but it also exemplifies the faithful potential of believing in God's sovereignty.

Both the Union and the Confederacy perceived themselves as fighting "God's fight." The Confederacy was defending the Bible and a divine social order; the Union was defending the Bible and God's command to obey the government. Throughout the war, each side interpreted events in light of this chosen status. As a result, defeats or failures were not causes for questioning this status but evidence of God's chastising judgment.[52]

Each side also grappled with their sense of national history and its relationship to God's divine plan—there was a raging debate not only about the Bible but about the meaning of founding American documents. What did contemporary distance from biblical history mean for interpreting the Bible? What did distance from the era of the founding mean for interpreting the Constitution?[53] Some melded those two questions into one. In a famous 1861 speech, Confederate leader Alexander Hamilton Stephens used the biblical image of the cornerstone (Mark 12:10) to judge America's founders: just as Jesus was the rejected cornerstone of the church—ridiculed by religious leaders but ultimately the foundation of the faith—so too was slavery, the foundation of the country, wrongly ridiculed by the founders.[54]

Biblical Ethics

Perhaps the most significant lesson from this period, however, is not about any one passage of Scripture but the way we think about ethics and the Bible. Both abolitionists and proslavery writers sought a hermeneutic that would produce timeless, universal principles. Abolitionists looked to moral intuition or general themes of Scripture to find abstract moral principles. Proslavery writers appealed to verses about slaves in the Old or New Testament as universal rules that could be applied in any context. Both sides were influenced by Enlightenment-era notions that "moral or spiritual perception could be crystal clear and that the means of moral action lay entirely within the grasp of well-meaning individuals."[55] In other words, moral action would be clear for rational humans, and we are not limited by sin or human finitude to know what is right and how to act on it.

By contrast, Black abolitionists were largely uninterested in abstract morals or deriving timeless immutable principles from Scripture.[56] Instead, they focused on particular stories and the ethics displayed in them. They saw themselves in the plight of the Israelites in Egypt, in David facing Goliath, in the oppressed faithful fighting off the devil in Revelation. When they heard biblical narratives that fit their experience of the world, it was natural to ask: What does *this* moment require of me now?

They recognized something we all need to recognize—that just as Scripture was given in particular circumstances, our own ethical questions will always be particular. This is the nature of all ethical reflection, that we evaluate the context we find ourselves in—including our social positions and resources, our various responsibilities and obligations, and the opportunities for meaningful action in front of us—and ask what is required of us in *this* time and place.

God did not reveal himself to us through *particular* stories, letters, and prophecies and then ask us to abstract them all into principles that can be applied in all times and places. The Bible is not a riddle to be solved, or a mess of historical stories we need to sift through to find gems of truth underneath. Scripture is given to us as a gift of particularity—a word given to a particular people at a particular place. The miracle is not that we can get rid of that particularity but that we are grafted into it. This is what enslaved people saw: themselves as the people of God suffering in Egypt or Babylon or Rome, with narratives and prophecies and letters that could help them navigate life under these conditions.

Of course, this does *not* mean that truth is relative or that systematic teaching derived from biblical accounts is bad. God has given creation a moral order—a good gift of absolute, unshakable truth about how we are meant to flourish in relationship to God and each other. But as finite, fallen creatures, our attempts at discerning that order will always be provisional and prone to error. We are time- and place-bound creatures, so of course all our ethics will be bound to a time and place.

Because we are finite creatures, we need help understanding the Bible, our contexts, and ourselves. Theology is the work of the church in response to the revelation of God. It seeks to harmonize, articulate, and apply the revelation given to God's people in God's Word. This is not about stripping off the outer garments of culture and particularity and finding the kernel of universal truth underneath but about seeking to grow in love and understanding of the God who has graciously revealed himself in human culture and particularity. Christians have always sought to harmonize the biblical account into theological truths. What do we do with the Old Testament worship of one God, the New Testament revelation of Jesus, and the gift of the Holy Spirit at Pentecost? We do theology. But we do not have to abstract these ideas away from the specific times and places God revealed himself in Scripture in order to do that.

Southern Presbyterian minister Joseph R. Wilson, in his defense of slavery, railed against those who treat the Bible as a "dead letter." The Bible is eternally relevant, he insisted, "intended for all times in all ages, and not for one period and a single country."[57]

He was correct that the Bible is not a dead letter. But what does it mean for it to be for "all times in all ages"? It surely cannot mean that any single verse pulled from Scripture is relevant to every and any circumstance. It cannot mean that a law given to the nation of Israel about slavery can be plucked out of its context and held up as a principle for all time.

And it cannot mean that Scripture offers us universal principles that absolve us of any responsibility to examine the specifics of the situation in front of us. We are not freed from the reality that in our fallen creation we will face challenging moral questions—challenging not only because we have to think hard but also because we might be asked to risk or sacrifice our own comfort and power.

If there is any universal moral prescription in Scripture, it's the one white slaveholders and slavery defenders most often missed: sin will warp our moral intuition and biblical interpretation. We need the stories of Scripture and the witness of marginalized and oppressed people today to help us see clearly and hear the Word of the Lord in our particular time and place. We will not know how we should now live without living in community with people who can help us see ourselves, our world, and Scripture clearly.

Your Kingdom Come

Social Gospel Hermeneutics

The social gospel looms large in evangelical criticisms of theology that motivate social reform or left-leaning activism. Theologian Walter Rauschenbusch was aware he needed to convince conservative readers that his work was truly biblical, defending that the social gospel was not some "alien or novel" idea but "built on the foundation of the apostles and prophets." The social gospel, he said, is actually "the oldest gospel of all."[1]

Evangelicals should have agreed with his assessment. Evangelicals have a long history of social reform that includes the work of abolitionists like Harriet Beecher Stowe and Charles Finney, national efforts toward prohibition and prison reform, and support of public education and welfare programs. How did the social gospel movement impact evangelicals' reading of the Bible (and of history)? And what are the possibilities and problems in that theology?

This chapter looks at a few examples of social gospel theology in order to better understand how we can apply eternal promises of flourishing to earthly reform. How do we articulate the political applications of the gospel without too closely identifying earthly politics with the kingdom of God? How do we know when we are responsible for creating change and when to recognize our own limitations and wait, in prayer and confession, for Christ's return? How do we know what the kingdom of God looks like and how to earnestly pray, "Your kingdom come"?

Social Gospel History

The term "social gospel" suffers from multiple misunderstandings. It can be defined in overly broad and overly narrow ways, its history is complex, and it has become a boogeyman in some circles. For some evangelicals, "social gospel" is a derogatory term that can be applied to any theology that *includes* social change as a part of the gospel message. For others, it's a negative term but with a narrower meaning: any theology that *reduces* the Christian message of cosmic salvation to social change. Then there's the tricky question of what *kind* of social change is intended. A famous 1921 definition of the social gospel is incredibly broad: "the application of the teaching of Jesus and the total message of the Christian salvation to society, the economic life, and social institutions such as the state, the family, as well as to individuals."[2] Even the conservative Christians who criticize the social gospel surely see their own efforts at faithfulness described in such a definition.

It's more helpful to define the social gospel as a Christian movement that came about in a specific context. As the previous chapters illustrate, no reading of Scripture comes from nowhere. Instead, communities interpret Scripture within the context of the pressing concerns of their time, with the tools and philosophical trends available to them, and with their own biases and community shaping their reading.

The social gospel movement came from a particular theological and historical context. According to scholar Christopher H. Evans, it "applied liberal theology to a range of social reform measures that would become associated with the political left."[3] In the late nineteenth and early twentieth centuries, in the post–Civil War political era of Progressivism, some theologians began searching for ways to reconcile Christian theological claims with new scientific knowledge and social reform efforts.[4]

The late nineteenth-century Progressive Era was a period of social reform and activism from within a variety of institutions and religious backgrounds. It was held together by shared beliefs about the progressive trajectory of society, the power of education and scientific advances to change the world, and greater confidence in government regulation. In this period of industrialization and urbanization, Americans were paying greater attention to social inequality and were confident that applying the scientific method to social problems would bring greater prosperity.

Many social gospel proponents shared two important experiences: theological training in institutions shaped by liberal theology and ministry in inner-city contexts. In this period, "liberal theology" refers to a theological tradition that included an emphasis on literary and historical criticism of the Bible, a prioritization of ethics above other doctrinal issues, a focus on human knowledge of God over God's transcendence, a high view of human goodness and progress, and a focus on the social life of the church.[5]

The social gospel movement largely developed as an outgrowth of the broader liberal theology project. But because the movement was less about doctrine and more about right action, it led to surprising friendships and coalitions. The movement included more than only liberal theologians and pastors. The Fundamentalist-Modernist controversy of the 1920s and '30s between "conservatives" and "liberals" was not yet full-blown, so there was more room for cooperation, especially because the issue of social reform had not yet become a defining difference between the two groups. Liberal theologians could have more conservative social thought, and vice versa.

All religion in America in this period was concerned about social issues like poverty, labor unions, alcohol, and housing.[6] When we look at the history of American Christianity, we can discern different traditions, denominations, and institutions with their own cultures and habits when it comes to reading the Bible, but we really can't draw strict lines between them—we have always had cross-pollination. Both liberal and conservative Christians at the time wanted to "win souls" and reform the social order, often explicitly articulating a desire to "Christianize" the nation.[7]

To this point, the social gospel movement was shaped by both liberal Protestantism and evangelicalism. First, evangelicalism was everywhere. The wide reach of the Great Awakenings meant that most of American religion was shaped by evangelicalism. Second, evangelicals' focus on personal conversion always had a social component. After the Civil War, evangelicals became involved in a range of issues: poverty, temperance, slum housing, racism, the labor movement. While evangelicals focused more on moral solutions to social problems, they recognized the communal nature of sin.[8] Even the social gospel movement's interest in God's involvement in human history was influenced by evangelicalism: as historian Timothy L. Smith describes it, if God felt close in nineteenth-century America, it was not because of theological trends among an elite group of scholars but because in revivals across the country "the 'tongue of fire' had descended on the disciples, freeing them from the bondage of sin and selfishness, and dedicating them to the task of making over the world."[9] "Awakenings," a hallmark of evangelicalism, have always had social, political, and economic elements.

Interest in social reform did not become a dividing line within the American church until the twentieth century. Here's why this is important: the social gospel is part of evangelical heritage too.[10] Not only did the social gospel movement include evangelicals, but the entire movement was shaped by zeal for mission and the drive of evangelism—characteristic traits of evangelicals.[11]

The movement was also always shaped by Scripture. There was great interest in the Old Testament prophets, the words and ministry of Jesus, and the economic and social elements of the early church. Special attention was paid to passages that emphasized God's work in human history, especially in using humans to accomplish larger purposes or "change the course of history."[12]

The Founder, the Nation, and the Kingdom

Washington Gladden

Walter Rauschenbusch became the social gospel's most famous theologian, but Washington Gladden is considered its "father." Gladden pastored several churches, served as the religious editor of the New York weekly magazine *The Independent*, and helped build several social gospel institutions. His approach shifted over time. He started with a more individual focus, encouraging the wealthy toward philanthropy and business owners to treat their workers better, but he slowly began thinking about structural barriers to justice. His approach to Scripture also developed throughout his life in a variety of ways.[13]

Gladden adopted tenets of higher biblical criticism and sought to reconcile Scripture with modern science, history, and philosophy. He argued that the Bible is "primarily" a book about human history and religious experience, and so it is historically, scientifically, and morally flawed. Gladden denied that the Bible was made up only of "tales and myths," affirming instead that the "treasure-truth of God" had mingled with the "moral-earthen vessel of man's historical experience."[14] He even incorporated biblical criticism into some of his sermons. He noted that some verses were missing from ancient manuscripts and said that portions of the Old Testament were "works of fiction." More than other ministers of his time who were taught higher criticism in seminary and then discarded the teaching in the pulpit, Gladden thought the church should be discussing higher criticism openly.[15]

He began one sermon on the final words of the Lord's Prayer in Matthew 6 ("for thine is the kingdom, and the power, and the glory, for ever" KJV) by saying, "My text is not in my Bible. It may be in yours, but it is not in mine. The oldest and best manuscript copies of the New Testament do not contain it." But then he added, "They are inspired words, for the spirit of truth is in them."[16] This is crucial for understanding Gladden's approach to the Bible: he denied infallibility and applied modern scientific and historical standards to test the texts' reliability. But he thought this could be done while still respecting Scripture. Instead of treating the whole text as entirely truthful and authoritative, however, he appealed to progressive revelation and religious development: revelation evolved over time, as successive generations more fully understood God's will.[17] You can tell that Matthew 6:13 is authoritative because you sense the spirit of truth in it, a moral standard apart from Scripture itself but applied to it.

Learning about Gladden's life and ministry is important to understand his theology, because it was shaped by his pastoral and political work. A good chunk of his public writing and work was done from his position as pastor of First Congregational Church in Columbus, Ohio, where he preached on "personal religion" on Sunday mornings and "social Christianity" on Sunday evenings.[18] Much of his writings are collections of these sermons. These two elements—personal spiritual change and social transformation— were always integrated for Gladden. "The end of Christianity is twofold," he wrote, "a perfect man in a perfect society." The gospel is addressed to individuals, but no person can be saved alone. This "vital and necessary relation" between the personal and the social is at the heart of the Christian faith.[19]

"The Nation and the Kingdom"

One of Gladden's sermons, "The Nation and the Kingdom," illustrates how the social gospel movement interpreted Scripture— and why later opponents rejected the approach.[20] In this 1909 sermon given at the American Board of Commissioners for Foreign Missions, Gladden preached from Isaiah on the central importance the nation plays in God's plan for creation. In one sense, this focus was natural for a sermon directed at a missions organization—it describes the Christian faith being spread from America to other countries. In another sense, however, it carries a strangely intense focus on the power of *America* to morally, economically, and socially shape the nations of the world.

Gladden goes to a familiar genre for this sermon: the exhortation of an Old Testament prophet. The two verses he selects as his text are part of a larger portion of Isaiah describing the coming

glory of Zion, a promise of prosperity in the midst of suffering
and judgment.

> Lift up your eyes and look about you:
>   All assemble and come to you;
> your sons come from afar,
>   and your daughters are carried on the hip.
> Then you will look and be radiant,
>   your heart will throb and swell with joy;
> the wealth on the seas will be brought to you,
>   to you the riches of the nations will come. (Isa. 60:4–5)

Isaiah expects "a regenerated society," Gladden says, "a society
from which injustice and oppression and misery and want and all
iniquity and wrong shall be put away; in which peace and good
will shall abide and order and security shall reign." This vision is
not for the religious community but for the *nation*. The prophets
had a message of the kingdom of God that was directed toward
nations. The prophets' "glowing promises" of future flourishing
are made "to the nation and not the church," and so "through the
nation" the kingdom of God will reign on earth. While the family represents some of the flourishing social life that God desires
for people and the church illustrates "certain of the gentler and
humbler" parts of the common life, "to know what Christianity
is, we must see it at work on the scale of the nation."[21]

Gladden says this "glorious society" has "irresistible attrac-
tion." Drawing on language of new creation from Isaiah and
Revelation, Gladden describes a good society that is universally
desired. Absent from this account is anything apocalyptic—there
is no coming judgment, no crisis or catastrophe that precedes the
newness, and very little emphasis on divine action. Unlike the civil
rights activists we'll hear from in the next chapter, Gladden strikes
a central social gospel note here: God is doing great things in the
world, but "He cannot do them without us."[22]

Even Jesus sounds fairly powerless to initiate the prophets' vision without help. Gladden says of the Sermon on the Mount:
"What would have happened if the social aim of Jesus could have

been realized then and there, if the society which is outlined in that great discourse could have been established in that little country of Palestine, we may faintly imagine." The world was not ready for Jesus's radical social vision, but it is now. Gladden echoes Rauschenbusch on this: the cultural context of the early church did not allow the apostles to enact Jesus's vision; they would have been killed by the emissaries of the Roman Empire. "This is the reason why the social aims of Jesus were not realized in his day," Gladden says.[23] The "seed" of his vision needed to grow in secret for generations before there was room for a "Christian social order" to bloom (never mind the centuries of "Christian emperors" and nations and state churches in between then and now). The time has come when the principles of Christianity might prevail.

America plays a special role in drawing other nations toward social reform. "The day is not distant" when nations will follow America's lead. Gladden says that the text of Isaiah sounds "like a transcript from a current history of the United States," which needed to be reformed in order to draw the other nations into social change as well. Immigration is proof that America embodies Christian principles irresistibly attractive to the "heart of universal humanity." The nations are recognizing America's greatness and turning "with wistful hope" to America for leadership. Toward the end of the sermon, Gladden says America could end international conflict and display the "glory of Christianity." We've sent great preachers into the world, he tells the missions board, but few are as effective as William McKinley and Theodore Roosevelt and William H. Taft. Gladden concedes there are some "evil tendencies" in American families, but those tendencies cannot compare with the tendencies in other societies (he mentions China, India, and Turkey) that permit abuse of women and a lack of education among children. [24]

Lots of social gospelers used the language of "Christianizing" a society. For many of them (Gladden included) this was about submitting the political, economic, and social life of a community to the power of Christ. Humans are responsible for "Christianizing" the nations, and Gladden is wildly optimistic about our chances of success. Like most social gospelers (and many theologians in this period in general), Gladden holds to a postmillennial eschatology—the expectation that increasing receptivity to the gospel will produce a period of faithfulness and prosperity before Christ returns. Everything was much worse even a hundred years ago, and in spite of the "pessimists" who point out current failures, the fact that Americans are shocked and saddened by the moral failures of the period proves that the nation's "moral forces" are stronger than they've ever been. (As a reminder, Gladden waxes poetic about the "rising standard of political morality" before the civil rights movement.) There are two tasks, then, for the listening audience: pour love and strength into preparing the way for Christ, and "make this nation fit to be a witness for Him, so that when the banner of our country and the banner of the cross are seen floating together, it shall be evident to all men that the day has come when mercy and truth are met together, and righteousness and peace have kissed each other."[25]

The End of the Social Gospel?

There's a popular history of the social gospel (and the Progressive Era more broadly) that says World War I dashed the movement's optimistic hopes for progress, dampening the goals of institutions, sounding a death knell for postmillennial theology, and chastening leaders convinced they were the saviors of the world. There's a lot of truth to this story. One former chaplain of the war said of himself and his fellow Christians, "We thought, at least many of us did, that we were fighting for great ideals, and that the winning of the war would give us a better world. Well, we know differently now."[26]

The story is also more complicated than that. The social gospel lived on in a variety of forms. World War II would pick back up on the movement's progressive idealism and blend it with patriotism, leading many Protestants to focus their attention on the power of American democratic institutions rather than the socially transformative power of the church.[27] The civil rights movement would draw on many of the same theological resources. While the optimism of the theology may have deflated, the social gospel lived on in the form of a great religious legacy: theological resources for political activism, hymns that spurred policies and protests, and lasting institutions.[28]

Theologian Reinhold Niebuhr's book *Moral Man and Immoral Society* exemplifies the judgment many theologians into the twentieth century had of the social gospel movement. Niebuhr shared much of the theological and ministry background of the social gospelers: he was trained in liberal theology, pastored a church in Detroit, and became passionate about economic and social justice. World War I and the economic collapse in the 1930s tempered his expectations for social reform. *Moral Man and Immoral Society* expresses concern over unwarranted optimism about the goodness of human societies.[29] In particular, Niebuhr was worried that people convinced of their own goodness and pure intentions were even *more* dangerous than people who openly acted from self-interest.[30] While Niebuhr's theology would develop throughout his career, he remained concerned about the unfettered optimism of his theological peers. He influenced generations of political theorists to take more seriously the power of sin to warp human communities and institutions.

The Hermeneutics of the Kingdom of God

The social gospelers have a lot to teach us about how to use Scripture well for political purposes. They identified biblical passages that went unnoticed or unappreciated in many churches, they took exhortations to care for the vulnerable seriously and *literally*, and in a time when some theological trends encouraged replacing Scripture with social science, they held to its importance.

They also can teach us through their problems and pitfalls. Many of them prioritized moral teaching in Scripture but minimized the teaching about Christ's work on the cross. Others appealed to Scripture when it suited them but undermined its authority by subordinating it to human moral judgments. Perhaps most importantly, many of these reformers sought to draw on specific texts (the Old Testament prophets especially) but abstracted the texts from their larger biblical narrative. They quoted Isaiah or Jeremiah but did not exegete them in the context of the whole story of Scripture. They referenced Jesus's ministry of healing the sick and feeding the hungry but didn't spend much time talking about the cross.

This era of preachers, theologians, and activists can help us think better about the theology of Scripture, the relationship between the nation and the Bible, and what it means to take the Bible "literally."

Theology of Scripture

The Bible was central to the social gospel movement: the passionate words of the prophets exhorted pastors and activists to work for justice, the life and ministry of Jesus prompted people to care for the vulnerable, and the story of Israel encouraged people to think about love and justice in communal terms. But as churches and denominations fought, splintered, or split between the Modernists and the Fundamentalists in the 1920s and '30s, a certain narrative was told: the conservatives take the Bible seriously, and the liberals don't.

This isn't accurate. It's more accurate to say that different theological camps emphasized different parts of the Bible and thought differently about what the Bible is. The liberals tended to emphasize the prophets and the life of Jesus; the conservatives emphasized the Old Testament law, Wisdom literature, and doctrinal teaching in the Epistles. When they did interpret the "other side's" favorite parts, they read them with a different hermeneutic. The conservatives often read texts as having purely or primarily individual or spiritual meanings; the liberals read them as having purely or primarily social and political meanings. Theological commitments always shape how we read Scripture, and everyone's theological emphases will be shaped by the failures or faults they identify in their current context.

One conservative, John Warwick Montgomery, saw the mutual failures of the conflict clearly: "But why don't we follow our own advice? The liberals use the visible scissors and paste of destructive biblical criticism while we employ the invisible scissors and paste of selective hermeneutics: we preach only those texts that do not make us socially uncomfortable."[31] Liberal theologians were disregarding the parts of the Bible that their higher criticism deemed questionable. But many conservative theologians claimed to believe the whole Bible while virtually ignoring portions of it that did not fit their politics.

We can learn at least two things from this larger conflict: (1) we need to examine our own theological frameworks, emphases, and biases, and (2) we need to read the *whole* Bible. We need to have honest conversations about the fact that rarely is any debate among orthodox Christians truly a debate between the clear teaching of the Bible and a position that has abandoned the Bible. Instead, we all read the Bible with inevitable glasses on. We've talked already about how we don't just read with our own biases—personal, cultural, racial, historical, and so on—but we also read (rightly!) with our theological frameworks. We look for how a particular verse can fit into our larger framework—whether we call it a "system" or a "story"—and fitting it into that larger framework will shape how we understand it.

We will need to spend time intentionally studying theology, specifically theology about our political life together, to do this well. But reading theologians and pastors from this period can help us clarify some good nonnegotiables.

In the story of Scripture, God is the main character. God is not just another agent in the universe, battling it out with slightly smaller human agents. God is sovereign over all of human history, the creator of everything that exists, and worthy of our worship and love. Scripture is also the story of God's characteristic way of entering history on behalf of creation: through humans, and most often on behalf of the poor and marginalized. God graciously allows us to work with him toward the flourishing communities he intends for humans.

Sin is both personal and communal. When we read Scripture and see only structural or systemic sin, we are missing something. When we read Scripture and see only personal or individual sin, we are missing something. Sin infects individual humans *and* communities and human-made structures. It has personal *and* cosmic effects.

These two important frameworks combine to highlight something crucially important for us to learn from the social gospel (both its proponents and opponents): *the depth of sin in the world requires divine action.* If our readings of Scripture diminish either the cosmic or communal effects of sin or the priority of divine action, we lose the power and significance of Jesus's work on the cross. The social gospel often forgot the cross; its opponents often forgot why the cross was necessary.

We will avoid some of these mistakes if we have the whole counsel of Scripture informing our political theology. Certain passages are more relevant to political and social questions, and some are more relevant to the contours of a particular pressing situation, but the whole of Scripture teaches about who God is, God's creation, and the nature of humans and human communities. We should notice when we are finding ourselves drawn primarily or exclusively to certain passages or genres of Scripture and examine *why* that might be. Does this moment need the passionate and firm words of a prophetic critique? Or do we enjoy imagining ourselves as the righteous truth-teller? These are not questions we can answer with a list of hermeneutical principles. These are questions we must ask repeatedly, within the context of community and with reliance on the Holy Spirit.

Christian Nationalism

The social gospel movement helps us straighten out how we use the Bible in relation to our *nation.* As we have already seen, Americans have always used biblical and theological language to talk about American identity and mission—but not always in the same way. The concept of Christian nationalism has become hotly debated post-2016, especially after the January 6, 2021, attacks on the US Capitol.

Sociologists Samuel Perry and Andrew Whitehead define Christian nationalism as "a cultural framework—a collective of myths, traditions, symbols, narratives, and value systems—that idealizes and advocates a fusion of Christianity with civic life."[32] There are significant differences between the social gospel movement and twenty-first-century Christian nationalism, but the two are connected. Many social gospelers spoke about "Christianizing" the nation—with mixed meaning and motives. They did not have in mind the right-wing politics of January 6 rioters; they usually had progressive economic policies in mind. But the social gospelers had their faults as well.

Gary Dorrien describes the well-known failures of the social gospel movement: it preached a "Jesus of middle-class idealism," was populated by middle- to upper-class preachers as its "prophets," was "culturally chauvinistic," baptized the ideology of Manifest Destiny, and justified American imperialism. It "fell short" of including racial justice or women's rights in its aims.[33]

The triumphs and failures of the social gospel should chasten our enthusiasm for our own "Christianizing" projects—whether of the right or the left. They should remind us that bringing Christian convictions to bear on political work is important, difficult, and potentially dangerous. We always risk covering our own cultural values or personal preferences with religious garb, and we always risk the allure of political power blunting our prophetic voice. Yet the real, material, influential work of the social gospelers should keep us from despair: they served the poor, advocated for social safety net policies, and articulated theology and built institutions that continue to do work on behalf of the poor and vulnerable today.

Taking the Bible "Literally"

Of all the things we say about the Bible, perhaps nothing is more confused and abused than the word "literally." In some communities, we pride ourselves on taking the Bible "literally"; in other communities, words like "biblicist" or "literalist" are insults. No one takes every word of the Bible "literally." The psalms are poetry, the Old Testament narratives use figurative language, and Jesus speaks in parables and riddles. A central debate between social gospelers and opponents (and between later conservatives and liberation theologians) was regarding what Jesus means when he talks about the "poor." Does he mean literal poor people, or is he using that language to describe the spiritual needs of all people?

You could argue that the social gospel takes Scripture more literally: the exhortations of the prophets should be heeded seriously; Jesus is serious when he tells the rich young ruler to give away all his possessions; the language James uses for the wealthy should be taken literally. Yet many social gospelers were influenced by liberal theology to be suspicious of Scripture when it describes miracles or to downplay the central place of the cross and atonement in the New Testament.

Rather than focusing on "literal" interpretations of Scripture, we should examine the hermeneutics we're bringing to the text. Why do we prioritize this passage over this other one? Why do we emphasize what we emphasize? Ultimately, the social gospel challenges us to take Scripture *seriously*. Does Jesus's ministry confront us with a radically different set of priorities than our own ministries? Does the communal life of Israel or the early church place an obligation on us to shape our lives differently? Do the words of the prophets—words like the following from Isaiah—convict and confront us?

> When you spread out your hands in prayer,
>   I hide my eyes from you;
> even when you offer many prayers,
>   I am not listening.
>
> Your hands are full of blood!
>
> Wash and make yourselves clean.
>   Take your evil deeds out of my sight;
>   stop doing wrong.
> Learn to do right; seek justice.
>   Defend the oppressed.
> Take up the cause of the fatherless;
>   plead the case of the widow. (Isa. 1:15–17)

Evangelical Legacy of Social Reform

Finally, it's worth reiterating that this is not a history distinct from evangelicalism. The history of biblical interpretation in America is not the history of distinct traditions inhabiting their own space, reading their Bibles together, and going their own ways. Evangelical Christians and social gospel Christians collaborated during this period, and the hermeneutical trends of this period shaped theologians across a variety of traditions. Evangelicals have a rich history of social and political work that predates the rise of the religious right in the latter half of the twentieth century. For evangelicals wary of the recent legacy of political engagement they have inherited, this history provides a very different posture and approach to political engagement from which to draw.

So why did evangelicals become so afraid of the "social gospel"? There were conservatives throughout this period expressing concern about the influence of liberal theological and historical-critical methods of biblical interpretation. But it wasn't until the Fundamentalist-Modernist split that people associated social reform with "liberal theology."[34] Timothy Smith famously called it the "great reversal": evangelical leaders who had supported the labor movement and other justice movements abandoned them after World War I, as evangelicals emphasized personal salvation over holistic revival.[35]

Eventually, the social gospel was linked to theological liberalism, and evangelicals felt it was important to distance themselves from it. "The sharp polarization that developed during the conflict made it politically impossible to remain both an evangelical and a social gospeler, and emotional involvements prevented Christians from recognizing the fallacies of being impaled upon the horns of a false dilemma," David Moberg writes.[36]

Many Protestant churches, evangelical and mainline, became richer and more secluded from the poor and the immigrants in the period following the Progressive Era. Their lack of exposure to the material needs of the most socially marginalized, the general pessimism about social reform after World War I, and shifting theological emphases (including eschatology, which we'll return to in chapter 7) all contributed to this great reversal. Additionally, the lack of emphasis on evangelism and spiritual questions in the social gospel churches pushed the conservatives toward *exclusive* emphasis on personal, spiritual solutions to social problems—and vice versa. The conservatives increasingly understood the "social gospel" as a "departure" from the real gospel—a substitution of biblical revelation for a different gospel.[37]

The history of the social gospel should be a reminder for all Christians to learn from our past with both a critical eye and a charitable heart. Not only might you discover that someone else's history is actually just as much your own, but that combination of criticism and generosity provides space to learn more widely and freely. For all its faults and failures, the social gospel movement in America emphasized biblical passages that had gone unnoticed, motivated institutions to create lasting change in communities, and continued the church's historic concern for social issues.

5

A Stick of Dynamite

Civil Rights and Scripture

Martin Luther King Jr.'s "I Have a Dream" speech is as much a feature of the American story as Winthrop's "city upon a hill." And just as Winthrop drew on biblical language to inspire a people, King's speech drew on biblical language for social and political work. King quoted from the Bible many times, most famously: "I have a dream that one day every valley shall be exalted, every hill and mountain shall be made low, the rough places will be made plain, and the crooked places will be made straight, and the glory of the Lord shall be revealed, and all flesh shall see it together."[1]

King's reference to Isaiah 40:4–5 exemplifies how much the civil rights movement was energized by Scripture. Leaders referenced the prophets, the exodus, and the message of Jesus. This chapter focuses on the liberating message of the prophets and how marginalized Christians have found comfort and courage to fight for political change. It also addresses the common responses by prosegregationist pastors, especially the "spiritualizing" impulse to deny the material implications of the gospel. Finally, it draws on this history to help us think about how we read the story of the Bible: how and where we hear the story, where we see ourselves in it, and whether that story shapes our work today.

The Bible and the Civil Rights Movement

Many chapters in the story of the civil rights movement have been forgotten, modified, or intentionally misrepresented. White Americans tend to imagine the movement as less controversial than it was, white resistance as less violent than it was, and the resolution more final and satisfying than it was. Many Americans also forget—or ignore—the significant role that religion played in motivating and strengthening both the movement and its opponents. The Bible unsurprisingly played a significant role.

In the Movement

Many scholars describe the civil rights movement as a political movement with religious dressing—useful for the movement's purposes but not central to the message. But the work of historian David L. Chappell, based on testimonies by civil rights activists and leaders, contradicts this. Their accounts indicate that "it was, for them, primarily a religious event."[2]

Black American Christians never had the option of separating their faith and political work. As biblical scholar Esau McCaulley says, "Due to the era into which it was born, the Black church found it necessary to protest a policy put in place by the state: slavery."[3] Other scholars trace the roots of Black church activism from secret churches during slavery to early Black denominations like the African Methodist Episcopal Church to the mobilizing role of the Black church in the civil rights movement. While formal denominational institutions and local churches were generally more conservative and less activist, the sermons, prayers, songs, and call-and-response interactions that formed those communities were central in animating and sustaining political action.[4]

Civil rights participants used biblical language to describe their motivations. One alluded to Joshua 24:15: "But as for me, I will serve the Civil Rights Movement. . . . As for me and my house, I will serve the Lord." Another said, "There is a scripture in the Bible, 'faith without works is dead.'" One activist, when met with the claim that the church "wasn't the place" for social activism, said, "I have read the Bible some. The Bible tells me 'out of one blood one nation came to dwell on all the face of the earth.' . . . That was in me, I couldn't get it out of me." Another referenced Jesus's words in Luke 4: "God is on the side of the oppressed."[5] Victoria Gray Adams, an activist from Mississippi, described joining the movement as a kind of conversion experience: she heard the words from Isaiah 6, "Whom shall I send, whom can we send and who will go for us?" and felt that "at that moment it was my word of truth." She responded, "Here I am, send me."[6]

In a speech to the World Council of Churches in 1954, Benjamin E. Mays, mentor to Martin Luther King Jr. and president of Morehouse College, quoted numerous scriptures in support of the civil rights movement. He began by addressing the misuse of Old Testament passages against intermarrying, highlighting that they are concerned with religious purity, not racial purity. When we pray as Jesus taught us, Mays notes, we affirm our common family: "*Our* Father," we pray. The Bible is full of examples of Jesus teaching and living this truth: the story of the good Samaritan, the faith of the Roman centurion, the reminder that Elijah and Elisha ministered outside the people of Israel in Luke 4. The story of Pentecost confronts any of our attempts to maintain strict racial or ethnic lines: "At Pentecost, a new community was created." Mays cites Galatians 3:28, Acts 14:24–26, and Acts 10:28 to describe the new unity of the church.[7]

The language in the early days of the Student Nonviolent Coordinating Committee (SNCC), a major organization of the movement, was "steeped in theology," says historian Paul Harvey. They were fighting for integration, but that was not the end goal—which was, instead, the "redeemed community" or the "kingdom of God." Unita Blackwell, who volunteered in voter-registration efforts with the SNCC, said of her work, "I had found it in my Bible that all men were created equal and I didn't understand that, how come that this was my constitutional right and I couldn't have that?"[8]

Sentiments like Blackwell's were common, mixing the language of the Bible with the language of civil religion. Fannie Lou Hamer, community organizer and cofounder and vice chair of the Freedom Democratic Party, turned "This Little Light of Mine" into a song for freedom. Referring to Georgia police chief Laurie Pritchett, she sang, "This little light of mine, I'm gonna let it shine, let it shine, let it shine, let it shine. We've got the light of freedom, we're gonna let it shine. . . . Tell Chief Pritchett, I'm gonna let it shine. . . . I'm voting for my freedom, I'm gonna let it shine."[9] We might criticize some mixing of the Bible with civil religion, but this history reminds us that doing so is not always "Christian nationalism" but is at times calling America to account, demanding it keep its promises.

Many white ministers and congregants opposed desegregation and other civil rights goals, and many more others were passive "moderates" who stalled the movement. Others supported and sacrificed for the cause. One minister in Little Rock, Marion A. Boggs, preached a sermon titled "The Crucial Test of Christian Citizenship" in 1957. He argued that the church's silence on civil rights was cowardly and a "neglect of urgent duty," because segregation is a "direct contradiction to the Christian Doctrine of the Dignity of man." He cited Acts 10:34–35 ("God is no respecter of persons"), Ephesians 2:11–20 (Jesus destroyed the "dividing wall of hostility"), and Galatians 2:11–14 (on discrimination between Jews and gentiles) to show that "passage after passage in the Bible confirms and supports this position."[10]

Everett Tilson wrote a book in 1958 directly addressing the supposed biblical evidence for racial segregation. *Segregation and the Bible* argued that the "Genesis myth" (the "curse of Ham" discussed in chap. 3) could not withstand serious analysis, that no real argument for segregation could be made from the passages in Ezekiel about intermixing plant and animal forms, and that the New Testament condemns racial prejudice.[11] Others went even further, arguing that segregation was one part of a larger social structure that Scripture condemned. One Congregational minister asked a question in 1945 that epitomizes this way of reading the Bible: "Will the churches of the South," he asked, "whose Holy Book is not a stick of candy but a stick of dynamite," bring to "the farm and factory worker a good wage, a decent house, a free assembly, a brotherhood enfolding all races?"[12]

Segregationist Arguments

Of course, the Bible also played a significant role in segregationist arguments. White churches and religious institutions—and the language and practices that formed them—both reproduced and reinforced the racial social life of the nineteenth and twentieth centuries.[13] Southerners carried resentment over the period known as Reconstruction—a short period of increasing racial equality and justice that had felt to them like "an overturning of a divinely ordered hierarchy." Fear of domination by Black Americans and concern about preserving racial and sexual purity fueled the racial politics of the period.[14]

The biblical "literalists" (again, this term is largely unhelpful, but it's how historians often describe white conservative Christians who made biblical arguments in support of slavery or Jim Crow) had a harder time making segregation an issue of biblical obedience than they had with slavery. There aren't short, simple verses to appeal to that clearly condone racial segregation. Instead, segregationists often paired verses with appeals to the unmistakable natural order of God's creation, larger theological themes, or cultural values. The state superintendent of education in North Carolina, for example, declared that any challenge to white supremacy was a "violation of God's eternal laws as fixed in the stars," and a church in Jackson, Mississippi, declared that "the facts of history make it plain that the development of civilization and of Christianity itself has rested in the hands of the white race."[15]

Segregationists also quoted Jesus's words "render unto Caesar," put forth absurd interpretations of obscure Old Testament passages, and described integration in apocalyptic terms.[16] Carey Daniel, pastor of First Baptist Church of West Dallas, Texas, cited the curse of Ham and Old Testament laws against intermarriage to support a biblical theology of segregation. Others appealed to the Tower of Babel in Genesis 11 as evidence that God intended the nations to be separated, argued that Jesus was a segregationist because he said that upon his return all nations would be gathered before him "and he will separate the people one from another" (Matt. 25:32), and claimed Philip the evangelist and the Ethiopian eunuch were only briefly together and then the Holy Spirit immediately "restored segregation."[17]

Many Southerners cited Acts 17:26–27, "He marked out their appointed times in history and the boundaries of their lands," as evidence of the divine ordination of segregation. For them, this verse perfectly described "God's Zion," the American South.[18] It didn't matter that theologians showed that these verses didn't apply to racial segregation in the South. In another dynamic familiar today, the loudest Christian voices in support of segregation were suspicious of "officially sanctioned modes of biblical interpretation."[19]

Church leaders and pastors struggled with if, when, and how they should challenge congregants' belief that segregation was divinely ordained. While church leaders were increasingly moving to support desegregation, they were often pastoring vehement opponents. Many described desegregation as a political issue that had no place in the church. One woman described her pastors: "Most hid their heads in the sand and spoke the language of the people in the church, even if they didn't believe it." It was more popular and common for people at all levels of church leadership to condemn "extremists on both sides."[20] The "white moderates" that King described in his "Letter from Birmingham Jail" were shaped by a theology of sin as solely individual, a view of social change as separate from the gospel, and ethics more formed by white, middle-class sensibilities than Scripture.

A Preacher Activist: Martin Luther King Jr.

Memory is a tricky thing. Whether it's our family memories or the shared stories of a larger community, remembering is a fraught endeavor that can distort as much as it represents, obscure as much as it illuminates.[21] When history becomes contested, caught up in divergent narratives about winners and losers, good guys and bad guys, it gets even more complicated. This is true of the civil rights movement, but it is especially true of one of its figureheads, Martin Luther King Jr.

Different people, with different interests and narratives, want to claim King—his words, work, and legacy. The dominant narrative in America often sanitizes him. We forget that King connected domestic racism with American imperialism, fought for labor rights, organized the Poor People's Campaign for economic justice, opposed the Vietnam War, and was assassinated as a political radical.[22]

King was born in 1929 in Atlanta, Georgia. He grew up in the church—in the language, ritual, story, and work of the gathered people of God. The Scripture that flows through his speeches and writings was learned from both academic study and during a childhood of memorizing passages, singing hymns, and listening to preachers (and imitating their sermons with his friends). The unique cadence of his later speeches was probably the fruit of memorizing so much Scripture in the King James Version.[23]

In seminary and graduate school, King "internalized the vocabulary and values of theological liberalism" but never fully accepted its tenets.[24] The Enlightenment account of humanity, nature, and God could not account for the depth of evil—or the redemption in suffering—that described his community's experience. King credits Rauschenbusch for leaving an "indelible imprint" on his thinking and giving him a theological foundation for the social and political work that was already central to his experience of Christianity. He criticizes Rauschenbusch, however, for falling victim to the "nineteenth-century cult of inevitable progress," being overly optimistic about human nature, and coming "perilously close" to identifying the kingdom of God with a particular political system.[25]

It is impossible to look at King's use of Scripture without thinking about his experience and understanding of the church. In church, King learned that the Word of God spoke directly to God's people: when the congregation verbally responds to the preacher, it confirms that the Lord is speaking through that preacher. Later, King would realize that this call-and-response was the "dress rehearsal" for the central performance of the Word—the social life of the people of God in the world.[26] When describing the Black church, King used a variety of images from the Old and New Testaments: "the least of these," "the chosen people," people in "Egyptian bondage."

In King's work on the church, the "most persistent single biblical symbol" is the exodus. Here his approach to Scripture and his theology of the church meet: the people of God are one community, their experiences are shared across time and space, and so King can take up the mantle of Moses standing in front of Pharaoh, crying, "Let my people go!"[27] King did not interpret Scripture in this way on his own, either. He intentionally drew on the interpretive legacy of enslaved people in America, insisting with his tradition that the exodus exemplified God's dealings with the poor and oppressed and that it provided a motivation for justice work in the present day. This was natural for a church community that was immersed in the language of Scripture, found itself described in the plights of Israel, and in the Bible discovered a divine mission for justice.

King posited that the civil rights movement was being hindered by incorrect interpretations of the Bible. In "Letter from Birmingham Jail," he describes churches that oppose or ignore social issues as committing themselves to the "un-Biblical distinction between body and soul, between the sacred and the secular." In a 1956 speech, he noted that "there is always the danger that religion and the Bible not properly interpreted can be used as forces to crystallize the status quo."[28]

King's biblical references are far too numerous to recount here, but a few examples should illustrate how thoroughly his words and work were shaped by Scripture. In his autobiography, he notes that it "was the Sermon on the Mount, rather than a doctrine of passive resistance," that inspired the Montgomery bus boycott.[29] The "Letter from Birmingham Jail" describes his work in terms of the Old Testament prophets and Paul: just as they "left their villages and carried their 'thus saith the Lord' far beyond the boundaries of their hometowns," so too was he called to carry the "gospel of freedom" beyond his home. King referenced prophetic promises of peace and flourishing often, especially the Promised Land. (In his famous 1968 "I've Been to the Mountaintop" speech, given the night before his assassination, he cited Numbers 27:12 and Deuteronomy 34.)

Perhaps most significant about King's hermeneutic was the way he enlisted the present-day people of God into the scriptural narrative. There was no sharp divide between the people of God in the Bible, the generations of Christians who came before him, and his own church. As a result, he could find in the Bible language for describing contemporary social and political concerns. The dangerous Jericho road in the parable of the good Samaritan became the price gouging in Chicago ghettos, and the injured man became a Memphis sanitation worker. Shadrach, Meshach, and Abednego were practicing "civil disobedience," just as members of the congregation where he was preaching had been when they were recently arrested.[30] In one particularly striking example, King delivered a sermon called "Paul's Letter to American Christians," in which he quite literally took up the mantle of Paul's letters ("Timothy is waiting to deliver this letter," he says toward the end) in order to tackle the "curse of Ham" segregation argument and instruct the faithful on persevering in the face of persecution.

King clearly saw himself in line with biblical prophets. "If Amos and Micah were prophets in the eighth century BC, Martin Luther King Jr. was a prophet in the twentieth century," Benjamin Mays describes him in his eulogy.[31] In one seminary paper, King describes Jeremiah in prescient terms: "If we judge Jeremiah by the ordinary standards of the world, his work was a failure. . . . But in after years his unheeded prophecies became the favorite book of the scattered Hebrew race."[32] As Jemar Tisby notes, while many Christians derided and resisted King during his lifetime, decades after his death "white evangelicals finally came to recognize King's contribution to American democracy and biblical justice."[33]

79

"I Have a Dream"

King's "I Have a Dream" speech is among the most famous in American history. Yet we are prone to miss many aspects of it. First, we often abstract the words of the speech away from its context. The March on Washington for Jobs and Freedom was enormously significant in the civil rights movement: the summer of 1963 march gathered nearly twenty-five thousand demonstrators to the Lincoln Memorial to protest racial and economic inequality. Its timing was strategic, intended to push President Kennedy toward more substantial legislation on civil rights. Organizer A. Philip Randolph had proposed a similar protest in 1941, prompting President Roosevelt to sign Executive Order 8802, which banned discrimination in hiring in the defense industry on the basis of race. Randolph planned another march in 1963 that merged with the planned demonstration of King and the Southern Christian Leadership Conference.

The speech that many Americans now remember with sentimental fondness was given at an event considered radical and unsavory by many Americans at the time. There were one hundred and fifty FBI agents monitoring the event, and the microphone King used was rigged to be turned off remotely if someone's speech got "too radical."[34] King's speech was not censored, but it was radical. King spoke about interpersonal relationships and idyllic communities, but he also directly demanded economic justice—in particular, compensation for the historic injustices perpetuated against Black Americans. In a move typical of American evangelicalism of this period, the "dream" was remembered, but the social and political mechanisms required to achieve it were not.[35]

King began by describing the economic condition of Black Americans one hundred years after the Emancipation Proclamation: "a lonely island of poverty in the midst of a vast ocean of material prosperity." He described the march as making a demand on the country—bringing a check to cash, a check that America had returned marked "insufficient funds." He refused the "tranquilizing drug of gradualism" and insisted on the urgency of enacting justice "for all of God's children" now. He cautioned against violence in protests and against the "new militancy" that would forsake building coalitions with white people. But, he maintained, the movement would not be pacified by anything short of justice.[36]

This is when his most famous biblical quotation comes: "No, no, we are not satisfied," King said, "and we will not be satisfied until 'justice rolls down like waters, and righteousness like a mighty stream'" (Amos 5:24). He continued this biblical language in the next line, acknowledging the "trials and tribulations" that many demonstrators had already endured and encouraging those "battled by the storms of persecution and staggered by the winds of police brutality" to return to their communities and continue the fight. "Let us not wallow in the valley of despair," he counseled.

At some point in his speech, gospel singer Mahalia Jackson yelled, "Tell 'em about the dream, Martin, tell 'em about the dream!" and King launched into the most famous part of the speech.[37] His dream, he said, was "deeply rooted in the American dream." But while his dream included the nation living up to its own ideals, that "all men are created equal," his dream sounded more like biblical prophecy than American exceptionalism. He dreamed about "brotherhood" across racial and economic divides. He dreamed of justice and freedom in place of injustice and oppression. He dreamed of segregation being turned into family. Finally, he dreamed that "one day every valley shall be exalted, and every hill and mountain shall be made low, the rough places will be made plain, and the crooked places will be made straight; and the glory of the Lord shall be revealed and all flesh shall see it together" (Isa. 40:4–5).

King was preaching. He wove the story of the civil rights movement into the biblical story—the story of an oppressed people, promised flourishing by God, awaiting God's redemptive work on behalf of all creation.[38] James Cone describes this approach to Scripture as "proclaiming with appropriate rhythm and passion the connection between the Bible and the history of black people. What has Scripture to do with our life in white society and the struggle to be *somebody* in it?"[39] King knew that the Word of God, spoken with authority and heard by the people of God, was effective to create change—he'd seen it in his father's church.[40]

Hermeneutics in the Civil Rights Movement

We've already covered some of the biblical hermeneutics used to uphold white supremacy, as well as the liberating hermeneutics of enslaved communities. Some of those themes continue here, but looking at the civil rights movement in relationship to the broader story of American history helps us see some unique lessons. Three important themes emerge from studying the sermons and speeches of the movement: the church is the proper location of biblical exegesis, we need caution in interpreting history, and where we see ourselves in Scripture shapes our interpretation. It is important to note that we are unavoidably speaking in generalizations. There is no single "Black church tradition" and no single perspective from the civil rights movement, but there are discernible distinctives of the loose tradition we call the Black church in America and habits of biblical interpretation more common during this period of civil rights work.

The Church's Book

King—and many other civil rights preachers and activists—first encountered Scripture in the context of the church community and felt bound to interpret it within that community. The words of the Bible are not open to any and every interpretation, in part because they are intended to be interpreted in a particular context: the gathered people of God. It's in the church that Scripture is read, sung, rehearsed, and embodied. King learned this as a child growing up in a church, but he also worked for justice in the context of church communities and collaborations and never left behind the language of the church.

His work grew out of church worship and community, and the church shaped his biblical interpretation. Despite the influence of academic theology on his thinking, King felt he must read Scripture within the bounds of the church's historical convictions.[41] This is part of what it means to read the Bible as "the church's book": you do not read it as an individual, with your own preferences, concerns, and questions guiding your interpretations; you read it as a book that belongs to a community beyond yourself. The work of the church, the history of the church, the diversity and difference within the church—all of these should shape the reading of Scripture. For King, reading the Bible as the church's book required holding to two things: the narrative of liberation and the precept of love. Read apart from the whole history and purpose of the church, the Bible could be used to defend unjust systems (as it was by many white Christians who may have read the Bible in a church building but did not read it as a book that belonged to the whole church) or to justify liberation by violence (as it sometimes was by activists who felt the institutional church was too passive or moderate).

Reading the Bible as the church's book means that passages cannot be abstracted away, because the church is a community made possible by the life, death, and resurrection of Christ; sustained by the Holy Spirit; oriented toward seeking the flourishing of God's creation while awaiting final restoration. Theologian John Webster identifies "the isolation of the text both from its place in God's revelatory activity and from its reception in the community" as one of the central disorders of the theology of the Bible.[42] Many of the social gospelers—and some civil rights activists as well—abstracted the text from its place in the community and then placed it within a new community: the nation. While King often appealed to the promises America had made, he also read Scripture *against* America.[43]

As Richard Lischer describes it, "Like the prophets in ancient Israel who debunked their own nation's false religiosity, King turned against the American covenant and began to demythologize it." There was never any "Christian America" to appeal to—there was never equality, never liberty and justice for *all*. King was clear on multiple occasions about the way biblical faith confronted America: "The judgement of God is on America now."[44]

While King was educated in historical criticism, the urgency of his community's context kept him from getting bogged down in those questions. Those methodologies were not relevant to his community. This should be instructive for us as well. Rigorous biblical and historical scholarship is not unnecessary or wrong, but it can lead us to forget the theological truth that the word of the Lord is speaking afresh in communities desperate for God's voice. King learned in church that the preacher needed to interpret the Scriptures so that the past and present were alive, accessible, and fresh with possibilities for social and individual transformation.

Stepping into the Book

The preeminence of the church in interpreting the Bible is closely related to the way Black churches thought about history, storytelling, and their own identity. In the gathered community of God, the preacher and the congregation are together brought into the biblical story: the Holy Spirit makes the words of the text alive for the church's present circumstances. From this perspective, there are no complicated exegetical methods required for understanding the meaning of the exodus. How or when or whether it happened is irrelevant when the cries of the Israelites enslaved in Egypt are the same as the cries of the oppressed in modern-day America. History does not work in the neat, linear, progressive way that enlightened modern people think it does, and a "people" is not defined merely by biology, geography, or nationality.

The African American tradition of biblical interpretation was shaped not by the philosophies of the Enlightenment but by the experience of suffering and the demands of injustice.[45] Rather than stepping *back* from the text and evaluating it from a supposed perspective of objectivity, Black preachers and congregants stepped *into* Scripture.[46]

Black churches were generally less interested in drawing out lessons or applications and were more interested in inhabiting the world of the Bible. When a white Methodist minister preached on Psalm 86 for a Black congregation ("Let God arise, let his enemies be scattered"), he was horrified by their enthusiastic response. "What was figurative, they interpreted literally," he lamented.[47] But as a people living into the world of the Bible, expecting God to act in history on behalf of his people, they believed God would arise and scatter his enemies—and theirs. This should complicate some of our easy associations of white conservatives with "literalism" against socially progressive Christian interpretive methods. Just as during the Civil War, the fights that white Christians have about the Bible often ignore Black Christians, who have historically taken Scripture seriously and *literally* in ways that discomfort people across the theological spectrum. Black Christians during the civil rights movement were not interested in defending the historical truth of the text as a disinterested theological exercise; they were immersed in worship of a God whom they believed consistently entered into human history on behalf of the oppressed—in Scripture and in the present.

In his speeches and sermons, King described the ordinary work of organizing and protesting in terms of the cosmic struggle for justice, the biblical story of captivity and liberation, and the divinely ordained plan for creation.[48] And yet King and other civil rights activists rejected the optimism of the social gospelers (or the Revolutionary or Civil War–era preachers).[49] The activists knew that God was on the side of justice, but they had little hope that society could be easily reformed through education or government policies.[50] They did not buy the view that history was moving on an unbroken path of progress. They expected opposition, and many of them sacrificed greatly because of the steady hope that God would eventually honor their efforts—whether on earth or in eternity.

For King, the civil rights movement fit within the "terms and framework of the biblical world," because all of history does. He refused to grant political or social events a "life of their own" outside God's providence. The church did not meet together to recount God's work in times past, as if God entered human affairs only during those special biblical times. The church community testified to the truth of the whole redemptive story of Scripture as it was unfolding in their own place and time. This meant that some political options—including accommodating white supremacy or fighting it with violence or separatism—were off the table.[51] Christians could not entertain political options predicated on a world where Jesus had not been crucified and risen from the dead.

Where Do You See Yourself?

King knew that "the same religious community which produced the prophets . . . stoned the prophets to death."[52] We are not, as we have seen throughout American history, always shaped by Scripture in the same ways. The civil-rights-era interpreters of Scripture teach us to ask this question: Where do you see yourself in the biblical story? The Black church in America read the story of the exodus and saw themselves in the oppressed Israelites, yet the white churches did not see themselves in Pharaoh.

This is an uncomfortable question for us to reflect on. When we read the Bible, where do we naturally see ourselves? Are we willing to be both comforted and confronted with the words of the Bible? Are we able to accurately determine who is playing what role? If there's anything we've learned, it's that communities can adopt the mantle of God's chosen people to justify their sin, that people can see themselves as the victorious warrior of God or the righteous prophet when they are in fact doing evil, and that fallen humans are prone to manipulate and distort Scripture for their own purposes. We need to become practiced in recognizing the signs of who is playing what role. Who is sacrificing for others rather than protecting themselves? Who has been shaped by suffering rather than comfort? Who keeps Jesus at the center of their political theology, and who sidelines him for their own glory?

King did not just read the Bible; he lived it.[53] He revealed the absurdity and depravity of unjust social conditions by sitting at lunch counters, marching with the poor and marginalized, and walking instead of riding segregated buses. He provoked mass public outrage, facing bomb threats, imprisonment, and eventually assassination. Why did people react with such vitriol at the marches or sit-ins? Lischer says that perhaps "Bible-believing southerners suspected what ancient Israel knew, that the actions of these prophets, just as surely as their words, are the signs of a new order that is rapidly approaching."[54]

Magic of the Market

The Hermeneutics of Small Government

While political slogans change every election cycle, one has consistently captured the imagination of conservative Christians: "Government that governs least governs best."[1] Variations of the phrase abound, but the "small government" drum has been beaten for decades in American politics.

The 1980s were a turning point for small-government enthusiasm—and a turning point for religion in America—after the counterculture of the 1960s and '70s, the '80s experienced an "awakening." This wasn't necessarily the spiritual revival of previous awakenings but a revival of interest in the Bible in public: reading the Bible in public schools, appealing to its authority in legal matters, and supporting politicians who openly quoted it. This was also a time when conservative Christians pushed for "limited government, free enterprise (particularly small business), and anticommunism."[2] The coherence that had long been created between the individualized theology of the American revivalist spirit and the political concern for individual freedom was easily adapted to 1980s politics. Concerns about biblical faith, small government, and economic freedom were deeply intertwined during these years—in ways that continue to exert significant influence on Christians today.

This chapter will explore the biblical justifications Christians have given for small government, focusing on the Christian support for Ronald Reagan and "Reaganomics" in the 1980s. Today, the firm sense that small government is a biblical principle guides Christian debates about economic policy. While the focus here will not be on biblical defenses of economic policy (a rich area of theological reflection), it will inevitably include biblical defenses and criticisms of general political economic theory.

Christians and Economics in the 1980s

Conservative politics—especially the supremacy of the free market, suspicion of labor unions, and fear of a powerful interventionist state—moved from a "marginal position" in the mid-twentieth century to the "reigning politics of the country" by the end of it.[3] Alongside the long and complicated story of that shift is the story of Christians working to reconcile these policies with Christian ethics.[4]

Christian theology has addressed economics in rich and complicated ways throughout its history—from the description of the early church in Acts sharing everything in common, to medieval denunciations of usury, to contemporary Christians who condemn consumerism and support fair-trade goods. Christians have disagreed about both personal financial ethics and economic policies. In the 1980s, however, the debate among American Christians about faith and economics was especially fierce.

Christian broadcaster Pat Robertson announced "A Christian Action Plan for the 1980s" in 1979. The plan was not about individual sin or conservative social issues. Rather, Robertson identified inflation, currency devaluation, productivity, government size, and communism as the most relevant issues for the country. He blamed the woes of the country on "flirtation with Marxism" and suggested that the solution was entreating God's favor and "a bold, dynamic plan" for economic recovery.[5]

Moral revival and political advocacy were working hand in hand here: the country needed spiritual revival that would cash out in Christians who would vote and lobby and write letters to politicians on behalf of conservative policies. Robertson alluded to a favorite verse for Christian political advocacy (2 Chron. 7:14): the "people who are called by His name" needed to pray and ask for a miracle. Wealth played a central role in this plea; Christians should "learn the ways of finance: stocks, bonds, banking, commodities, real estates, taxes," and they should "apply the principles of God's kingdom dealing with the acquisition and use of wealth." When they "accumulated material resources," they would be able to do "enormous good" in unity with other Christians around the world.[6]

We can't neatly separate economics and a general theory of government. A concern for the "free market" was not merely a domestic economic question but a moral question (freedom against unjust tyranny), a foreign policy question (against encroaching communism), and a theological question (the power of the state was a threat to the church). Robertson and others taught that any growth in state power hampered the power of the market and the church.[7]

In May 1978, Jerry Falwell started a newspaper, first called *Journal-Champion* and then *Moral Majority Report*. The June 1978 issue included a short article titled "America Threatened by Creeping Bureaucracy: Freedom's Greatest Threat." The greatest threat was not "Communist aggression, crime in the decaying cities, or any other external cause," the article argued. "It comes from the growing internal encroachments of government bureaucrats as they limit the freedom of Americans through distribution of rules and regulations."[8]

Fears of government overreach were connected to fears of infringement on religious freedom. In a period of American history where conservative Christians felt culturally under attack, the fear was heightened that if the government became too powerful, it would naturally be used against Christians. These fears did not arise from nowhere, but they were often exaggerated or misplaced. For example, two California professors started a small movement petitioning the FCC to freeze religious broadcasts until they investigated noncommercial radio and television stations. The FCC declined, but it contributed to general suspicion of federal regulation. Often, cultural changes were translated into government intervention in the minds of conservative Christians. Events like a 1973 Securities and Exchange Commission court challenge of Falwell stirred fear that government agencies were targeting religious organizations (although in Falwell's case he was cleared of intentional wrongdoing). In the late 1970s, the IRS enforced federal desegregation law, requiring private schools to meet the same desegregation requirements as public schools in order to maintain their tax-exempt status.[9] That this decision helped catalyze the religious right has been well documented, but it was the combination of white supremacy and fear of government intrusion that made it so politically powerful.

Reaganomics and the Bible

No president is more burned into the collective consciousness of American Christians than Ronald Reagan. While George W. Bush was lauded as "the most aggressively religious president Americans have ever had" and early presidents like Washington or Jefferson hold special places in America's religious history, Reagan is the president within recent memory who took on a unique mythology that excused his various sins and deviations from the conservative Christian norm.[10]

Reagan enjoyed broad appeal to Christians—especially white "born-again" Christians—in his presidential elections (63 percent voted for him in 1980, and 81 percent voted for him in 1984), but his status as heroic defender of conservative American values would only grow among that demographic in later years.[11] He was an unlikely choice for religious voters in many ways: he signed the most liberal abortion bill in the country as California governor, he was divorced, and he didn't always support their social issues. But he hammered home the need for small government. This combined their economic concerns (government spending and the welfare state) with their fears of government interference (intrusion in Christian schools or churches, regulation of school prayer or Bible teaching, and other religious freedom issues).[12]

Reagan's famous "Time for Choosing" speech, given on behalf of Barry Goldwater's presidential run in 1964, catapulted him into national politics and resulted in his run for California governor two years later. It evidences some of the themes that would characterize his influential presidency. He began by narrating his move from lifelong Democrat to enthusiastic Republican as rooted in concern over the size of the national "tax burden," unbalanced budget, and bungling of the Vietnam War.

He described the government as a dangerously metastasizing agent: it will never "voluntarily" reduce itself in size. "Actually, a government bureau is the nearest thing to eternal life we'll ever see on this earth," he quipped. He described the "Great Society" ambitions of liberalism as veiled attempts to dehumanize and control people: "A government can't control the economy without controlling people." He characterized Goldwater's opponents as "those who would trade our freedom for the soup kitchen of the welfare state" and government programs as "compulsory" and "utopian." The "issue of this election," he said, was "whether we believe in our capacity for self-government" or we "abandon the American Revolution" and put faith in a small "intellectual elite in a far-distant capital."[13]

At the end of his 1980s presidential acceptance speech, the president-elect admitted, "I confess that I've been a little afraid to suggest what I'm going to suggest." But then he said, "I'm more afraid not to." He dramatically asked the crowd, "Can we begin our crusade, joined together, in a moment of silent prayer?" He paused for thirteen seconds, then became the first president to invoke the iconic phrase in an acceptance speech: "God bless America." Not only did Reagan begin a strong tradition of presidents proudly acknowledging God—asking blessing for the country, declaring their dependence, articulating their campaign as a calling—but in his hesitance he nodded to Christian fears about cultural change and government overreach.[14]

It's up for debate how genuine these religious displays were, but they were certainly effective. One of Reagan's speechwriters left a note to his staff members during his first campaign, warning them about the "awful lot of code words, religious allusions and whatnot" in his speech but saying that it wasn't important for Reagan to understand all of them because "his audience will. Boy, will they ever!"[15] He was not wrong.

In one campaign speech a few months before the 1980 election, Reagan described politics—working in campaigns, running for office, voting—as a Christian responsibility. If God has "blessed America with liberty," then voting is a "duty." The American people had an opportunity, just as the Israelites entering the Promised Land did, to make their government and laws "models to other nations, showing to the world the wisdom and mercy of their God." He finished by recounting a question a reporter had asked him about what book he would choose to have with him if he were shipwrecked on an island and could read only one book for the rest of his life. His answer: "The Bible, the Old and New Testaments." Then he explained, "It is an incontrovertible fact that all the complex and horrendous questions confronting us at home and worldwide have their answer in that single Book."[16]

Reagan was sworn into office with his hand on his mother's Bible, open to 2 Chronicles 7:14: "If my people, who are called by my name, will humble themselves and pray and seek my face and turn from their wicked ways, then I will hear from heaven, and I will forgive their sin and will heal their land." The reference might have been lost on many Americans, but for the Moral Majority, it signaled that Reagan was on their team.[17]

Being on their team meant fighting for their economic policies and couching them in biblical terms. A few years into his presidency, Reagan spoke to the National Religious Broadcasters Convention and contrasted government programs and the guidance of Scripture. "Government bureaucracies spend billions for problems related to drugs, alcoholism, and disease," he said. "How much of that money could we save, how much better off might Americans be if all of us tried a little harder to live by the Ten Commandments and the Golden Rule?"[18] Similarly, in a Conservative Political Action Conference speech in 1984, he contrasted faith in God with faith in government programs.[19]

Reagan named 1983 the "Year of the Bible," describing the social and political work the Bible inspired: "For centuries the Bible's emphasis on compassion and love for our neighbor has inspired institutional and governmental expressions of benevolent outreach such as private charity, the establishment of schools and hospitals, and the abolition of slavery."[20]

Reagan masterfully combined descriptions of America as specially favored by God with biblical justifications for small government. He described government intervention as a breaking of the nation's covenant with God, with economic consequences. To be sure, Reagan would intervene in the market as much as his predecessors—he was still "manipulating the tax code to induce social change." Even still, he articulated these policies as a lack of intervention, as leaving what God had created in its natural state.[21]

Christian Defenses of Small Government

"Reaganomics" looms large in the imagination of many conservative Christians today.[22] And while Reagan played a significant role in molding the particular relationship between faith and economics in the United States, he was aided by pastors and theologians.[23] Before we look into what we can learn about political hermeneutics from this period, we'll look at some examples of the political theological disagreements that blossomed into full-blown battles in this period.

Ronald Nash: Poverty and Wealth

Theologian Ronald H. Nash wrote a number of influential books and articles on Christian economics in this period. In 1986 he published *Poverty and Wealth: The Christian Debate over Capitalism.*

For both Nash and many (if not the majority) of conservative Christians in this period, there was a significant difference between private charity and government "planning" of the market. Nearly all the Christian defenses of capitalism in this period describe the importance of caring for the poor and vulnerable—personally or through the church—and many Christians who supported Reaganomics were personally very generous. Unlike other proponents of unfettered capitalism, many of these Christians were critical of consumerism and unabashed glorying in self-interest.[24] In *Poverty and Wealth*, Nash argues that the desire to help the poor is good, but liberal Christians have poor "philosophical, political, and economic" knowledge.[25]

Nash claims to make "no effort to deduce a system of economics from the Bible" but rather combines biblical principles with the economic principles learned from "scientific economics."[26] This is central to Nash's argument: his chapters about "basic economic concepts" are distinct from his "biblical principles" chapters— the lesson being that the Bible teaches general ethical themes and science teaches neutral economic principles. He describes his approach as first acquiring "a clear and complete picture of the Christian world view" on questions of human nature, communities, society, and God, and then putting his "best effort into discovering the truth about economic and political systems."

On that second step, Nash recommends that Christians avoid "assorted propagandists." While left-leaning Christians might have good intentions, the question as to whether capitalism is harmful is "an empirical and not a normative matter." In other words, this is not a question for theology or philosophy, not a question about what is right and good in the world, but a question for the science of economics, a question about math. "The Leftists simply have their facts wrong."[27]

Nash does describe some biblical principles for *personal* economics: Christians should use resources with dedication and judgment (Luke 16:9), shouldn't have "single-minded concern" for wealth (Luke 12:16–21), and should seek the financial resources required to meet God's obligations (he draws on parables, citing

Luke 16:1–3 and Matt. 25:24). While he acknowledges that money can "have a negative effect on people's character and spiritual relationships," he notes that Jesus does not condemn wealth (as his opponents would say). Jesus was concerned about spiritual conditions, not money.[28]

Nash says that the Bible has "no systematic teaching on economics" but does have "important things to say about economic matters."[29] He explains that the Bible does teach stewardship, that Christians are only stewards and God owns everything (Ps. 24:1 and Job 41:11), but this doctrine is "misused" by Christian leftists because the New Testament says nothing about state coercion for the sake of economic justice. The reasons Nash gives against this are not biblical (finding direct biblical support either for or against a modern liberal democracy using the state to redistribute resources is impossible): welfare encourages dependence, diminishes incentives to work, traps people in poverty, and is not a form of genuine compassion.[30]

Ronald Sider: Rich Christians in an Age of Hunger

Reaganomics Christians were far from the only Christians—even the only evangelicals. There were alternative viewpoints, expressed by evangelical theologians and housed in evangelical institutions, that grew out of the evangelicalism of the progressive movement. Magazines like *The Other Side* (1965) or Jim Wallis's *The Post American* (1971, later *Sojourners*) articulated the continuing tradition of evangelical concern for social reform, while groups like Evangelicals for Social Action (1978) and the Evangelical Environmental Network (1993) worked to educate and mobilize Christians to action.[31]

One crucial book in that broader movement was Ronald Sider's *Rich Christians in an Age of Hunger*. Sider, theologian and founder of Evangelicals for Social Action, published six editions of the rallying-cry book over nearly thirty years. Sider made some large policy suggestions (the last section of the first edition makes suggestions on North American food policy, international trade, and military spending), but the policy prescriptions changed over the course of the many editions. The parts of the book that stayed the most consistent are Sider's biblical cases for "equalizing mechanisms" in a community (like the Jubilee in Exod. 23:10–11 and Lev. 25:2–7), for individuals to prioritize the needs of their neighbors over profit-seeking, and for individuals to adopt a "graduated tithe" that would require them to give greater amounts as their wealth increases beyond their immediate realistic needs.[32]

The book has had many critics. *Christianity Today* published a review in 1977 that argued that Sider was impractical or misguided in his policy recommendations (and Sider's changes over the course of the many editions evidence his learning from such criticisms). Other criticisms were harsher and more holistically attacked Sider's biblical theology. One critic of Sider's book, theologian David Chilton, wrote a book-length response to *Rich Christians in an Age of Hunger* titled *Productive Christians in an Age of Guilt-Manipulators*. Chilton was an advocate for Christian reconstructionism, a movement that believes that biblical law should stipulate national legal code, and his criticism of Sider was scathing.[33] He refers to Sider as a false prophet in sheep's clothing (Matt. 7:15–16), probably a Marxist even though he denies it, and a "legalist" for requiring Christians to obey "Old Testament ceremonial law" and "manmade regulations."[34] He misrepresents Sider's positions: he claims that Sider "strongly hints" that the Bible requires repudiation of private property, that he sees no limits on the power of government, and that he advocates for socialism.[35]

In a line that sums up his tone, Chilton says that Sider's theology "more closely resembles Marx's *Communist Manifesto* than it does the book of Deuteronomy."[36] Like most of the conservative authors in this period, Chilton agrees that wealth is not the ultimate good and that Christians should serve God with the resources they are given. Even still, while he calls Sider's application of Old Testament law "legalism," he relies on citations from Proverbs to defend "dominion" in the economic sphere and interprets the eighth commandment ("You shall not steal") as prohibiting "fraud and coercion in the marketplace" and establishing "the conditions for a free market."[37]

Political Hermeneutics

We don't have the space to systematically evaluate the various arguments made for or against policy proposals in these works—and in many cases it would be a trivial exercise since the policy proposals and the global economic context have changed in many ways since the 1970s and '80s. We can, however, learn a few important truths from these examples.

First, the Bible is concerned with the spiritual and the material. Many of the Christians writing for one side or the other in this debate diverge along two important lines: the spiritual/literal and the individual/social. Are biblical descriptions of freedom, flourishing, or redemption intended to be interpreted spiritually or materially? Are biblical condemnations of greed and oppression intended to condemn individuals or communities?

Different passages will have different emphases: some really do emphasize the material, some the spiritual, some the individual, and some the communal. When the Old Testament law describes the poor and vulnerable, it's hard to argue that it is referring to the spiritually poor—the categories of orphan, widow, and foreigner that it describes are material conditions of poverty. On the other hand, John Jefferson Davis, another defender of capitalism in this period, in order to defend the "virtue of individual responsibility" cited Galatians 6:7 and 2 Corinthians 5:10—passages whose contexts clearly describe the spiritual condition of a person before God, not the value of a society that thinks primarily in terms of atomized individuals.[38]

But there are some general guidelines we can keep in mind for all passages. The Bible never gives us reason to disregard the physical body or material creation. God calls his creation good, and he promises to redeem and perfect it as a home where he will dwell with his people in eternity (Gen. 1–2; Rev. 21). The human body is never denigrated but is honored as a gift from God (the early centuries of the church already hashed this question out for us). Pitting the spiritual and the material against each other ignores the scriptural harmony between them. When one theologian of the period says that the "priority" for the prophets is "spiritual repentance" and not "socio-economic reform," that assumes the spiritual and material are separated in a way they are clearly not by the prophets.[39] Isaiah 1 urges socioeconomic reform ("Learn to do right; seek justice. Defend the oppressed. Take up the cause of the fatherless; plead the case of the widow") *and* spiritual repentance ("Though your sins are like scarlet, they shall be as white as snow") in the span of two verses (vv. 17–18).

Even those who want to emphasize one over the other are rarely consistent. Many Reaganomics Christians cited biblical passages about "freedom" in support of their own conception of political or economic freedom, but in other contexts they accused "leftist" or "liberationist" Christians of confusing the spiritual meaning of "freedom" with political liberation. Meanwhile, many of the Christians committed to a "literal" interpretation of Scripture described poverty in the Gospels as a metaphor for "spiritual bankruptcy."[40]

We are often inconsistent with the choices we make, but these inconsistencies teach us a valuable lesson: there is no neat dividing of the spiritual and the material. When we try to claim that the Bible favors one over the other, we will accidentally undermine ourselves somewhere else.

Second, the Bible is directed to both individuals and communities. We find a similar dynamic at play when we try to interpret passages as individual commands or corporate directions. Do Old Testament laws demand that individuals care for the poor or that a community does so? If it's a community demand, which community is it—the church or the government? And if the Bible does give direction for whole human communities, what kind of direction is it—general moral principles or specific laws?

There are pitfalls in multiple directions here. One side will say that these commands are for the people of God, so today they apply to us only as individuals or churches. Another side will say that the commands were given to a political body, the nation of Israel, so the whole body of Old Testament law should guide national laws today. Neither represents the whole counsel of Scripture; both ignore different genres, different audiences, different commands.

For example, one theologian writing in this period cited Proverbs 11:14, "in an abundance of counselors there is safety" (RSV), in support of a free-market system that "distributes the decision-making process over a vast number of buyers and sellers."[41] This ignores the genre and the audience: the proverbs were written not as universal moral commands but as sayings that generally describe how things work in the world, and they were not directed toward social structure or national policy. Applying them to national policy is even more ridiculous than plucking Old Testament law out of its religious and political context and trying to implement it as national law.

But other descriptions in Scripture are explicitly given to nations—prophecies in the Old Testament condemn nations for violence, exploiting the poor, enslaving humans made in God's image, and rebelling against God's rule.[42] The Old Testament's instructions given to the nation of Israel also give us some political instruction today. Nash and others are correct that these instructions cannot be explicit blueprints for us (America is still not the chosen people of God and exists in a vastly different political and economic context than Israel), but they do indicate how God desires human communities to function. They describe perennial problems of human communities—unjust accumulation of wealth, dynamics of exploitation and abuse, moral decay—and God's desire for communal rhythms, structures, and laws that address those problems.

Third, the Bible does not give us a blueprint for government, but it does leave us with some direction. Can we find in Scripture general "principles" that can guide contemporary policy or specific moral demands of what policy should look like? Many of these authors criticize Christians who take a wild jump from a biblical citation to a social or economic program. These Christians, they argue, should not transmute the Jubilee—the Old Testament practice of returning land to its original owners in an attempt to prevent uneven generational accumulation of wealth—into a policy of wealth redistribution today.

Yet some of these authors make similar moves: Davis and Chilton argue from 1 Samuel 8 that any tax of 10 percent or more is, in Chilton's words, "regarded by Scripture as *tyranny* explicitly prohibited by God."[43] Nash argues that Old Testament laws against moving a neighbor's landmark or delaying payment to a worker support personal property and capitalism, and Chilton argues that verses like Proverbs 11:1 ("The LORD detests dishonest scales") and Micah 6:11 ("Shall I acquit someone with dishonest scales . . . ?") are "absolute biblical prohibitions" against inflation.[44] In a similar way, they have selected Old Testament verses, abstracted them from their context, and turned them into biblical demands for specific policy.

Oftentimes these authors rely on the *silence* of the text more than its overt meaning. A "modern welfare state," Nash notes, is not described in Scripture, and Davis argues that the Old Testament laws about leaving the edges of your fields unharvested so that the poor can pick and eat from them were personal provisions that "created no administrative bureaucracies."[45]

True, Scripture does not describe modern political arrangements (how could it?). But it does describe God's intention for human communities to care for the vulnerable. We should take the words of both Testaments as challenging, daunting, and sometimes terrifying instructions for our own political work. The Old Testament describes the land, and even the agricultural product of human labor, as God's—not the individual's, as we think today, and not the king's, as the surrounding nations believed at the time. God's people accepted the notion that God was the giver of all good gifts and so could demand not only that individuals give generously but also that communities be organized to care for the poor. God gave his people explicit instructions for a cycle of restoring land and for interrupting cycles of injustice, instructions that were not subject to questions of practicality or convenience.[46]

Even when we agree on general biblical principles, we apply them in different (and often selective) ways. One of the significant arguments during this period was that capitalism is more biblical because it recognizes the reality of sin in its evaluation of human life. In comparison to socialism, which assumes the best intentions of the humans who would plan the economic life of a whole community, capitalism recognizes that humans will sin and are limited in their knowledge, so it puts limits on government and spreads out decision-making across the whole community.[47] But the same could easily be said against capitalism. It disregards the sinful motives of powerful businesspeople and puts them in positions of unaccountable power. As Eric Crouse notes, "Christian leftists found it inconsistent that conservative Christians apparently saw sin everywhere but in the marketplace."[48]

We are always making decisions—about which verses apply to which situations, and about what general biblical principles apply in what kinds of ways. Rather than claiming that our side is taking the Bible seriously and the other side is playing fast and loose with it, we need to be honest about which verses we prioritize and why, and reason together (with people who disagree with us) about what God demands of us in the here and now.

Fourth, the Bible is not the only source of truth, but it should shape how we interpret other sources. At the heart of these debates is a concern not only about what the Bible teaches but also about what economic theory and social science teach. Two factors are in tension here: common grace means we can learn from a variety of sources, but no theory is neutral.

Nash often describes the economic principles he holds as neutral, scientific facts. Christians might interpret the Bible differently, but his opponents are just wrong about the economic facts. Nash represents a common way of thinking about economics in modern American life: it is a machine that works according to certain absolute laws and is separate from moral considerations.

Nash rightly recognizes that Christians can learn from all kinds of sources—atheist economists included. He uses economic concepts along with Scripture because Christians are "required to believe many things, not because they are taught *explicitly* in the Bible, but *simply because they are true!*"[49] This is true, and crucially important for our conversations about the Bible in political work; depending on the question we're asking, the answer might be

101

found in social science or political theory or epidemiology rather than the Bible. If we're wondering whether our education system is adequately serving the poorest students in our country, social science gives us better answers than the Bible. If we're wondering whether it *matters* if our education system is adequately serving the poorest students in our country, the Bible gives us a better answer than any social theory. Updated versions of Sider's *Rich Christians in an Age of Hunger* include insights from economists and social scientists, recognizing that biblical study alone doesn't make for great policy.

Nash is misguided, however, to think of economics as a *neutral* science. Humans have not always thought about economics this way. During the Industrial Revolution, the idea of machinelike precision was exciting, and advances in technology and science made us want to describe *all* of human life in their terms. But humans are not machines, and neither is there "magic" in the market or a godlike hand of providence directing everything for the ultimate good.[50] There are no neutral economic laws directing everything regardless of culture and time, and the economy does not operate outside broader society. This is true of all social science. While there is much we can learn, and must learn, to do faithful work in the world, we should also examine the underlying assumptions in that work—assumptions about human communities, what kinds of creatures humans are, and the ultimate good and end of creation.

Crucially, the Bible describes a vision of the human that is counter to a libertarian vision of humans. From the Garden of Eden through to the end of the story in the new Jerusalem, humans are *relational*. The image of God as given to human creatures is inherently relational: male and female he created them, with a commission to be fruitful and increase in number. This is not merely a picture of nuclear family life but a picture of the kind of life all humans were intended for: community. The end of the story is not about individuals going to heaven but about a community reconciled to God, living together in a city: a communal life where humans have taken the good gifts of God's creation and collaborated to build something new. These authors are right to be wary of economic projects that are seemingly lifted straight out of Scripture, applying Levitical laws directly to contemporary policy. Scripture does, however, give us a robust account of the kinds of creatures humans are, an account at odds with the underlying assumptions of much of contemporary economic theory.

Fifth, the Bible does not fit in predetermined political boxes. Many writers from this period ask this question: Does the Bible favor capitalism or socialism? The writers then line up the biblical arguments for capitalism and the biblical arguments for socialism, using these predetermined categories for seeing what the Bible says about economic life. Rather than coming to the Bible with the expectation that *every* political position and identity will be confronted and challenged, this approach decides in advance what *kind* of message the Bible will give. It forces different genres, cultural contexts, and theological purposes into a chart that can help Christians answer a question the Bible never asks or answers.

This has broader implications than how we frame the debate. When we begin with political categories and questions—Who should I vote for? Which party is more Christian? Which economic system is more biblical?—we will miss biblical commands that do not fit our predetermined questions. Our binary thinking blinds us to the ways Scripture confronts our favored party or policy. It becomes easier to pick and choose which verses will shape our political work. And it often ends up yielding our spiritual formation to a political party or television network: suddenly we have moved from biblical defenses of a free-market system to doing hermeneutical gymnastics to defend unbridled self-interest as a virtue.

Sixth, the clearest teaching of the Bible regarding politics is that we treat our opponents fairly. I hope the examples in this chapter have highlighted another problem of political hermeneutics in American churches: the hermeneutics of how we interpret *each other*. Many of the positions in this period were firm and fiery—on both sides. There were often good reasons for this. When Jim Wallis wrote "A Wolf in Sheep's Clothing" to describe the political right, he was describing what he perceived to be a serious threat to the gospel witness.[51] When people like Nash and Davis warned of encroaching Marxism in churches, they really meant it too.

Yet we can strive, perhaps above all else, to accurately describe the positions of other Christians, assume good motives from them until given evidence otherwise, and take seriously their concerns rather than ridiculing them. In an early part of *Productive Christians in an Age of Guilt-Manipulators*, Chilton turns to Elijah to defend his mockery of Sider: "I stand firmly with the prophet of Elijah; that which is ridiculous deserves ridicule."[52] We have biblical warrant to speak firmly and passionately about people who misuse God's name, abuse image bearers, or lead God's people astray. But we cannot claim prophetic fire without also claiming prophetic humility: "Woe to me!" Isaiah cried. "I am ruined! For I am a man of unclean lips, and I live among a people of unclean lips, and my eyes have seen the King, the LORD Almighty" (Isa. 6:5). Our use of the Bible in political arguments should evidence conviction and humility.

Late Great United States

Biblical Eschatology in the Cold War

Growing up, did you ever come home from school or soccer practice to find an empty house, a kettle boiling over, maybe some discarded clothes draped over a couch, and fear that your faithful family had been raptured away and you'd been left behind? If so, you had rapture anxiety. Infatuation with biblical prophecy, confident predictions about the end times, and political posturing motivated by eschatology are nothing new. But in Cold War America, they took on renewed vigor and a new shape.

The *New York Times* declared Hal Lindsey's *The Late Great Planet Earth* the number-one nonfiction bestseller of the 1970s. The book shaped the imagination of many American Christians and sparked a widespread interest in biblical prophecy and its application to politics. Lindsey himself said, "As world events develop, prophecy becomes more and more exciting," and more people are given insight into prophecy. In addition, Lindsey argued: "this is one reason you will find on Christian bookshelves an increasing number of books on the subject of Bible prophecy."[1] His book applied passages from Revelation to modern events, making interpretive claims about the Bible with geopolitical applications.

This chapter explores the way apocalyptic literature in Scripture can motivate political action—in faithful and unfaithful ways. Biblical prophecy along with end-times theology has always had political meaning: revealing the corruption of leaders and the evil of nations, comforting the oppressed, and motivating resistance to broken systems. How can we know its *true* political meaning in our specific moment in time? How can we rehabilitate the political power of Revelation in the light of its fraught American legacy? What does faithful interpretation of such a tricky text look like?

American Apocalypse

Americans have always wanted to find their country in biblical prophecy. John Winthrop's "A Model of Christian Charity" predicted the nation's coming judgment in the face of moral decline. Fears of ultimate judgment have fueled religious revivals and political action. Some historians have argued that apocalypticism— the warning of sudden, approaching end times—defines American religion.[2]

The period after World War II was especially ripe for this kind of thinking. Church attendance drastically increased as Americans looked to both religion and "traditional American values" in the wake of great loss and fear.[3] After a global war, genocide, and threat of nuclear annihilation, people were deeply aware of evil in the world and desperate for answers and hope. As the United States progressed further into the Cold War—the conflict between the United States and the Soviet Union that would dominate international politics for forty years—American Christianity became a comfort for those fearful of nuclear war.[4]

Americans have often imagined themselves living in the "center of history." The extreme threat of nuclear destruction heightened this sense. It was easy to connect nuclear annihilation to biblical descriptions of fiery destruction.[5] The effects of a thermonuclear blast were described in Zechariah, the falling stars and locusts of

Revelation were warheads descending from space and helicopters spraying nerve gas, and the deadly fire throughout biblical prophecy was actually a description of unleashed radiation.[6]

Christianity was also tightly tied to American nationalism in the fight against atheistic communism. Eschatology was a form of comfort *and* political maneuvering: America's foreign enemies were not regular opponents but evil players in a cosmic battle. Tapping into American religion for the fight against communism was also good politics; Congress added "under God" to the Pledge of Allegiance in 1954 and "In God we trust" to US currency in 1955. Evangelicals were helpful allies in this period, giving moral weight and urgency to the fight against communism.[7]

The Cold War was *full* of biblical imagery and language in politics. "What is our battle against communism if it is not a fight against anti-God and a belief in the Almighty?" President Dwight Eisenhower asked.[8] Billy Graham said at a 1949 revival that the Bible was the foundation of Western culture, while communism "has decided against God, against Christ, against the Bible, and against all religion."[9]

Up through the decades, biblical-prophecy fiction became wildly popular: the Left Behind book series by Jerry Jenkins and Tim LaHaye sold tens of millions of copies, spawning children's books, comic books, and movies—as well as popularizing a specific method of biblical interpretation. While this chapter will focus on biblical interpretation in *The Late Great Planet Earth*, you cannot think about biblical prophecy in American history without considering the effect of prophecy fiction. Prophecy fiction was incredibly popular because it engaged the imagination and emotion, allowed for speculation outside biblical texts, and provided the entryway for many readers into the wider world of prophecy.[10]

Before we look at a crucially important text of prophetic interpretation in the Cold War era, we should ask: Why would people obsessed with prophecies about the end of the world spend so much time and energy on *politics*? If cultural decay is a sign that Jesus is returning soon, why would you want to stop it? If the

Bible promises that your efforts are ultimately futile, why organize politically—and so effectively?[11]

For one thing, people are complicated. Our politics are not easily disconnected from our theology or morals. People are driven by emotion and imagination: even if the world is destined to fall apart before Christ's return, fear of suffering can easily animate political advocacy.[12] Add in the increasing sense of cultural stigma and isolation that evangelicals felt, and political advocacy might be necessary merely to maintain the ability to evangelize people before it is too late. Global events in this period also contributed to Christian political activism: it seemed as if biblical prophecies were being fulfilled before people's eyes, and this shaped how they felt about American foreign policy. Armed with increased political power and fresh confidence in the truthfulness of biblical prophecies, evangelicals fought for policies that seem confusing if not contradictory today.

Confident that international developments were preparing the way for Armageddon, many conservative Christians supported a stronger nuclear force and an increased military budget for the United States. Further, their belief that biblical prophecy foretold the Soviet Union's role in the coming cosmic battle made them suspicious of any attempts at compromise.[13]

The creation of the modern state of Israel in 1948 also played a significant role.[14] Christian interest in Israel has had long-term effects in US foreign policy and Christian theology, but it also impacted how many saw the applicability of prophetic texts to current events. Once this significant event they saw foretold in eschatological prophecy occurred, they started focusing on the order of events *before* the rapture, specific "signs of the times."

Perceived moral decline was also politically motivating. The sexual revolution, fears of encroaching communism, and a sense of Christian marginalization all fueled political work. Attaching prophetic significance to American politics would not stay contained to specific premillennial scenarios: the imaginative and affective power of biblical imagery and language would light a fire under politicians and preachers alike, even if the theological details got muddled. And when Americans appealed to biblical prophecy, they usually resurrected notions of America as a covenanted nation with special significance for God's global plans.[15]

Late Great Planet Earth

Hal Lindsey popularized a strand of evangelical theology through dozens of bestselling books in the 1970s, '80s, and '90s. Lindsey was a former agnostic who cited a 1956 sermon on prophecy for motivating his lifelong interest in the topic. He went to Dallas Theological Seminary, the flagship seminary for dispensational theology, and worked for Campus Crusade for Christ in California before publishing his most popular work, the astronomically successful *The Late Great Planet Earth*, in 1970.[16] The book has sold upwards of forty million copies, has been translated into fifty languages, and has spawned twelve sequels.[17] Lindsey's work shaped a generation's approach to biblical prophecy.[18]

As we've already noted, this is not the first time that Americans had enthusiastic expectations of Christ's imminent return. But unlike other prophetic movements, Lindsey and other interpreters of this period generally avoided precise date setting. Yet many were convinced that Christ's return would happen within the coming decades—Lindsey claimed that it would happen sometime in the 1980s, then later updated his prediction to the year 2000. The lack of specificity served a spiritual goal of the movement: uncertainty about the exact time combined with deep certainty that it was coming *soon* engendered reflection, repentance, and evangelization.[19]

Lindsey was popularizing (and sensationalizing) dispensational theology. To be sure, his book did not necessarily reflect the detailed views of many dispensationalists of the time, nor does it represent the views of many dispensationalist theologians today. But his perspective comes out of this theological tradition, so we should say a word about it.

Dispensationalism found its roots in the theology of nineteenth-century British preacher John Nelson Darby and spread mostly through lay teachers and Bible schools in nineteenth- and twentieth-century America. It produced the Bible church movement and theological institutions like Dallas Theological Seminary and Moody Bible Institute.[20] It teaches that human history has been divided into "dispensations" in which God deals with people differently—affecting understandings of how to interpret the Old and New Testaments and of the relationship between the church and Israel.[21]

Most relevant to our concerns here is its eschatology. Dispensationalism teaches a secret rapture of the church that will occur before a seven-year tribulation, the return of Christ to earth to reign over it for a thousand years (the millennium), and the final judgment. Some Christians have held to a "premillennial" eschatology—that Christ will return and reign on earth for a thousand years before the final judgment—for all of Christian history, but it's worth noting that dispensationalism as a system is a relatively new theological tradition.

Central to this theology is concern for the "literal" interpretation of Scripture. Interpreters focus on the historical and grammatical meaning of the text, avoiding allegorical interpretations common in the early church as well as modern forms of biblical scholarship. This explains some of the appeal at the time: in comparison to modern biblical criticism that often questioned the traditional authorship, dating, and meaning of the Bible, dispensationalists read the Bible in a "straightforward" way. They insisted that the Bible was not an incomprehensible ancient document but a gift to everyday believers, who could read, understand, and apply it to their lives.[22]

Dispensationalists claim to stick to a "plain reading" of the text, but their framework for interpreting Scripture must be taught. Dispensationalism became so popular in part because of the Scofield Reference Bible, a Bible published in 1909 that featured copious footnotes, charts, and cross-references to other biblical texts. Many people reading a Scofield Bible did not distinguish between the biblical text and the notes.[23] When people picked up a copy of *The Late Great Planet Earth*, many of them were already familiar with Lindsey's way of reading the Bible, and many others were unaware there was anything distinctive about it. "We're just reading the Bible," many pastors and Bible-study teachers said at the time.

In the book, Lindsey attempts to cover the timeline of biblical prophecy: from the rapture of the church, through the tribulation, until the return of Christ. While he spends one short chapter on the return—Christ's return to earth, thousand-year reign, final judgment, and the new heavens and earth—the vast majority of the book is dedicated to the lead-up to the rapture and the tribulation. Lindsey doesn't predict *when* the rapture will happen, but he is specific about the order of events, the role nations play, and how prophetic details will translate into contemporary technology.[24]

Lindsey begins the book by stacking the deck for his position with confidence: while people might go to lots of places to find truth, in this book, he says, "let's give God a chance to present His views."[25] These are not Lindsey's views, apparently, but *God's*. Lindsey uses this rhetorical tactic throughout: he doesn't present his views as one *interpretation* of the Bible among other valid options, but he describes his position as God's.

Early in the book, he argues that people misunderstood Jesus's mission on earth and the messianic prophecies he fulfilled because people "didn't bother to do any investigation for themselves."[26] He draws on what now sound like conspiracy theory tactics: casting doubt on the wisdom of "experts" and encouraging people to "do their own research." He makes repeated reference to "religious leaders" in the Bible who led people astray and religious leaders in the present who "dilute" what God has to say. He also highlights biblical references that say people will be deceived and teach false-hood in the last days. It is an effective rhetorical strategy: now your critics are not just wrong, but their opposition proves the justice of your cause because they are confirming biblical prophecy.[27]

We don't have the space to work through all the interpretive claims Lindsey makes, but we can identify key themes he shares with other writers and theologians of the time. These themes shape our reading of Scripture.

Themes of Lindsey's Prophetic Interpretation

The Bible is "definite" about the roles particular nations will play in the coming cosmic drama. Lindsey argues that it is incredibly important that we map biblical prophecies onto modern-day nations. The data in the biblical text is sufficient for us to understand which nations play which roles in the end times, as long as we apply the right hermeneutical rules.

Scripture is interpreted from a position of American superiority. Lindsey makes derogatory comments about Asian and Middle Eastern nations and peoples, describing them as "backwards" and writing about Islamic head coverings with suspicion.[28] In short, Lindsey approaches questions of biblical interpretation with an explicit yet uninterrogated cultural bias (a bias that we will see with more political flair in his later work).

Scripture is a puzzle or riddle to be deciphered. Lindsey insists that he isn't reading current events *into* the Bible; he's merely reading the Bible and watching its predictions unfold in real time. While Lindsey does have some evangelistic goals (securing your salvation before the coming crisis), much of the book reads the Bible like a puzzle God knew would stump us. The prophets do not challenge us by drawing attention to our sins or calling us to repentance. Rather, they outline dramatic events that we can puzzle together as informed spectators.

Scripture should be interpreted "literally" (sometimes). Lindsey highly values faithfulness to Scripture. He decries pastors who "explain away" prophecy, and claims to take it seriously and literally. Of course, no one interprets every word of the Bible as if it intends a physical or historical meaning. Even Lindsey says that some parts are figurative and some parts (like the "revived Roman Empire" in Daniel 7) must be metaphors because they don't make sense in light of current international affairs. One proponent defined dispensational theology by noting that they "believe what the Bible literally teaches" while their opponents allow for allegorical or spiritual interpretations by which you "can invent any kind of 'interpretation' you want."[29]

This disdain for allegorical readings of Scripture is itself a problem: there are legitimate concerns about allegorical readings, but to condemn them is to condemn the biblical interpretation of wide swaths of the historic church, including theologians who helped cement the foundational doctrines of the faith against heresies and schisms. Many critics also misrepresent allegorical readings. They do not come from a lack of discipline (theologians work out and argue with each other about the "rules" of interpretation), and they do not avoid what the Bible teaches.[30] When early Christians read the Old Testament allegorically, they were doing what they saw the apostles who wrote the New Testament doing: seeing in Old Testament passages truths more fully expressed in the New.[31]

No one reads the Bible entirely literally. The Bible is full of figural language, different genres, and somewhat bizarre cross-references from our perspective (who would have thought to cite Hosea 11:1 as a prophecy about baby Jesus in Egypt?). Most Christians recognize that everyone is making judgments about when to take things in a physical or historical way and when to understand them in a spiritual way. Obviously the Pharisees are not literal whitewashed tombs, and Israel understood that God's "mighty hand and outstretched arm" was a way to describe God's power, not his body. Other references are more contentious: Is "one day" literally one day or a "thousand years" a literal millennium? Was the story of Jonah intended to be understood as a historical account or a parable about God's love?

Important for our purposes, some of the most popular prophecy interpreters of this period denied that they were making decisions like this and thus did not explain their rationale for those decisions.[32] Why do we think Daniel or Revelation was intended to describe physical events in human history (or not)? How do we distinguish figurative language from plain-sense language? These questions are harder than those interpreters made them seem. We are not without tools for answering them—the history of the church in particular gives us guides—but ignoring the questions themselves by claiming that our interpretation is *the* straightforward one is dangerous and unhelpful.

This moment in history has special prophetic significance—and only now can we understand what the Bible means. "We have lived in the most significant period of prophetic history," Lindsey says.[33] About twelve years earlier, Billy Graham said something similar, that the present moment was the "climax" of history.[34] But for all the ways that international developments and technological advances made this period feel full of prophetic significance, other generations at other moments of instability and change have felt this same way. The rhetorical effect, however, is powerful.

Lindsey says that as members of the "prophetic 'now' generation," we have special insight into the biblical text. He cites Daniel 12:9, "The words are rolled up and sealed until the time of the end," in support of this. Until the end times, we couldn't understand these texts, but now we can. The "key" that will "unlock the prophetic book" is not Scripture or a hermeneutical method but "the current events that would begin to fit into the predicted pattern."[35] While biblical interpreters of the past might have been confounded by Revelation's "locust with the face of a man," modern interpreters recognize that this refers to a helicopter.

America's Place in the Prophetic Imagination

How does any of this translate into political activism? In *The Late Great Planet Earth*, amid foreboding descriptions of international players in the coming conflict, hope surfaces that a "widespread spiritual awakening" might avert America's decline. Lindsey takes on a more explicitly political form in his 1982 book, *The 1980s: Countdown to Armageddon*. Lindsey had already argued that the '80s were a significant decade: if a "biblical generation" is forty years, and a kind of "countdown" began after the Six Days War and Israeli statehood in 1948, then the cosmic "final battle" should occur no later than 1988.[36]

In this book, Lindsey looks back at predictions he made in *The Late Great Planet Earth* and is satisfied: the Soviet Union had indeed become more powerful, the Middle East was as volatile as ever, Israel had survived conflict and maintained statehood, the

United States faced energy instability because of powerful Middle Eastern countries, and Lindsey sees in European economics signs of a coming ten-nation confederacy described in Daniel. (Of course, other events fit his predictions less neatly, but he doesn't dwell on those.)[37] In many respects, Lindsey's general prophetic timeline between the two books stayed the same, bolstered by apparent confirmation in world events—with one striking difference.

The Late Great Planet Earth had almost entirely low expectations for American prosperity because the Bible predicts that power will shift to Rome, and the United States and other countries will inevitably cease to be world powers. In *The 1980s* Lindsey blames not divine ordering of human history for this decline but weak American foreign policy, liberalism, a "free lunch" mentality and state welfare, and the encroaching corruption of communism.[38] This by itself is consistent—God could use these developments to accomplish the preordained decline—but Lindsey goes on to describe the "critical and difficult choices" the American people must make "*right now*" in order to maintain American dominance.

While Lindsey says he isn't a "political writer," he is not afraid of giving political solutions to these problems. "I believe that the Bible supports building a powerful military force," Lindsey argues. "And the Bible is telling the US to become strong again."[39] Lindsey does not mince words: "We need to clean house in Washington and elect a Congress and a President who believe in the capitalist system," he says. If people act now, "America will survive this perilous situation and endure until the Lord comes to evacuate his people."[40] In many ways, Lindsey's exhortations were modeled after the Republican program and the Reagan administration.

Eschatology and the Bible

It is easy to look back on this theology and this political period and find it all to be ridiculous. It's easy to scoff at prophetic predictions that turned out to be wrong, ridicule evangelicals' confidence in their timelines, and criticize a hermeneutic based on current events. But we should also be chastened by recalling the long and diverse tradition of Christian expectations of the end times—from the early church's expectations that are corrected in 1 and 2 Thessalonians to Joachim of Fiore in twelfth-century Italy to the Millerites in nineteenth-century America.[41] In Lindsey's period, millennial expectations had largely tapered, but communism, the threat of nuclear destruction, and the creation of the United Nations (a kind of "world government") suddenly made a dispensational eschatology seem more possible.[42]

For people who did not live through the creation of the nuclear bomb (or don't remember it), it's hard to recapture the sense of terror. This new technology presented a realistic situation of global destruction that prompted fearful people to seek refuge in a rapture. Many readers of the Left Behind books, for example, were not necessarily convinced of dispensational theology but found the books comforting or edifying.[43] Looking for Jesus to fix the world made even more sense under "the shadow of nuclear weaponry."[44]

This approach to the Bible also met a more personal spiritual need. Does this ancient text apply to my life? Do these strange and confusing passages say something to me today? This approach made Scripture clearly relevant to politics and individual behavior. In the face of a political situation that felt hopeless, this interpretation ironically gave people a sense of renewed agency: they could make a choice to avoid the coming tribulation, and even if they did not get raptured out of it, they would have a guidebook for survival.[45] Many Christians in this period experienced a real zeal for evangelism, and while we might criticize their efforts as overly individualistic today, they were genuinely concerned with their neighbor's well-being. Whereas historical criticism focused on the text as a "window to an ancient world," the Scofield Bible was a window into the past and the future—and a guide for the present.[46]

So how can we read prophecy with an eye toward the past, present, and future? How can we find spiritual exhortation and even political instructions in the Bible, without succumbing to the methods that produced *The Late Great Planet Earth*? Here are some things to keep in mind.

Prophecy is not only predictive but also intended to provide critique, comfort, and confrontation. Dispensationalism is not the only Christian tradition that views the prophets as primarily predictive. Some of the earliest Bible interpreters, like Justin Martyr and Irenaeus, read the prophets this way, and all Christian traditions take many biblical prophecies to be predictive: the Apostles' Creed says that we all expect Jesus to return to "judge the living and the dead" and that we all expect the resurrection of the body and the "life everlasting." But not *all* prophecy is predictive, and not all of it is predictive in the same way. Much of Old Testament prophecy condemns the people of God for abusing and exploiting the vulnerable, giving colorful threats of judgment to emphasize how seriously God takes the abuse of creatures made in his image. The same is true of Revelation: as biblical scholar Michael J. Gorman describes it, Revelation is a "prophetic critique" of political idolatry and injustice.[47]

Oppressed peoples throughout Christian history have read Revelation in a similar way. Gerrard Winstanley, an English radical who criticized economic exploitation in the mid-1600s, drew extensively on biblical prophecy.[48] Allan A. Boesak, South African pastor and anti-apartheid activist, wrote a commentary on Revelation in 1987 that called the book a form of "underground protest literature."[49] Even early dispensationalists applied their theology against the evils of materialism and capitalist exploitation.[50]

Both Revelation and Daniel were intended to sustain the people of God in times of instability and crisis, and both express hope by pulling back the curtain on the ordinary functions of life and showing God's ultimate judgment against oppressors. These are *apocalypses*: a genre of literature in which revelation of a transcendent reality is mediated to a human from some kind of supernatural being. As such, they give language and imagery of resistance to oppressed peoples.[51]

Read for the whole redemptive story; don't search for a hidden narrative. There is a fine line between seeing connections between different parts of Scripture—across genres, time periods, and human authors—and moving into date setting, conspiracy theory, or heresy territory. One way to avoid this fate is to reflect on your reading *habits*. One scholar notes that many of the people she studied who spent hours absorbing Left Behind novels read them very differently than they read their Bibles. Their Bible reading was characterized by "formal repetition and discipline"—in short, daily doses—but they read Left Behind books for hours, leaving dishes and family responsibilities neglected by their total absorption into the story.[52]

Many twenty-first-century American Christians were taught that a "daily quiet time" was the mark of a faithful Christian, and so one way of reading the Bible (a reasonable, daily habit) turned into the *only* form. Reading Scripture the way we would read a story—sitting with it for longer periods, allowing ourselves to be engrossed in the story instead of getting hung up on how each small piece applies to our own lives—might help us read the prophetic and apocalyptic parts more faithfully.

Practice hermeneutic humility. It is ironic that Revelation, a book that so colorfully describes the pervasiveness of evil in human hearts and communities, has often attracted such *confident* interpreters. Our attention to the reality of evil in the world should include attention to the sin inside ourselves: our wayward motives, disordered desires, and learned prejudices. This is a posture of the heart more than a hermeneutical rule, but the former often drives more of our interpretations (especially our political ones) than the latter.

Remember that Revelation was given to the church, not to an individual. The book of Revelation is a strange "hybrid document." It's an apocalypse, prophecy, liturgical guide, and political text. It is also, foundationally, a *letter*. It was written to specific communities in the early days of the church, for their instruction and edification. The entire structure of the book counteracts our tendency to skip over the Bible's instructions for everyday faithful living and go straight to the juicy details of conquest and battle. Eugene Peterson says of the seven letters that begin the book, "We would prefer to go directly from the awesome vision of Christ (Revelation 1) to the glorious ecstasies of heaven (Revelation 4, 5) and then on to the grand victorious battles against dragon wickedness (Revelation 12–14) but we can't do it. The church has to be negotiated first. The only way from Christ to heaven and the battles against sin is through the church."[53] Our response to this wild and wonderful book should not be to shut ourselves into a basement room with some red string and photocopied Bible pages, piecing together our country's role in the final battle. Our response should be *worship* with the gathered people of God. In the face of civil religion in the Roman Empire, Revelation offers a call to right worship in the midst of wayward worship.[54]

Pay attention to your feelings. We'd be wrong to assume that the dispensationalists of the Cold War era were alone in having politics and emotions shape biblical interpretation. Both shape Bible interpretation for us all. The political and social context we live in, the moral demands of our moment, and the feelings shaping our hearts and communities will all influence how we read the Bible. This doesn't make politics or emotions bad; it makes our ignorance of their power dangerous. We need to examine what feelings we might bring with us to the biblical text—fear we are looking to inflame, anger we are looking to justify, sadness we are looking to heal—so that we can be aware of how they might influence our reading. And we should examine the emotions the text is *intended* to form in us. Biblical scholar Richard Bauckham says that the book of Revelation is supposed to "purge and refurbish the Christian imagination."[55] We are supposed to have our wayward loves and loyalties confronted, examined, and changed into love for God and his coming kingdom.

This attention to emotions will also help us have better conversations with people who interpret the Bible—and our political context—differently. Similar conversations about the meaning of Revelation happened during the height of the COVID-19 pandemic. Conspiracy theories and references to end-times theology increased during this time of great fear and instability. Some churches and Christian leaders circulated conspiracy theories that the COVID vaccine contains fetal tissue or implants a tracking microchip in your body, that chemicals or herbal supplements from the internet are better treatments than those provided by hospitals, or that the vaccine is the "mark of the beast" described in Revelation.[56] We have to ask where these theories come from—bad theology, unexamined emotions, shallow spiritual formation—if we are going to have more productive conversations about our responsibility to our neighbors and to the biblical text.

New Heavens and New Earth

While many prophecy interpreters at this time placed a huge emphasis on the rapture, the details of the tribulation, and present indicators of the "end times," they often placed very little emphasis on the parts of Christian eschatological hope that have enjoyed the most agreement among Christians across time and geography. While Revelation is unclear about many things, it is clear that Jesus Christ will ultimately exercise complete, just, and merciful rule over all creation, that God will dwell directly with his people and "wipe every tear from their eyes," and that, in the end, God will make everything new (Rev. 21).

8

Prayer, Politics, and Personal Faith

George W. Bush's and Barack Obama's Use of Scripture

Inauguration Day is full of ceremonies and celebrations, quiet moments where one president (and often their family) welcomes a new president and their family to the White House, and sometimes a church service. The day celebrates a peaceful transfer of power and gives the president an opportunity to cast a vision for the nation. It also features a swearing-in: a formal acceptance of authority that has almost always included placing a hand on the Bible.

The Bible is deeply entangled with the American presidency. A nation formed with no state church or official religion would nevertheless find great significance in the faith of its leaders. Biblical language still shapes our political rhetoric, and many voters still want to know that their president attends church, prays to God, and looks to Scripture for guidance. Campaign speeches, election debates, and presidential speeches quote the Bible regularly, with varying degrees of faithfulness.

This chapter explores the role Scripture continues to play in our political imaginations. It looks at some of the speeches two recent presidents gave—their National Prayer Breakfast speeches—in order to think better about the relationship between faith and public policy.[1] We won't get into many of the policies either president supported but instead will explore a number of questions: What does it mean that Christians in America want their politicians to display Christian faith but often recoil when their politicians explicitly use the Bible in policymaking? What is the appropriate role for Scripture in political advocacy? Do we care more about Christian *identity* than Christian *action*?

Religion and the American Presidency

The American presidency plays a unique role in the religion of the nation. Without a state church yet full of religious people, America developed a distinct religious tradition, a tradition in which the faith of the rulers still mattered to voters.[2] One scholar calls American presidents the "high priests of the American civil religion."[3] Others have described presidential speeches as "perhaps *the* central factor" promoting civil religion in American life. Presidents are among the few leaders who can both appeal to biblical language and command the attention of most citizens.[4] American presidents have always used religious language, with varying degrees of specificity and frequency. But phrases like doing "the Lord's work," building the "kingdom of God," or honoring the "covenant of the nation" have always been popular.[5]

Modern evangelicals have had a rocky relationship with presidents. Many pinned their hopes on Richard Nixon, who turned out to be an embarrassment. Evangelicals were initially interested in Jimmy Carter, who spoke their language and made "born again" part of the national vocabulary, but he did not support their social policies and made public missteps that turned off evangelicals.[6] Prior to the 1970s, conservative Protestants were more likely to be Democrats, but Reagan's presidency solidified the relationship between the emerging religious right and the Republican Party.

This history informed evangelical Christians' attitudes about both George W. Bush and Barack Obama. The standards for these presidents were vastly different: one had a reputation of religiosity but rarely quoted Scripture; the other used language from the Bible often, but rumors about his faith were so frequent that his campaign staff had to add a page to his website clarifying that he was not a Muslim.

George W. Bush

A Personal Jesus

While Bush was known as "the most openly religious president in generations," he was also a remarkably *private* religious leader, believing in what one magazine called his "personal Jesus." He did not attend a DC church, he did not publicize his spiritual advisors or pastors, and while it was well reported that the White House was full of Bible studies, his own study and spiritual practices were "as guarded as a state secret."[7]

In many ways, this fit the expectations and desires of his primary religious constituency. Bush had a personal conversion story that evangelicals understood: a fall from grace, a moment of illumination, a new life moving forward.[8] He used evangelical language to describe it: "I searched my heart and recommitted my life to Jesus Christ." He credits a conversation with Billy Graham for "sparking" a change in his heart, and his conversion prompted him to give up drinking alcohol.[9] By the 1990s, he was even more well versed in evangelical Christianity, citing *The One Year Bible*, Oswald Chambers's *My Utmost for His Highest*, and books by Charles Spurgeon and Charles Stanley as favorite reading materials.[10] He became a kind of ambassador to religious-right leaders during his father's presidency and described his later decision to run for president as a call from God during a sermon at his Texas church.[11]

In comparison to his opponents in the 2000 election, Bush made less explicit connections between his faith and his policy positions. Al Gore used much more biblical language: he drew on the story of Cain and Abel and the Golden Rule to talk about gun reform, on Psalm 24 in the context of environmental policy, and on Jesus's parable of the seeds when talking about violence in media. He cited 2 Thessalonians and Galatians, "Be not weary in well-doing," in the context of continuing President Clinton's legacy.[12]

In comparison, Bush made few biblical references but made clear that he shared Christians' *personal faith*. Many of his religious statements focused on personal conviction or inner comfort. In a 1999 primary debate, he famously cited Jesus Christ as his favorite philosopher, "because he changed my heart." Explaining the answer later, he did not point to any of Christ's teachings or philosophy but said he shared his admiration for Jesus to let people know "the kind of person I am."[13]

On rare occasions Bush invoked religious beliefs on behalf of actual policies, and most of them were symbolic cultural issues. He supported teaching creationism along with evolution in public schools, the public display of the Ten Commandments, and prayer in public schools. Some of the few actual policies he engaged with religious motivations were increasing government support for faith-based nonprofits and preventing federal funding of stem cell research. Most of the time, the religious influence was indirect: he talked about going to God for guidance, having his faith strengthen him personally, or finding comfort in the Bible.[14]

In Bush's 2001 inauguration speech, he only briefly touched on religious themes. He noted that religious organizations could address needs that government does not, and then he made a biblical allusion: "When we see that wounded traveler on the road to Jericho, we will not pass to the other side." There wasn't anything overtly *Christian* about the speech, other than the reference to the good Samaritan. Even still, Richard Land, then-president of the Southern Baptist Convention's Ethics and Religious Liberty Commission, described the speech as the "most overtly religious speech in its tone of any inaugural address in living memory." Land said he felt that the speech signaled that "President George W. Bush is not going to be intimidated by the media elites into pretending that we are a secular nation. We are not."[15] These responses drew on a decades-long narrative that conservative Christians were socially and politically marginalized, a narrative (like most) that featured some truth and some fiction.[16]

By the time of Bush's inauguration, evangelicals had a strong national presence and a solid relationship with the Republican Party. But central to their identity was a remaining sense of cultural stigma. We saw this dynamic already with Reagan: evangelicals identified with him because he appeared *afraid* it was unacceptable to express religious devotion in public. We'll see the same dynamic at play in Bush's presidency—the strange combination of self-conscious cultural isolation combined with great political power.

Evangelicals were initially pleased with the new president: cabinet meetings opened with prayer, there were weekly Bible studies for the staff, and the National Day of Prayer was observed with flourish.[17] He quickly cut off federal funding for overseas groups providing abortions and announced on his ninth day in office a White House Office of Faith-Based and Community Initiatives that would end "a legacy of discrimination against faith-based charities."[18]

For many, however, the allure of Bush was his *individual experience of faith*, the very fact that he was a Christian and could talk genuinely about his relationship with Jesus. Too much theology, doctrine, or direct relationship between faith and policy was just "bad politics."[19] For many Christians, a president with personal faith could automatically be trusted. If God guides genuine Christians, a president who confesses real faith will ultimately make the right decisions. This gives a president a lot of "leeway" with leaders when it comes to specific policies, because the most important thing is that he has a personal relationship with the sovereign God.[20]

Bush's staff was clear that the rarity of biblical language was intentional. The director of White House communications told a journalist shortly after the 2004 election, "The president divorces policymaking from personal faith." His personal faith gives him clarity, comfort, and assurance in God's ultimate plan. But "George W. Bush believes in a secular state," Dan Bartlett emphasized. He went further, noting that the president was not instituting a theocracy, adding, "I can tell you that George Bush is not making decisions based on his own personal faith." The journalist who got these lines summed it up this way: "For George Bush, thus, everything is dependent upon spirituality, and at the same time nothing is dependent upon spirituality."[21]

Many White House insiders, journalists, and scholars agree: the important thing for Bush was to *identify with evangelicals*, not necessarily to make Christian decisions about policy. Doug Wead, who worked with the younger Bush on helping his father communicate with evangelicals, put it bluntly: "There is nothing more thrilling for an evangelical than to believe their president is reading the Bible." It matters less that his policies come from Scripture than it does to know that their leader is "hearing the word of God." Land said something similar in a 2004 interview: he knew Bush was "an evangelical Christian," without any doubt, because he "believes in the truth of the Bible, with a capital T."[22]

Prayer Breakfast Speeches

We're going to devote special attention to the National Prayer Breakfast speeches of Bush and Obama because they are the president's annual opportunity to address religious people and articulate the relationship between the president's faith and public role.[23] The speeches are also a good way to compare these two presidents: they each gave eight Prayer Breakfast speeches across their two terms, and the general themes of their presidencies are exemplified in these speeches.[24]

Unlike his successor, Bush never said the name of Jesus Christ in any of his eight speeches and made relatively few references to Scripture. In his first Prayer Breakfast speech, he cited James 3:11 ("Fresh water and salt water cannot flow from the same spring") and quoted Harry Truman alluding to Matthew 25:23: "I ask only to be a good and faithful servant of my Lord and my people." In

2005 and 2006, his only biblical references were to loving your neighbor as yourself, cited once as a commandment and the second time as a "universal call." In 2008 he asked God to "bring about the day when His peace shall reign across the world and every tear shall be wiped away."

Bush made lots of references to "faith" without any Christian content: "Faith crosses every border and touches every heart in every nation" (2001), or "The promise of faith is not the absence of suffering; it is the presence of grace" (2002). Like many of his predecessors, he called America "a nation of prayer" frequently and described prayer as something "universal" the country shares (2001). He used general terms for God, like "Providence" (2003 and 2004), and used vaguely covenantal language, like the "testing" of the nation (2003 and 2004).

Many of his religious references were either about his support for faith-based nonprofits or about how his personal faith sustains him. To him, faith teaches humility (2001), helps him recognize human limits (2004), brings people together (2005), and reminds politicians that their power is temporary (2005). At the first Prayer Breakfast, he noted that faith had motivated opposition to slavery, support for the civil rights movement, and work in prisons, hospitals, and homeless shelters.

Like his successor, Bush also made frequent references to pluralism and religious freedom. In his speech after 9/11, amid inflamed religious tensions nationwide, he said, "Every religion is welcomed in our country; all are practiced here." In 2004 he talked about the "great American tradition of religious tolerance" and called Christians, Jews, and Muslims to overcome their historic divisions and act like "sons and daughters of Abraham." In 2006 he mentioned Americans with "no faith at all." In 2007 and 2008 he made similar attempts at interfaith unity: "We come from many different faiths, yet we share this profound conviction: We believe that God listens to the voice of His children and pours His grace upon those who seek Him in prayer."

Bush's successor would draw on many of the same themes, but with some marked differences.

Barack Obama

The Joshua Generation

In some ways, Bush and Obama were remarkably similar: both were Bible-believing Christians who found identity and comfort in the church. Both claimed that the Bible shaped them personally, and both confessed their faith in Jesus as they campaigned and led the country.[25] But Obama had a different reputation among conservative evangelicals, even though he frequently and explicitly referenced his Christian faith. He spoke in terms of personal conversion, belonging to a church and tradition, and spiritual practices.[26] It became especially important for him during elections to describe his Christian faith openly and often because of the persistent false belief that he was a Muslim.[27] He responded in direct, clear, orthodox language in an interview for the evangelical magazine *Christianity Today*: "I am a Christian, and I am a devout Christian. I believe in the redemptive death and resurrection of Jesus Christ. I believe that that faith gives me a path to be cleansed of sin and have eternal life."[28] He had to walk a fine line, however, both because of the relative discomfort his own party had with religious language and because of controversies surrounding his former pastor, Jeremiah Wright.[29]

Obama became a Christian after working with Black churches in Chicago as a community organizer.[30] He learned about both politics and faith in the context of a tradition that has always drawn on biblical language to describe political work. A few weeks after announcing his candidacy for president, he spoke at the commemoration of the Selma Voting Rights March in Alabama, honoring the "Moseses" who "challenged Pharaoh, the princes, powers who said that some are on top and others are at the bottom, and that's how it's always going to be."[31]

He said the civil rights generation took people "across the sea that folks thought could not be parted" by "always knowing that God was with them." Drawing on a common approach in Black churches, he intertwined this biblical story with his own—the Moses generation's faithfulness allowed him to thrive, changing the circumstances of his life from the limited opportunities available to his father or grandfather. He led his charge by continuing the biblical story: "I thank the Moses generation; but we've got to remember, now, that Joshua still had a job to do."[32]

He often answered questions about faith in language that *would* have been more appealing to evangelicals if not for their strong relationship with the other party. When asked about prayer, he said that he prayed for "forgiveness for my sins and flaws," and when asked if the kingdom of God was attainable by human effort, he said, "I don't believe that the Kingdom of God is achievable on Earth without God's intervention, and without God's return through Jesus Christ, but I do believe in improvement."[33] In the 2004 Democratic National Convention speech that catapulted him to national attention, he blamed the "pundits" who "slice-and-dice" America into Red States and Blue States for ignoring that Democrats "worship an awesome God" too.[34]

Prayer Breakfast Speeches

Obama said Christ's name in all of his Prayer Breakfast speeches but one. He said that he placed his faith in the "nail-scarred hands of Jesus Christ" (2013), narrated how he "came to know Jesus Christ" as his "Lord and Savior" (2011), and talked about relying on Jesus in tumultuous times (2016). Like Bush, he used more generally spiritual language as well, saying that the country needed to be "empowered by faith" (2010), that the gathered group was kneeling "before the Eternal" (2011) and "pausing for fellowship and prayer" (2015) as "people of faith" (2013). Both Bush and Obama talked about people of faith serving the country by feeding the poor or caring for vulnerable people, and both used the language of "children of God" frequently.

Obama referenced religion being used for divisive or even radical ends a bit more than Bush did in these speeches. "Far too often," he said in his first Prayer Breakfast speech, "we have seen faith wielded as a tool to divide us from one another" or "an excuse for prejudice and intolerance." In 2014 and 2015 he referenced faith being betrayed or twisted by people with nefarious intentions. And while he talked about pluralism about as much as Bush did, he used different terms. Where Bush often referenced generic "faith," Obama was more likely to talk about specific *faiths* and their real differences. In his first speech he said, "We read from different texts. We follow different edicts. We subscribe to different accounts of how we came to be here and where we're going next—and some subscribe to no faith at all."

He often quoted from the Bible, Torah, and Koran to support a religious idea the three major faiths could agree on. He mentioned more religions than Bush, like Hinduism and Sikhism, and more often acknowledged nonreligious people. Obama's descriptions of pluralism were likely shaped by his childhood: he was born in Hawaii but spent several years of his childhood in Indonesia with his anthropologist mother, whom he remembers "dragging" him to church on Christian holidays but also exposing him to Buddhism, Shinto religion, and other traditions.[35] His nods to pluralism and his frequent naming of Jesus and quotations of Scripture weren't accidental. Where Bush often relied on general civic religion, Obama named particular religious traditions. By acknowledging religious differences, Obama was able to be more specific about his own beliefs. He did not appeal to general religiosity but named theological differences, honored other beliefs, and then confidently invoked his own.

In his final Prayer Breakfast speech, Obama described it as a regular habit to include in the speech a passage from Scripture that had "sustained" him throughout the year. His 2013 speech featured an extended account of the Bibles of Martin Luther King Jr. and Abraham Lincoln, and how they both found comfort and strength for their respective challenges from the pages of their Bibles. Sometimes the language was mere allusions: in 2010 he talked about political "contests for power" as a "Tower of Babel" where we "lose the sound of God's voice." Other times he quoted directly: "Seek first His kingdom" (2011); "Those who wait on the Lord will soar on wings like eagles" (2011); "Do not claim to be wiser than you are" (2014); "Do justice, love kindness, walk humbly with our God" (2015); "For God has not given us a spirit of fear, but of power and of love and of a sound mind" (2016). He frequently mentioned the biblical command to care for the poor and vulnerable, and the humility that Scripture should instill in us (twice he quoted 1 Cor. 13:12, "For now we see through a glass darkly").

Obama was more likely to directly address policy issues in these speeches as well, a feature of his belief that faith and politics were not strictly separated. He talked about poverty and LGBTQ rights in 2010, climate change and environmental issues in 2014 and 2016, and economic policy in a 2012 speech that enraged some conservative commentators.

His 2012 speech hit some familiar notes. He stressed that living in a religiously pluralistic society meant that "personal religious beliefs alone" couldn't dictate policy, but he also noted that religion couldn't be "left at the door." He again referenced the many religiously motivated social reformers in American history. He made clear that his faith, like theirs, could not be contained in "personal moments of prayer or private conversations with pastors" but must motivate his leadership as president, even if imperfectly.

Obama said that regulating financial institutions and insurance companies upheld God's command to "love thy neighbor as thyself." He defended higher taxes for the wealthy by citing Jesus's teaching: "For unto whom much is given, much shall be required." He couched his support for foreign aid and intervention for human rights abuses in the "Biblical call to care for the least of these, for the poor, for those at the margins of our society" and Proverbs 31: "Speak up for those who cannot speak for themselves, for the rights of all who are destitute."

He quoted C. S. Lewis, saying, "Christianity is not, and does not profess to have a detailed political program," but also said that he hoped people of "good will" could pursue places of common ground on the basis of their religious beliefs. He praised the recent Passion Conference, where students had gathered to "worship the God who set the captives free" and worked to end modern-day slavery. He highlighted the White House's partnership with religious organizations like Catholic Charities and World Vision (as well as Jewish and Islamic organizations). He exhorted that the Bible teaches Christians to be "doers of the word and not merely hearers" (James 1:22–25) and to live out their faith in not only word but deed.

He acknowledged that government policy alone could not solve the country's problems and encouraged people of faith to join together in acts of kindness and courage, citing 1 John 3:17–18, "If anyone has material possessions and sees his brother in need but has no pity on him, how can the love of God be in him? Dear children, let us not love with words or tongue but with actions and in truth."

Conservative political commentators tore apart this speech.[36] Peter Wehner, speechwriter for Reagan, George H. W. Bush, and George W. Bush, wrote a scathing piece for *Commentary*, calling the speech "divisive theology." He criticized Obama for moving from the general biblical commandment to specific policy: "Perhaps the argument being made by the president is that if we read the book of Acts carefully enough, we'll find that God's preferred tax rate just happens to be the one championed by Obama."[37] Faith and Freedom Coalition founder Ralph Reed called the connection between tax policy and Scripture "theologically threadbare and straining credulity," and he said any policy talk in the breakfast was "over the line."[38]

Wehner's argument exemplifies the difference between Obama and Bush we are interested in. He criticized Obama for "using the Scriptures to advance a transparently partisan political agenda." While Wehner said he has "long argued" that faith should shape an individual's political ethics, "Scripture does not provide a governing blueprint." He cited Christian ethicist Paul Ramsey on this point, that identifying Christian ethics with "specific partisan proposals that clearly are not the only ones that may be characterized as Christian" is akin to heresy. He said that Obama was as "eager to vulgarize and dumb down Christianity as Jerry Falwell was."[39]

Presidential Faith: Personal or Public?

These two examples help us think about the way biblical passages should be used in the public forum of our pluralistic country. What do we *say* we want our politicians to believe or do or say, and what do we *actually* want? Is it appropriate for politicians to use biblical passages for political purposes? Is it appropriate for them to appeal to Christian identity without being committed to distinctly Christian politics? These are questions we cannot entirely answer. But the recent examples of Presidents Bush and Obama can help us begin to articulate a few answers.

Bush tended toward identifying faith, prayer, and Scripture as internal, personal motivations for his political work. Obama was more likely to draw on the social-reform tradition of the church and point to that legacy as the legacy of faith in America. Obama was also more likely to draw biblical language than Bush, but he often used it more as part of the moral language of America than as a source of moral commandments. Bush was more in line with conservative Christians on social issues (and economic and military issues); Obama was more in line with progressive religious commitments to economic and racial justice. In short, Bush's public Christianity was mostly commitment to a social and religious *identity*; Obama's was more about speaking the *language* of the Christian faith. With that summary in mind, let's think more deeply about the meaning and purpose of faith in public.

We need to examine what influences are shaping our voting habits. Bush and Obama had strikingly divergent reputations. If you didn't know the history of the religious right, it would be unintelligible why one of these presidents still has the reputation as *the* Christian president and the other worked for eight years to prove he was a Christian. So why did evangelicals respond so differently to Obama than they did to Bush?

First, Obama came from a different religious tradition than white evangelicalism, and while he used familiar Christian language, his public work and personal faith did not match their expectations. His conversion was foreign to them. Not only did he become a Christian in the context of community organizing with Black churches, but he described his conversion in terms of the church and social action, not as a personal moment. In a speech to progressive leaders as a senator, he described his conversion as realizing that he needed community, a "vessel for my beliefs," and an opportunity to join the social work of the church. It was "not an epiphany" but a "choice." Yet there remained a deeply evangelical sense of conversion: "Kneeling beneath that cross on the South Side, I felt that I heard God's spirit beckoning me. I submitted myself to His will and dedicated myself to discovering His truth."[40]

Second, we can't ignore the racism behind some evangelicals' disdain for President Obama. While there were legitimate policy and theological disagreements, many not only criticized his policies but also questioned his American citizenship and his Christian identity. In the 2012 election, Latter-Day Saint Mitt Romney was considered the "Christian" choice by Protestants—who would normally distance themselves from the LDS church—in comparison to the Protestant nondenominational Obama.[41]

Last, and perhaps most obvious, Obama was a Democrat. By the time of Bush's first election (and certainly by the time of Obama's), the relationship between white evangelicalism and the Republican Party was so tight that untangling theological and political reasons for their rejection of Obama is difficult. Some of these political motivations were consistent and genuine: abortion was a central political issue for evangelicals, and Obama had a terrible record on that count. He voted against the Induced Infant Liability Act in 2002 in Illinois, then voted against similar federal legislation (the Born-Alive Infants Protection Act) even when extremely pro-choice groups had no objection to it.[42] In his first term, he reversed two important Bush policies that evangelicals favored: the executive order ending federal funding for embryonic stem cell research and the prohibition on funding for international family-planning NGOs that provided contraceptives or abortion.

But as we've seen, some conservative Christians vehemently criticized his entire approach to faith and politics—a surprise given their joy over Bush's public faith. There are plenty of legitimate reasons Christians could have voted for Bush and not supported Obama, but with a little bit of distance and the benefit of hindsight, we see how different influences—discomfort with a different tradition of Christianity, racism that has been strongly embedded in American history and churches, and partisan identity overtaking Christian identity—may have shaped our votes.

And then it's worth reflecting on the present. What sources most influence our interpretation of candidates? What standards do we hold these sources to, and are they good and faithful? Do we care more about a candidate publicly claiming our "team" or using our language than we do about the faithfulness of their policies and personal life?

We need to be cautious—but not suspicious—about biblical language in public life. Obama was deeply concerned that his party stop avoiding religion—and stop forfeiting that space to the Republican Party. In 2006, then-Senator Obama spoke at the Call to Renewal conference for progressive faith leaders. He described the "mutual suspicion" between "religious America and secular America" and said "secularists" were wrong to ask believers to "leave their religion at the door before entering into the public square." He listed important social reformers like Frederick Douglass and Dorothy Day who were motivated by faith *and* used biblical terms to describe their cause. He called it an "absurdity" for people not to bring personal religious beliefs to public policy debates.[43]

He also described what the left lost when they avoided religion: the moral language of the country. If progressives "scrub language of all religious content," he said, "we forfeit the imagery and terminology through which millions of Americans understand both their personal morality and social justice." Imagine Lincoln's second inaugural address without "judgments of the Lord," he said, or Martin Luther King Jr.'s "I Have a Dream" speech without "all of God's children." He went on to describe not only the rhetorical loss but also the way some in his party ignored the genuine religious motivations of the majority of Americans—to the party's political and moral detriment.

Obama's insight is important: American public life throughout history has been shaped by biblical language. It is an important part of our shared history and sense of community. But there are dangers with thinking of biblical language this way: when the Bible is merely a reservoir of helpful moral and political language, it is easily abused. Recent examples have clarified that for us. Think of Florida governor Ron DeSantis referencing imagery of spiritual warfare during an election season ("Put on the full armor of God, stand up to the left's schemes") or President Biden citing Isaiah 6:8 ("Here I am, Lord, send me") when talking about American military service. Biblical language is powerful. It gives our words a sense of transcendence and moral obligation—and that can be easily abused.

We do not need to avoid Christian convictions in public life because others have misused or abused them. We should persist in bringing our faith, both public and private, to bear on politics, regardless of whether others have done it poorly or in ways we disagree with. The conservative commentators who criticized Obama's 2012 Prayer Breakfast speech were wrong to say that Scripture cannot inform policies or be cited as a public reason for supporting certain ones.

The ethicist that Peter Wehner cited above did not say that distinctly Christian reasons—such as biblical passages—could not be used for political goals, but he said that identifying one political position as *the* Christian position (and thus calling any political opponents unchristian) was akin to heresy. We struggle to find the space between avoiding *all* biblical arguments and identifying *one* policy as the only Christian one, but such space exists! Citing biblical passages about caring for the poor and vulnerable in support of tax policy that is intended to serve those people can be a faithful way of engaging in public life. Claiming that your tax policy is the only Christian option is not.

Obama cited his own religious beliefs more often *because* he acknowledged the importance of pluralism. He could openly acknowledge the "nail-scarred hands of Jesus" because he also referenced the faith of Jewish, Muslim, and other Americans. Rather than using vague language to paint the country as religiously monolithic, by recognizing our diversity we actually give space for specificity. Part of respecting our differences is being honest about them. If Christians want to have our politics informed by the Bible, we should not misrepresent ourselves in public by pretending we came to our positions apart from the Bible. Instead of treating the Bible like a trump card that invalidates all other positions or invoking divine support of our specific policies, we can faithfully engage in public with our own convictions and compassion for others who think differently.

Obama's arguments are an important reminder for Christians weary of the misuse of biblical arguments in politics. There are pitfalls, to be sure, but ignoring the power of biblical language in our public life ignores the rich history of social reform and faithful political work that came before us.

Scripture in Public

These two recent presidents are not perfect foils for each other. They both relied on Christian identity to make voters feel as if they could identify with them, they both quoted Scripture when it suited their political purposes, and neither of them should be held up as the ultimate example of faithful witness. Yet their crucial differences help us think more critically and carefully about what we expect of our leaders, the ways we ourselves are shaped and formed to participate politically, and how the Bible should or should not be used in public life.

"Give unto Caesar
What Is Caesar's"

Evangelicals and Donald Trump

Donald Trump was not the original evangelical favorite. Early in the 2016 primaries, there were many more palatable candidates, and evangelicals had no universal pick. One key player in uniting evangelicals around Trump was one of the few leaders who endorsed him early in the primary: Jerry Falwell Jr. The president of Liberty University constantly praised Trump, often invoking the words of Jesus to defend the candidate against naysayers concerned about his language, behavior, or morals: "Give unto Caesar what is Caesar's and to God what is God's."

Falwell joins a long history of using this passage for political purposes, but the verse took on a unique life during the 2016 election. Christian leaders used it to explain a warped version of "two kingdoms" theology that separated a person's interpersonal moral obligations and their public political obligations. Christians were free to make political decisions that were entirely contrary to their faith's moral teaching because the "rules" in the two kingdoms were different. Giving to Caesar what is Caesar's meant playing by the rules of the world when it came to politics, and giving to God what is God's meant acting faithfully in your church, family, or immediate community.

After the 2016 election, evangelicals would grapple with that biblical interpretation and would search for alternative ways of allowing Scripture to fuel their political imagination.

"We Take the Bible All the Way": Donald Trump and Scripture

Trump's presidency was marked by a confusing relationship with the Bible. At a 2015 rally in Mobile, Alabama, Trump said the Bible was his favorite book, adding, "We take the Bible all the way."[1] Later that year, in a famous TV clip, Trump was asked about his favorite Bible verse and he responded that it was "very personal" and that he didn't "want to get into verses." "The Bible means a lot to me, but I don't want to get into specifics." Another interviewer pressed him, asking if he prefers the Old Testament or New Testament. "Probably . . . equal," Trump responded.[2]

Easily, Trump's most famous Bible reference was the St. John's Episcopal Church debacle. Media coverage that Trump had briefly stayed in an underground bunker during the 2020 racial justice protests angered the president, and the administration had him give a speech in the Rose Garden along with a photo op at St. John's. After a "law and order" speech in which Trump threatened to deploy the military to areas where police failed to adequately respond to the protests, Trump told the press, "Now I am going to pay my respects to a very, very special place."[3]

Tear gas and other riot-control measures were used to clear Lafayette Square to prepare a path for the president to walk from the White House to the church.[4] In the course of his seventeen-minute-long photo op, Trump awkwardly bounced a Bible in his hands, held it up for the cameras, and said little. Asked "Is that your Bible?" by a reporter, he quickly replied, "It's *a* Bible." When directly asked about the protests, Trump responded, "We have a great country. That's my thoughts. Best country in the world. It's great, and we will make it even greater, and it won't take long."[5]

Writer Elizabeth Bruenig describes the whole affair as "vulgar" and "blunt." Trump didn't open the Bible, read from it, or take it with him into the church building to hear a sermon about it. It was a prop. As Bruenig notes, "He seemed to know, as he positioned himself as the defender of the Christian faith, that he needed to imbue his presidency with some renewed moral purpose; Christianity was simply a convenient vein to tap."[6]

It was a convenient vein for many of Trump's defenders as well. Christians formulated a variety of theological justifications for Trump—from direct prophecies, to comparisons with biblical kings who had moral failings but helped God's people (David, Cyrus, Nebuchadnezzar), to claims that Trump's surprising win proved God's favor.[7] Vaguely biblical language was constant, often divorced from larger biblical narratives or theological context: Trump was in power "for such a time as this" (Esther 4:14), evangelical naysayers had forgotten that God's thoughts are not our thoughts and his ways not our ways (Isa. 55:8), and one pastor compared Trump's daughter and son-in-law to Mary and Joseph: "It's just like God to use a young Jewish couple to help Christians in the United States."[8] Not only did the January 6 rioters use Christian language and biblical references in their signs and chants, but the protest was described by participants as a new march around Jericho.[9]

The days of the shining city on a hill were over. Trump was the first US president since JFK *not* to use the language from the Sermon on the Mount, and his campaign was defended by Christians intent on sidelining Jesus's language. "We aren't electing a pastor" was a constant refrain of evangelical Trump supporters. Robert Jeffress, senior pastor of First Baptist Dallas and a regular Fox News contributor, reminded voters in 2016 of the 1980 election: one candidate was a "born-again Christian, Sunday school teacher in a Baptist church, who was faithfully married to one woman" (Jimmy Carter), and the other was "a twice-married Hollywood actor who as governor of California had signed the most liberal abortion bill in California history, and whose wife practiced astrology" (Ronald Reagan).[10] When asked if he wanted a candidate who followed the teachings of Jesus, Jeffress replied, "Heck no. I would run from that candidate as far as possible, because the Sermon on the Mount was not given as a governing principle for this nation." The government is supposed to "be a strongman to protect its citizens against evildoers," not turn the other cheek.[11] It wasn't a far jump from wanting a country that didn't turn the other cheek to enthusiastically supporting a candidate who hit back.

Marchers and Ministers

Jerry Falwell Jr. appealed to his father's authority in defending his decision to endorse Trump: "When he walked into a voting booth, he wasn't electing a Sunday school teacher or a pastor or even a president who shared his theological beliefs; he was electing the president of the United States with the talents, abilities, and experience required to lead a nation." Later he added, "Jimmy Carter was a great Sunday school teacher, but look at what happened to our nation with him in the presidency."[12] This appeal to his father's authority was important. To understand the significant role that Jerry Falwell Jr. played in Trump's election, we first need to understand the significant role Jerry Falwell Sr. played in evangelical political engagement.

Falwell Sr. was central to the Moral Majority, a political coalition of conservative Christians associated with the religious right. The pastor of Thomas Road Baptist Church and founder of Liberty University in Lynchburg, Virginia, Falwell was initially politically disinterested. In a March 1965 speech titled "Ministers and Marches," Falwell discouraged Christian involvement in direct political action, particularly the marches led by civil rights leaders with "left-wing associations" like Martin Luther King Jr. The church had a "message of redeeming grace" designed to meet humanity's "spiritual need," Falwell preached. "Nowhere are we commissioned to reform the externals." He criticized people ("not acquainted with the Bible") who see in the exodus an impetus for leading people out of bondage in the present day.[13]

The "key verse" in this whole matter of the church and the world, he said in the sermon, was Philippians 3:20, "But our citizenship is in heaven." Close behind it, though, was a verse that his son would rely on, in very different ways: "We are told to 'render unto Caesar, the things that are Caesar's," Falwell said. The "true interpretation," he insisted, was that Christians "have very few ties on this earth." Later he emphasized the cruelty of the Roman government. In the context of the oppression of his people, "surely [Jesus] would take some political stand here," he wondered. "But he did not." Instead Jesus gives apolitical spiritual counsel: "Pay your taxes, forget politics, and serve Me with all your heart."

Unsurprisingly, Falwell made the argument in terms of biblical fidelity: "Believing the Bible as I do," he said, he needed to preach the gospel, not battle communism or fight for civil rights.[14] "Preachers are not called to be politicians but to be soul winners." If preachers just preached the gospel, it would cause revival, and social problems would disappear. While this initially seems entirely counter to the position he and his son would later adopt, toward the end of the sermon he begins to sound a bit more like Jr.: Jesus "was not here to reform the Roman Empire."

Falwell Sr.'s position on politics would change drastically. Falwell Sr. played a significant role in a narrative about American evangelical political engagement: evangelicals were politically inactive and culturally isolated until the sexual revolution (and *Roe v. Wade* in particular) propelled them into the voting booth.[15] The Moral Majority, founded in 1979, would register millions of new voters, change the terms of debate in the Republican party, and shape the political theology of the American church. As the founder, Falwell became the "face of Christian political involvement."[16] While the "shift" argument is deeply overstated (the story of evangelical political involvement is more complicated) and at least partially misplaced (abortion was less the flashpoint than desegregation of schools), there is some truth in it. Evangelicalism's ideas about political influence, and the group's relative importance in American politics, did change.

Falwell Sr. articulated the change in a way that aligned with this later narrative. Religious conservatives have not "politicized the gospel," but "liberals" have turned the moral foundations of the country into political issues that conservatives have no choice but to address.[17] Falwell Sr. described his activism as a "divine mandate" to fight for leaders who would "save America."[18] His son's later work would echo these themes: the government is not supposed to be "Christian" (at least in the "turn the other cheek" sense), but the country's demise demands that Christians fight for their nation.

Liberty became an important institution in the Moral Majority milieu, hosting Reagan in 1980 to talk about prayer in public schools, John McCain in 2006 to make friendly with evangelical voters suspicious of him, and Romney to talk about marriage in 2012.

Trump's 2016 appearance at Liberty exemplified his relationship with evangelicals: "We're going to protect Christianity," he said, "and I can say that. I don't have to be politically correct." It was in line with Trump's previous appearance in 2012, when he advised students to "get even" if someone wronged them and Falwell defended the comments as compatible with the "tough side" of Christian doctrine and "the ministry of Christ."[19]

"Give unto Caesar . . ."

After Falwell Sr.'s passing in 2007, one of his sons took over the church and the other son took over the university. The son who took over the university, Jerry Falwell Jr., would also take up the mantle of his father's political activity in the 2016 election. Liberty hosted Senator Ted Cruz when he announced his campaign for president, brought a variety of pundits to campus, and on January 18, 2016, hosted Donald Trump. Falwell endorsed the then-candidate about a week later, though his introduction at the Liberty event left little question about his support. "In my opinion,

Donald Trump lives a life of loving and helping others as Jesus taught in the great commandment," Falwell gushed.[20]

Unlike some Christian leaders who were more restrained or even apologetic in defending Trump, Falwell was enthusiastic. One Bible verse played a crucial role: "Then Jesus said to them, 'Give back to Caesar what is Caesar's and to God what is God's'" (Mark 12:17, as well as Matt. 22:21 and Luke 20:25). Falwell cited the verse regularly, usually without very much explanation. It could even be shortened further: "Give unto Caesar what is Caesar's" was enough, shorthand for a larger political theology, an easy way of gesturing to his larger approach to politics without getting into the details.

In August 2016, Falwell wrote a *Washington Post* op-ed defending his support of Trump, titled "Trump Is the Churchillian Leader We Need." While he didn't reference the verse in the article, Falwell's understanding of "give unto Caesar" is discernible throughout the piece. It is not moral strength or Christian conviction that determines the choice in the 2016 election but the political needs of the moment. The country is on the "precipice" of international conflict because Obama "breathed life" into the Islamic State, the administration "demonized" law enforcement, and "anarchy is erupting" in American cities. In this moment, the "first priority" must be "saving our nation."[21]

Trump had the courage to put the country first and stand up to a world "hostile to our values." Falwell also referenced Supreme Court justices, arguing that Trump-appointed justices would protect the Second Amendment and stop "activist judges" from rewriting the Constitution. According to Falwell, "our nation's future truly hangs in the balance."[22] There wasn't a recognizably Christian argument in the article, but that is consistent with his larger theology of government. In the personal realm, Christian virtues or practices might be required, but in the realm of government, the rules are different. Even earlier in the election season, in January 2016, Falwell explained his decision to endorse Trump in exactly these terms: "When Jesus said 'render unto Caesar the things that are Caesar's,'" he told us not to elect someone who would make a good Sunday school teacher or pastor, but "when we step into our role as citizens, we need to elect the most experienced and capable leaders."[23]

After the election, Falwell continued his passionate support. Tweeting in January 2018, he referred to Caesar again. "Jesus said love our neighbors as ourselves but never told Caesar how to run Rome—he never said Roman soldiers should turn the other cheek in battle or that Caesar should allow all the barbarians to be Roman citizens or that Caesar should tax the rich to help [the] poor. That's our job."[24] Between this and previous comments, we can piece together Falwell's political theology. "Give unto Caesar what is Caesar's" essentially means that the rules of politics and the rules of Christian life are different.[25]

Falwell Jr. combined the thrust of his father's pre–Moral Majority days (Jesus never told Caesar how to run Rome) with his later fervent involvement in politics (Christians need to be politically active in order to save the country). Christian political involvement does not mean holding rulers to Christian values or advocating for Christian policies; it means fighting for the military or economic strength of the nation. Christian values of compassion and charity are ethics reserved for private life.

Falwell Jr. more fully fleshed out this position in a 2019 interview.[26] He criticized Democrats who quoted Jesus's statement "Let the little children come to me" in support of relaxing immigration restrictions, calling it a "distortion" of the teachings of Jesus, because his ethic cannot be "imputed on a nation." He repeated his argument about Jesus never telling Caesar how to run Rome, adding, "He went out of his way to say that's the earthly kingdom, I'm about the heavenly kingdom." Falwell clarified further what that meant: "I'm here to teach you how to treat others, how to help others, but when it comes to serving your country, you render unto Caesar what is Caesar's." Forgiveness and love are not for politics.

Lest you think that we're reading too much into Falwell's largely unarticulated theology of this verse, he went on in this interview to describe a version of Luther's teaching on "two kingdoms." When asked if it was hypocritical for evangelical leaders to support an immoral leader, Falwell responded, "There's two kingdoms." In the heavenly kingdom, you are instructed to treat others well, but in the earthly kingdom, Falwell says, you must "choose leaders who will do what's best for your country." When asked if Trump could do *anything* to risk Falwell's support, he responded, "No." When pressed, he added, "Only because I know that he only wants what's best for this country. . . . I can't imagine him doing anything that's not good for the country."

Falwell was not the only person to make a connection between Trump and Luther in the 2016 election. Some, such as a *Nation* article titled "How Martin Luther Paved the Way for Donald Trump," blamed Luther for the political sins of evangelicals.[27] The article connected Luther to Trump because of his harsh language toward opponents, love of the Bible, and "two kingdoms" theology. According to the author, Luther's two kingdoms theology was the "rigorous" separation of the secular and the spiritual. In that context, the gospel "was to apply only in the spiritual realm," and in the secular realm the government has a role to "maintain order and punish evildoers, not to show compassion and mercy."

One commentator called Luther the "Donald Trump of 1517," and another asked, "Did Martin Luther spawn Donald Trump?"[28] Many of the comparisons were patently silly. American evangelicalism has a more complicated heritage than one reformer, neither Luther nor Trump were true "outsiders" to their respective institutions, and their shared brash attitude does not make Trump's tweets and Luther's Ninety-Five Theses similar. But the comparisons suggested that Luther's two kingdoms theology was part of the Trump era.

In making a Trump-Luther connection, some were harkening back to criticisms of Lutheran theology as *quietist*—unable to properly criticize or confront unjust political orders.[29] While Luther's position was more complicated than this, Lutheran history does include inaction in the face of political evil, in part because of this strict separation between the earthly and heavenly kingdoms.[30] Luther was most deeply concerned with the doctrine of grace by faith alone. He needed to distinguish, then, spiritual righteousness that required the inner work of the Holy Spirit from civil righteousness that could be compelled by human governments. He needed to articulate how someone could be coerced into right behavior without the spiritual change that true righteousness requires.

This is a theological problem that predates Luther. Christians have always struggled with how to think about the relationship between spiritual and earthly authority. They've had various ways of grappling with the reality that Christians live under the rule of Christ and also under the rule of human governments. Most theologians have described two rules: church and civil authority, divine and earthly rule, national and religious communities.

Luther also distinguished between the "inner" and "outer" person—something that is susceptible to misinterpretation. He wanted to distinguish between outer good works that all humans were capable of and inner piety that only regenerated believers possessed. Some Christians today have warped that distinction into a different one: my inner piety is wholly distinct from my outer political action. On one hand, this is true and good: how you vote does not determine your salvation. On the other hand, it risks severing us into spiritual and political parts and ignoring the clear words of the Bible: faith without works is dead.

It is also important to understand how deeply connected the doctrine of two kingdoms was to the rest of Luther's theology, particularly his theology of human nature and salvation. Human sinfulness and "faith alone" led him to place less authority in the church and more authority in the government. While the church could lead people astray in ways that impacted their eternal destiny, the misdeeds of the government could harm the body but not the soul. Before God, moral achievement means nothing; but in relationship to other people, it matters. Luther's political theology was more nuanced and set in the context of these other theological concerns.[31]

Luther's theology is not above criticism, but Falwell's implicit appeal to it is also not faithful to the larger theological context. Instead, Falwell used some similar language but relied on a distinctly

148

modern, evangelical, American way of reading the Bible for his position: using repeated and insistent references to the words of the text, as if they were easily or automatically self-interpreting.

"What Is Caesar's . . ."

The phrase "Give unto Caesar what is Caesar's" has taken on a life of its own. Like referencing "Romans 13" without needing to specify the verse numbers or explain the context, "give unto Caesar" seemingly requires no exegesis, no context, no reasoned application. It's an easy way to slip in an important and contestable political theology without explaining or defending it. Before we examine the hermeneutics animating Falwell's use of the passage, we should try to understand what Jesus meant.

In all three Synoptic Gospels, Jesus confronts religious authorities over paying taxes to Caesar (Mark 12:13–17, as well as Matt. 22:15–22 and Luke 20:20–26), with minor differences. Luke describes the confrontation with generic religious authorities, but Mark and Matthew both specify Pharisees and Herodians, an interesting mix of people to ask Jesus about the relationship between religious and civil authorities. The Pharisees held religious authority, and scholars describe them as of a "mixed mind" about Roman occupation. Some supported rebellion against the Roman Empire, others opposed it, but all were against the occupation. Their political and religious beliefs were incompatible with Roman political rule and the influence of Roman religion. The Herodians, on the other hand, were more sympathetic to Rome.[32]

It's not entirely clear, historically, who the Herodians were or what that meant for their involvement in this dispute with Jesus (they aren't mentioned often in the Bible, and there's been historical debate about the meaning of the term). What is clear is that by framing the question as coming from the Pharisees *and* the Herodians, the texts are emphasizing the fraught nature of the question. These two surprising groups come together in order to trick Jesus by asking him, "Is it right for us to pay taxes to Caesar or not?" (Luke 20:22). The central question puts Jesus into a bind: if he says yes, he angers Rome's critics and many in Judea will condemn him; if he says no, he is in open rebellion of Rome and may be charged with sedition.[33]

Jesus flips the question and asks another one. "Show me the coin used for paying the tax," he says, and then asks, "Whose image is this? And whose inscription?" (Matt. 22:19–20). The Pharisees and Herodians answer, "Caesar's." Before we think about Jesus's response, it's important to imagine this conversation with a little more color. In our own context, we can skip right over this portion—our coins often have images of historical figures or politicians, and they function as symbols of a national identity. That is similar to Jesus's context, but with some differences.

The coin the Pharisees and Herodians presented would have had the image of the current emperor, Tiberius, and an inscription that probably ascribed divinity to him (something like "Caesar Augustus Tiberius, son of the Divine High Priest Augustus").[34] The coins were "portable billboards," propaganda for the empire that reminded people of Caesar's political power and divine authority.[35] Some coins also featured images that evoked Rome's national narrative of prosperity and peace, like the Roman goddess of peace.[36] The coins reminded foreigners of their subjugation. Jesus asks them for a coin, and they pull out of their own pockets an idolatrous image that symbolizes the humiliation of God's people.[37]

Then Jesus says, "Give back to Caesar what is Caesar's, and to God what is God's" (Luke 20:25). With the added context of imperial rule, of the conflict between different factions about the right response to this rule, and of the visual power of the image, it's easier to see what Jesus was doing. While he might be differentiating civil and religious obligations, he is also highlighting their inherent *confrontation*. Paying the tax is giving Caesar his own coin back. But giving God what is God's, in light of Caesar's false claims to divinity, is to give God *everything*—including those things that Caesar might wrongfully require. Many biblical scholars describe this as a "nonviolent subversion of the oppressive power" that neither provokes open political rebellion nor acquiesces to Caesar's all-encompassing claims to sovereignty.[38]

As such, this story is less about justifying Caesar's authority and more about emphasizing God's claims over us. Early church theologian Tertullian said, "Thus, we render our money to Caesar and ourselves to God." For him, the story was another way of seeing the gospel: "What do I owe God as I owe a denarius to Caesar, except the blood that his Son poured out for me?"[39] Similarly, Augustine noted that if Caesar's image is found on his coin, God's image is found on humans, those made in his image (Gen. 1:27). We are "like coins that have wandered away from the treasury," and the image stamped on us has been "worn down" by our wandering—so just as Caesar seeks the coins with his image, so too does God seek out those stamped with his image.[40]

Compared with Caesar's, God's demand on humans is far greater, total, and prior—and it takes precedence whenever it conflicts with Caesar's claims. Nothing *ultimately* belongs to Caesar.[41] But Jesus does not deny the question entirely or imply that it is illegitimate to ask what might be owed to leaders. Rome's claims to authority are relativized, but not to the point of ignoring them. It's clear that Jesus is not telling his followers to forgo the political and economic world.[42] While the "claims of Caesar are always subsumed under the fundamental claims of God," loyalty to God does not require total disavowal of political authority. Loyalty to God is not compromised by submission to earthly authorities.[43]

We glimpse in this little phrase a biblical political theology, a picture of two kinds of rule. This interpretation has a similar early history, especially as early church leaders began to grapple with new problems of civil and ecclesial authority in a newly "Christian" empire. Athanasius of Alexandra and Ambrose of Milan both saw in Jesus's words a picture of different obligations and kinds of rule. "Palaces belong to the emperor, churches to the bishop," Ambrose said.[44]

There's tension here. The tradition has frequently gone to this pithy phrase in a paradigmatic way: as a short summary of Christian teaching on government, as an image or parable of a larger theology taught throughout Scripture, or, in contemporary politics, as shorthand for an unarticulated and underdeveloped political theology. Yet Jesus was not giving a sermon on the question of government authority, nor answering a theological question with a systematic answer.[45] He was addressing a particular, pressing question—but not acquiescing to the terms of the debate as given.

He did not ignore the question, but he used that question to draw attention to larger dynamics of the relationship between religious and civil obligations. He did not allow anyone listening to think *either* that paying their taxes fulfills their most serious moral obligations (they may have given back to Caesar, but have they given to God what God is owed?) *or* that their various obligations are entirely separate questions (the question about taxes cannot be answered without reference to God).

In short, it is far from illegitimate to see in this one phrase something about larger questions of civil and religious authority. It is less legitimate, however, to see a clear picture of two separate spheres in this one cryptic reply, and it is entirely illegitimate to see in the text a divide between "sacred" obligations and "secular" political ones.[46] While Caesar has legitimate authority, when his authority conflicts with God's, there's no question about whose authority wins. In fact, in every account of this story in the Synoptic Gospels, Jesus's announcement of the destruction of the temple and of the signs of the end times is right around the corner from this story. The coming kingdom of God demotes all earthly power. As many have said of New Testament political theology, "If Christ is Lord, then Caesar is not."[47]

"And to God What Is God's"

Falwell was far from alone in using Jesus's words to justify not only distinct realms of human life but different moral requirements in each. References to "Render unto Caesar what is Caesar's and to God what is God's" are plentiful—in popular books, sermons, political speeches, academic works, commentaries, and regular conversations between Christians. The phrase "render unto Caesar" has taken on a life of its own. You don't even need to finish the sentence or exegete the verse. Depending on the context, you might mean that the church and state should be separate, that Jesus validated earthly authorities, or that people should pay their taxes. But you can support any of these points with this one phrase, without even explaining it.

We should be concerned with understanding what Jesus actually meant, not merely picking up useful language for our predetermined political projects. We should also think more critically about the ways we have learned to think about our spiritual and political lives. We can get the nuances of this verse right while still operating in the world with an ingrained instinct that the "rules" in one realm of our lives are different from the "rules" in another. In one sense, that instinct is right. Our obligations to our families, churches, immediate communities, and broader political communities are different—but not unrelated. The standards we hold for a pastor and a politician are different—but not unrelated. God's demands on our lives in a church pew and a voting booth are different—but not unrelated.

In her study of evangelical sermons during the 2016 election, Stephanie A. Martin notes the prevalence of what she calls "active-passivism": emphasizing *hating* the political process and the available options, reiterating that politics should be based in the Bible, and skirting around what that specifically means.[48] While some conservative preachers veered into explicitly partisan territory, it was more common for them to encourage people to "rise above the fray" and focus on the eternal over the temporal. While there's a version of that teaching that is important, true, and obviously rooted in biblical teaching, there's a version of it that justifies a non-Christian political engagement. As one preacher she studied said, "Listen, it doesn't matter who's in the White House" because "God rules the universe with his feet up."[49] It's not too far of a jump from "Politics doesn't matter because God is in control" to "so do whatever you want in the earthly kingdom."

These preachers were not entirely wrong. But their preaching fits within a larger evangelical impulse to sharply separate our spiritual and political obligations. It is important for Christians not to merely ask: What does "Caesar" require of me, and what does God require of me? They must also ask: What might my ultimate obligation to God require me to demand of Caesar? What might the redemptive narrative in Scripture demand of my political life? How might the Holy Spirit be moving in our political world today?

Seek the Peace and Prosperity of the City

Jeremiah 29 and Political Theology

I was in college at the beginning of the 2016 election—and it felt as if the world was crumbling around me. I had spent the first few years of college doing what we might call "deconstructing"— working through questions about my faith, including questions about what my faith required of me in the political and ethical realms. None of that was particularly disillusioning, in part because it was slow, ongoing, and met mostly with calm care by people I trusted.

As the 2016 election gained speed, however, things felt more disastrous. I watched people I trusted churn out stomach-turning defenses of the sexual misdeeds of then-candidate Trump. I watched church communities wrenched apart by a reckoning with the idolatrous relationship evangelicals had cultivated with the Republican Party. I saw the fruit of a malnourished *political theology*—theological reflection on the meaning, shape, and purpose of human communities.

In the midst of this crumbling, I was introduced to a passage from Jeremiah:

This is what the LORD Almighty, the God of Israel, says to all those I carried into exile from Jerusalem to Babylon: "Build houses and settle down; plant gardens and eat what they produce. Marry and have sons and daughters; find wives for your sons and give your daughters in marriage, so that they too may have sons and daughters. Increase in number there; do not decrease. Also, seek the peace and prosperity of the city to which I have carried you into exile. Pray to the LORD for it, because if it prospers, you too will prosper." (Jer. 29:4–7)

There was something both comforting and thrilling about this passage. On the one hand, it described life in the world that looked slower and simpler than the "change the world" rhetoric I had heard growing up (and seen exaggerated to disastrous effect). On the other hand, it described a radical mission for the people of God: to seek prosperity even in exile, to seek the good of even their captors.

Tired of culture war and a utilitarian politics that seemingly justified evil for some greater good, I found Jeremiah's vision refreshing. Disillusioned with the political legacy I'd inherited but still searching for a way to participate in politics, I was encouraged by Jeremiah's instructions to build, plant, and seek the peace. This passage shaped my interest in political theology, my love of the Old Testament prophets, and my desire to root my political participation in deep spiritual formation. I even named my college blog *Letters from the Exile* after Jeremiah's letter. It turns out I was far from alone in my interest in this passage.

Contemporary treatments of the passage abound. The Acton Institute produced a video curriculum called *For the Life of the World* that centered on Jeremiah's language (the subtitle is *Letters to the Exiles*). An organization advocating for immigrants and refugees draws its name, Seek the Peace, from the passage. The passage is frequently referenced in the context of conversations about immigration or refugee policy.[1] Tim Keller, the founding pastor of Redeemer Presbyterian Church in New York City, helped popularize the language of Jeremiah 29 for describing a Christian's life in the world.

His curriculum video series *Gospel in Life* begins with a session called "City" that exegetes the passage. Keller describes the plight of the Israelites in language general enough to allow his audience to make easy connections with their own context: the people of God are in a context that is religiously, morally, and culturally different from what they knew. The Babylonians want them to assimilate to the city's cultural and spiritual norms; their own false prophets want them to fight against their captivity in an attempt to keep their spiritual identity. But God says instead, "Move into the city and keep your spiritual identity." Keller says that cities are places of unique cultural and political significance, as well as places of great spiritual searching. The "density and diversity" of the city is a good that turns sour with sin, causing racism and violence. Keller's use of the passage contributed to a larger resurgence of interest in it, particularly among evangelicals interested in a more holistic and less belligerent approach to culture and politics.[2]

It's hard to find a book about culture or politics in recent years that doesn't at least mention the passage or use its language: books on urban ministry, political theology, benefactors in the early church, and culture-making all take Jeremiah's language for their titles.[3] Even when books or sermons don't explicitly reference Jeremiah 29, they often rely on the language and framework of exile, prophetic presence, or planting and building. It's especially appealing language when many Christians who once felt relatively comfortable in America have begun to feel marginalized or scorned in popular culture.

In the aftermath of the 2016 election, the passage became even more enticing. Christians who were tired of "culture war" approaches to politics and were more aware of the corrupting potential of political power were drawn to language that sounded more like cultivating than combat. Leaders who were tired of partisan posturing searched for a political theology more focused on creating a faithful life within the church than battling it out in the public square.

Jeremiah's letter to the exiles has a much longer history, however, than our contemporary appropriations. We've seen how pressing political moments in American history shaped biblical interpretation, but we also need to zoom out and think more broadly about how different theological and political contexts shape interpretation. As we said at the beginning, we will be more faithful readers of Scripture if we understand how the church in our immediate context has read it. We also will be more faithful readers of Scripture if we understand that our contemporary readings are not universal or neutral but conditioned by the demands of our time and place.

To that end, this chapter describes the long journey of interpretation that this crucial passage has had. Jeremiah 29 has not only motivated particular policies but has been used to describe a whole theology of government and faithful Christian witness. Thinking about this passage across a much longer history than the American experiment can help settle us into this kind of thinking.

We will examine how this crucial passage has been handled in various historical situations (from the time of the Babylonian exile to the present day), political contexts (from ancient empires to modern liberal democracies), and theological traditions (Jewish faith, patristic theologians, reformers, and modern theological debates). Because Jeremiah 29 is used to describe a whole political theology, it's an important passage for highlighting the reality that all of our biblical interpretation is shaped by our political theology.

The Power of Exile

Long before contemporary Christians saw in the Babylonian exile an analogue for their isolation, the *actual* exile deeply shaped the imagination of the Jewish people and, later, the early church.

Many intertestamental texts (writings from the period in between the writings of the Old and New Testaments) describe Israel's condition as if the nation is still in exile: while the people are no longer held captive by Babylon, they remain subject to foreign control and, in the case of those scattered abroad, alienated from their homeland.[4] "Exile" was already a flexible concept, referring not merely to a distinct event but also to the Jewish people's continued oppression and alienation.[5]

The New Testament uses the language and image of exile and diaspora—the dispersion of a people—to describe the ongoing condition of the people of God: James begins his letter, "To the twelve tribes scattered among the nations," and 1 Peter begins, "To God's elect, exiles scattered throughout the provinces of Pontus, Galatia, Cappadocia, Asia and Bithynia." Later in his letter, Peter writes, "Dear friends, I urge you, as foreigners and exiles, to abstain from sinful desires, which wage war against your soul. Live such good lives among the pagans that, though they accuse you of doing wrong, they may see your good deeds and glorify God on the day he visits us" (1 Pet. 2:11–12).

Seeking the "prosperity of the city" was good advice not only for the literally exiled people of God but also for the displaced and oppressed people of God throughout time and around the world. New Testament scholar Bruce W. Winter argues that the concept overlapped well with Greco-Roman ideas about citizens' responsibility to seek the common good. Jeremiah's instructions provided the Jewish people with a paradigm for civic participation that mirrored political expectations in their context.[6]

Two Cities: Augustine's Interpretation of Jeremiah 29

Jeremiah 29 was important for the early church, primarily because of the work of theologian and bishop Augustine of Hippo and his *City of God*. This sprawling book covers theology, philosophy, political theory, history, and spiritual formation.

Augustine's Context

Augustine was writing in a time of great political instability.[7] Military campaigns, slavery, and traveling workers led to high levels of migration in the empire, and the increased migration caused fear and suspicion to reign in communities. As a whole, it was a society "lurching drunkenly from one disaster to the next."[8]

In this political and social context, Augustine reached for the metaphor of migration to describe the Christian life: the church was a community traveling together on a fraught journey. The metaphor both distanced the people of God from overidentification with earthly affairs and increased a sense of belonging in the church. When you do not share geography with your people, you find greater identification with your shared purpose and identity. This metaphor was often connected to ethical action in Augustine's sermons, such as practicing hospitality and welcoming foreigners.

Augustine was also writing with apocalyptic expectations about Rome in mind. Many of his contemporaries expected the year 500 CE to inaugurate the end times, and many interpreted the sack of Rome as an apocalyptic event. When the great empire was revealed as fragile, it felt as if the entire world were crumbling. In contrast to apocalyptic expectations that could fuel withdrawal from the world, Augustine repeatedly insisted that the political instability they were experiencing was instead a reminder of the inherent instability of the temporal world. Ironically, Augustine's hope for Rome was rooted in recognition of its mortality, in awareness that it would experience decay. Rather than focusing on apocalyptic endings, such ruin would be an impetus for renewal. After the sack of Rome in 410, he preached about the coming ultimate judgment of all cities and exhorted the church to respond well to hardships. He finished by emphasizing "how unsteady and fragile are all worldly trivialities and all deceitful madness."[9] He encouraged the church to neither despair nor place ultimate hopes in the empire. The political turmoil they experienced didn't signal the end times, nor did it give Christians an excuse to withdraw from the world.

Augustine's Political Theology

It is in this political and theological context that Augustine wrote, over the course of at least a decade, the extensive *City of God*. The book describes the whole of human history through the lens of the "two cities." This is not a divide between church and state the way we typically think of it today, but it is a divide between two communities united by their "common objects of love." The city of God is the community of all beings united by their love of God, and the earthly city is the community of all beings united by their *disordered* love of earthly things above love of God. For Augustine, all communities—the church, the government, neighborhoods, families, and businesses—are a mix of these two cities, an intermingling of peoples divided by their divergent loves.[10]

Jeremiah 29 plays a significant role in book 19 of *City of God*, where Augustine distills his political thinking. Book 19 describes the "ends" of the two cities—not only the ends of their stories but their purposes, meanings, or ends to which they are oriented. In contrast to the various philosophies of the day, the Christian view is that ultimate good and ultimate evil are not found in this present life. The ultimate good is eternal life, and the ultimate evil is eternal death. In agreement with the philosophers, however, the Christian view of the good life is inescapably *social*. Augustine did not write about two kinds of people but two cities.

This flows into a discussion of the true nature of peace: what is the relationship between earthly peace (the absence of military conflict, the ability of human communities to procure the necessary material goods for their physical flourishing) and eternal peace (the true flourishing of human communities oriented in their love toward God and in ultimate reconciliation with each other)? Augustine's answer to this question is similar to his answer about the nature of love: the important thing is how we *order* our loves, how we order earthly peace to eternal peace. People whose lives are based on faith look forward "to the blessings which are promised as eternal in the future, making use of earthly and temporal things like a pilgrim in a foreign land," not being distracted by them but treating them as supports for earthly living.[11]

The earthly city and the city of God, then, share overlapping concerns and conflicts. This is where Augustine compares Jeremiah's exile and the Christian life in any social and political context: members of the city of God have "what we may call a life of captivity in this earthly city as in a foreign land."[12] While Christians have already received the promise of redemption, they remain temporarily in "captivity" living among the earthly city. While they do not share ultimate goals, both cities share a desire for basic temporal goods—safety and flourishing on earth—and so work together for those goods.

This is when Augustine gives his famous definition of a "commonwealth"—a definition so stirring that President Joe Biden referenced it in his 2021 inaugural address, to the delight of theology nerds everywhere.[13] A people is "the association of a multitude of rational beings united by a common agreement on the objects of their love."[14] Unlike Biden's optimistic quotation of it, Augustine was not saying that a community *should* be united by its common loves but that all communities *are* united by their common loves, including a common love of evil things.

Toward the end of this important section, Augustine cites Jeremiah 29 to describe the way of life for the city of God: "So long as the two cities are intermingled we also make use of the peace of Babylon." In other words, the members of the city of God are to seek peace together with the earthly city. Augustine's biblical supports are 1 Timothy 2:1–2 and Jeremiah 29:7:

> I urge, then, first of all, that petitions, prayers, intercession and thanksgiving be made for all people—for kings and all those in authority, that we may live peaceful and quiet lives in all godliness and holiness.

> Also, seek the peace and prosperity of the city to which I have carried you into exile. Pray to the LORD for it, because if it prospers, you too will prosper.

And thus begins the "canonization" of this passage in the history of political theology. The experience of Israel in Babylon became the paradigmatic example of the people of God, living under both earthly and divine rule, subject to two sovereignties and seeking two kinds of peace.[15] As we will see, however, the shared importance of this passage has not translated into shared interpretation.

Augustine's Biblical Interpretation

To understand Augustine's interpretation of the passage, it's important to understand his larger theology and his approach to interpreting the Bible. Augustine was pastoring and teaching during a period of intense theological deliberation in the church, when doctrines we receive today were first hammered out under the pressures of pastoral concerns, harmful heresies, and changing circumstances for the church.

Augustine details his long and wandering journey to Christianity in one of the most famous books of all time, his *Confessions*. He describes his interest in other religions, like the dualist and gnostic Manichaeanism, and philosophies, like the popular Neoplatonic philosophy in Rome. While his mother, Monica, prayed fervently for him over his lifetime, he remained unconvinced of the Christian faith. A key concern for Augustine was aversion to the Old Testament—these earthy, violent, and commonplace stories could not be considered great literary or philosophical works.[16] Eventually, however, Monica's faithful prayers and deep theological discussions with Augustine would bear fruit.

Under the preaching of the bishop Ambrose, Augustine learned to read the Old Testament allegorically, seeing eternal truths in the earthly vessels of these commonplace stories. By the time he wrote *City of God*, Augustine did not think that the *whole* of the Old Testament could or should be taken allegorically, but this approach shaped his theology.

In book 17, he describes the layers of meaning that prophecies can have: the earthly, the spiritual, or both. When the prophets write about Jerusalem, they are talking about the earthly Jerusalem and also about spiritual realities: the city of God, the true Jerusalem. Prophecies can have multiple references and images, and their language can contain more than one meaning, especially a historical meaning and a greater spiritual meaning. Augustine argues that it is a "complete mistake" to think a passage of Scripture is merely historical record *or* to think the Bible contains only allegories with no historical truth.[17]

The prophet's mission is to keep the people from fixating on the earthly things that were meant to point toward eternal, spiritual (but also material) promises. The people of God often fail to distinguish between the earthly city and the city of God, confusing the earthly kingdom and the heavenly kingdom it points to.[18] And yet, to Augustine, the earthly still matters: the earthly city is often an instrument of God, serving divine purposes of punishment and redemption. The Babylonian exile is one such example (Nebuchadnezzar was used by God for his purposes, for God says, "*I carried you into exile*," in Jer. 29), and the Roman persecution of the church still led to its growth.[19]

In another writing, Augustine returns to this passage, saying that the exile in Babylon and the instructions to pray for the peace of the city prefigured the people of God's journey into the kingdoms of the gentiles to make disciples. First Timothy 2:1–4, which contains the phrase "that we may live peaceful and quiet lives," is "repeating" Jeremiah's instructions. In Augustine's allegorical reading, the church is also called to build houses (churches) and plant vineyards (groups of believers) in anticipation of their return to Jerusalem (new creation).[20] In a later sermon, he says that the prophecy "in their peace shall be your peace" has finally been fulfilled: "The prayers of the Church have been heard, and the kings have become Christian."[21] Augustine was no triumphalist, no Christian nationalist of his time. He wanted the church to hold Christian leaders to high standards, and he held no illusions about Rome becoming the kingdom of God. He did, however, rejoice at the peace of churches that could worship without persecution, of Christians who could serve God without martyrdom. It was natural for him, in his context, to see in Jeremiah's words a promise of peace that might look like the eventual Christianization of the empire. This reminds us that context always deeply informs how one interprets Scripture, not least Jeremiah 29.

Augustine's work has generated many different interpretations, especially when it comes to applying his work to politics.[22] But his use of Jeremiah 29 to describe this "two cities" theology has had a unique and lasting impact on Christian theology. In Augustine's context, Jeremiah 29 helped make sense of the changing political dynamics of the Roman Empire and the changing social and political status of Christians.

"Reverence and Dutifulness": Calvin's Interpretation of Jeremiah 29

Jumping forward through a thousand years of theology and politics, we come to John Calvin. The French reformer's context couldn't be more different from Augustine's in many ways: the once-fledgling church is now a wealthy and powerful institution rivaling the secular rulers it is intertwined with, the printing press has allowed theological treatises to spread throughout communities, and Calvin is preoccupied with the errors of the medieval church. Yet Augustine and Calvin share some foundational conditions that make Jeremiah 29 a captivating passage: they both lived in times of intense political and religious turmoil, they both spent their time combating theological errors, and they both led communities struggling to discern between earthly and eternal peace.

Calvin's Context

Toward the end of his life, Calvin delivered a series of lectures on Jeremiah.[23] These hour-long lectures were given in Latin to students and pastors in the Geneva Academy, and Calvin was characteristically confident in them. "If Jeremiah himself were now alive on earth," he said, "he would, if I am not mistaken, add his own recommendation."[24] Calvin not only thought his interpretation consistent with Jeremiah's intent but also thought he had correctly applied the prophet's words to his contemporary situation.

Calvin identified with Jeremiah. The prophet combated corruption and theological error as Calvin did ("Every one invented errors to suit his own humour," he writes of Jeremiah's context), his God-given task was "hard and arduous," and it required great endurance to stay the course of ministry.[25] Calvin also saw his own community in Jeremiah's community. Calvin had fled his own home country of France in the 1530s out of fear of retribution for his opposition to the Roman Catholic Church, and by the time he published the first edition of his *Institutes*, he was housing refugees from the religious conflicts of the Reformation in Geneva. Some of his fellow refugees, in fact, were in the midst of Bible translation projects, making the famous "Geneva Bible" itself the product of a community of exiles. Calvin interpreted Scripture about exile with intimate experience of displacement.[26]

Calvin's context, like Augustine's, was one of political, social, and religious turmoil. Unlike Augustine, Calvin was the recipient of a long tradition of close relationships between civil and church powers. While the reformers differed greatly on questions of political theology, most of them assumed that reforming the church would require reforming the whole public order—and that required government aid. Calvin struggled to balance criticisms of corrupt church hierarchy with the maintenance of church and government authority. He did not want the Roman Catholic Church, but he was also concerned about rejection of civil authority.[27]

Calvin's Political Theology

This was not just a political question; it was a theological question as well. The Reformation emphasized Christian liberty, but most of the reformers still wanted to defend authority—the authority of the church to discipline people and the authority of the state to punish evil. Calvin needed a theology that could contain both the spiritual freedom at the heart of the gospel and the command to obey government authorities.[28] He went to great lengths to nuance his account of Christian liberty, clarifying that it should not be used as a cover for sin.[29] He vehemently condemned those who would "erroneously transfer" the doctrine of spiritual liberty to the political order.[30]

For Calvin, the state is divinely commissioned, given authority by God to maintain earthly peace by protecting the vulnerable and punishing the wicked. Calvin gave very limited allowance for resisting the government, because the state gains its legitimate authority not from the consent of the people but from God. There are mutual obligations, of course, between the state and the people, but even when the state does not meet those obligations (to protect, justly punish, maintain peace), the people's obedience to their leaders is a form of obedience to God.[31]

Calvin described government as "twofold": there is spiritual government and civil government. The spiritual government of the church trains people toward piety and worship; civil government instructs them in their duties to their earthly community.[32] He was pretty strict about the difference between these two authorities: when we are considering one kind of government, Calvin counsels, "we should call off our minds, and not allow them to think of the other."[33] But while there is a kind of dichotomy in Calvin, he thinks of all of life as under the sovereign control of God. Reformed theologians since Calvin have often emphasized this sovereignty to elevate the value of faithful Christian work in politics, culture, art, and science.

While his writing can sound to the modern mind like a harsh distinction between the civil and spiritual authorities, many scholars agree that Calvin's distinction between the two authorities was not so strict in *practice*.[34] Calvin promoted more than a theological reformation in the city of Geneva; he wrote and advocated for political and social reform as well. More than maintaining an abstract distinction between the two powers, Calvin was responding to the problems he perceived in his context, struggling to assert the authority of the church in the face of government powers accustomed to interference in religious matters. While he was writing about the harsh line between political and ecclesiastical power, it is clear today that in reality the two were deeply entangled in Geneva, especially from the perspective of modern citizens. In ways similar to other legal codes of the time, Calvin thought the state should enforce the Ten Commandments and punish people for idolatry and blasphemy. He even went so far as to advocate for the execution of Michael Servetus for heresy.[35]

Calvin's Biblical Interpretation

Before we look at the ways Calvin employed Jeremiah 29 in his work, it's important to briefly think about how his approach to biblical interpretation differed from Augustine's. Calvin was especially concerned with prioritizing and honoring the historical and grammatical sense of the text, as many in his period were.[36] Calvin prioritized reading the Bible in its original languages, setting the text in its historical context, and working to understand the intent of the original human author. But unlike some later Protestant interpreters, he also relied on the broader Christian tradition, citing patristic theologians and recognizing himself as part of a larger community of faith. Like Augustine before him, he asked an important question we need to ask as well: How do these ancient texts relate to pressing theological questions of the day?

For Calvin, reading the Bible required that the present not eclipse the past. Where Augustine saw in Jeremiah 29 a picture of human life before Christ's return, an image full of meaning for Christians in the present, Calvin would be more restrained. General moral rules might be found in the letter to the exiles, but only to the extent that there was a clear parallel between the situation in the past and that in the present. Contemporary readers might see something instructive or meaningful for their own moment in the text, but only because the situations were similar enough that the same rules might be followed. Calvin used the image of the mirror to describe how Scripture speaks to contemporary situations: the people of God see themselves in sacred history and thus discern an instructive word for their moment.[37]

This isn't to say that Calvin didn't see the significance of prophecies beyond their historical referent. When Calvin read the prophets, he saw references to historical events, to Christ, and to the whole history of Christ's kingdom. He saw the Old and New Testaments as one continuous story pointing to Christ. This included the exile, which was an image of the redemption of the whole people of God by Christ's work on the cross. When Calvin wrote about the prophets' promises of return from exile, he often said, "The prophet is speaking about the restoration of the Church."[38]

Calvin and Jeremiah 29

In Calvin's most focused reflection on politics, "On Civil Government," he cites Jeremiah 29:7. Rather than seeing a universal image of Christian political engagement, Calvin sees a parallel situation between the Israelites in exile and Christians subject to civil authorities in the present. He also sees a general moral teaching: the Israelites were "despoiled of all their goods, expelled from their homes, carried off into exile, cast down into a wretched bondage," and yet they were still commanded to pray for the good of their captors.[39] This must teach us something about our duty in the present. God's people are instructed to pray for their leaders' peace and safety, as a form of duty to God.

Calvin acknowledges the reality of tyrannical leaders but also prioritizes the doctrine of God's providence and tries to discern how such leaders could be a punishment from God. Private citizens still have no right to protest against these leaders (the citizens are not even allowed to discuss among themselves what kind of government is best), but God occasionally raises up "avengers" to punish tyranny, such as Moses against Pharaoh. The one exception to this command, as you might expect, is if the demands of a leader directly contradict God's law.

In his commentary on Jeremiah, Calvin says that the prophet had two goals in this letter to the exiles: comforting them and breaking their "obstinacy."[40] Jeremiah wants to direct their vision toward the end of their captivity, holding on to the promise God has made them, but in the meantime he exhorts them to be patient, to be "quiet and peaceable," and not to "raise tumults" until God delivers them.[41] It's perhaps unsurprising that in Calvin's political context in Geneva and in the context of his larger theology of government he would see in Jeremiah 29 a command to obey government authorities.

While Calvin was usually resistant to move to direct application of these kinds of texts, in this case he does. There is a "very useful doctrine" found in this passage. Christians should obey the rulers they live under and pray for their prosperity.[42] Calvin's words should sound strange to us after reading Augustine's account of the passage. Calvin does not focus on the image of Israel in Babylon or on the work that the people should do—planting gardens, building houses, having families—but on obedience to Babylon.

Exile as Mission: Contemporary Exilic Theology

We're taking another big jump here: from the sixteenth century to the twentieth century, from the Reformation to modern theology, from the rule of empires to the rule of nation-states. We need a little less context, politically and historically, for this interpretation—because we share much of it. And unlike the former two interpretations of Jeremiah, we're not going to look at one person but rather at a tradition of thinking about theology and politics that some have called "exilic theology."

This loose tradition—rooted in pacifism, rejection of political power, and the priority of the social life of the church—is shared by biblical scholars and theologians like Stanley Hauerwas, John Howard Yoder, and Walter Brueggemann.[43] They share a concern for the "otherness" of the church, a distinctive communal life shaped by social practices and in some sense separate from the rest of the world. We're going to focus on Brueggemann's work on Jeremiah 29.

Brueggemann writes not only as a biblical scholar—thinking through the grammar and vocabulary, literary structure, and historical context of the text—but also as a preacher interested in the spiritual formation of the people of God. He's written multiple commentaries, theological works, and books about preaching on Jeremiah.

He frequently connects the historical context of the book to contemporary circumstances, as both Augustine and Calvin did. The state of Israel was a "remarkable experiment" in the ancient Near East, a community committed to one God that often sent prophets to critique or condemn the government of the nation.[44] Brueggemann describes the same political instability that Calvin and Augustine emphasized, but he also describes the exile as the "defining trauma" of the people. The Israelite leaders brought to Babylon were the elite of their community, and the exile was a serious loss in status for them: they went from being political leaders to peasants farming someone else's land.[45]

For Brueggemann, this defining trauma is comparable to the "traumatic loss of the old certitude of American closeness to privilege and dominance."[46] This sense of exceptionalism is tied to white supremacy, economic inequality, and militarism. The task for the preacher today is similar to Jeremiah's: gather the remnant of faithful believers, uproot the evil among them, and go about the work of "planting and building" something new. The metaphor of exile gives the church a fresh way of thinking and living, rooted in the scriptural witness.[47]

The exile is instructive not only because of the parallel circumstances of the people of God in Babylon and the people of God in America; it also has similar instructions for faithful living. In a context where people feel as if their way of life is threatened, Jeremiah's instructions offer an alternative to both despairing escapism and culture warring: build homes; plant gardens; live quiet but powerfully different, faithful lives. The power and privilege the people of God enjoyed is judged faithless, but there is hope in their communal life in exile.[48]

Just as Augustine's and Calvin's uses of Jeremiah 29 had their pitfalls and blind spots, the exilic theology tradition is often criticized as withdrawing from the broader life of the community. An overemphasis on the internal life of the church can discount the power of common grace and the work of God outside the church. Exilic language understandably lends itself to thinking of the church as an embattled, isolated community. If the church is Israel and "the world" is Babylon, the church is taking on the role of the smaller, weaker, defeated one. That made more sense to say of the early church than it does of today's, when most Western nations have a political tradition deeply shaped by Christian theology and Christians still exert significant political power in places like the United States.[49] However, while many proponents of "exilic theology" are white, upper-class Americans, other theological traditions from more marginal perspectives have also found hope and strength in Jeremiah's letter to the exiles.[50]

But this is also an important word for Christians infatuated with political power: Jeremiah, according to Brueggemann, protests against a "civic-sacred enterprise remote from the will of

YHWH." He does not protest against a relationship between faith and politics but against a relationship that is counter to God's will for creation.[51]

Folks like Brueggemann and Hauerwas have a vision for countercultural churches that remain concerned with their larger communities. Some influenced by them do not. Interest in Rod Dreher's "Benedict Option"—a strategic withdrawal from public life for the sake of cultivating strong Christian communities—is evidence of a trend toward isolation. An overemphasis on the internal life of the church can lead to actual withdrawal: paying little attention to social and political life, discounting the power of common grace and the work of God outside the church, avoiding political work for fear of dirtying one's hands. Christian nationalism has a parallel error of pious withdrawal.

In the aftermath of chaotic election seasons and discouraging periods of church conflict, a withdrawal option is appealing. Many Christians watched their friends and family members show up to protest school-board meetings, pass out "biblical" voter guides at church, or post about the January 6 insurrection approvingly on social media. And yet there is a pitfall on the other side, a pitfall that looks strangely similar to the "culture warrior" approach. Both approaches see the larger social and political world as external and "other" to themselves—one wants to fight, and the other wants to withdraw.

But as theologian David Fitch says, "Church community must mold character and form families as well as shape the skills necessary for discerning and participating in Christ's work in the world."[52] Jeremiah's letter to the exiles does not separate the commands to build houses and plant gardens (that internal work of cultivation) from the command to "seek the peace and prosperity of the city." The commands are intimately connected. The flourishing of a countercultural community is crucial for faithful witness in the world, in part because it provides a space for practicing that witness among brothers and sisters in the faith. Faced with a decision between culture warring and withdrawing, Jeremiah's letter to the exiles gives us another way.

A Letter to the Exiles

Where does all of this leave us, as people struggling to apply the Bible to our political questions? It can be tempting to view this short zip through interpretive history as a progression (we've gone from worse readings to increasingly better ones) or a declension (we used to have it figured out, but it's become a mess and we have to go back to the beginning). It's neither. Throughout church history, our various perspectives, emphases, and contexts have given us a mix of good, bad, and in-between. Augustine got some of it right, certainly Calvin had some good points, and contemporary theologians aren't hopelessly lost either.

The goal of this final chapter was to highlight a crucially important passage for political thinking and to show some of the factors that affect how we read. As we think about America's history with the Bible, it's important to see how one passage could be interpreted so differently across time and political context. We are shaped by the contours of American political history, just as Augustine and Calvin were shaped by their political contexts. Just as Calvin and Augustine and Brueggemann brought their theological systems or stories to the text, we do too. Just as their experiences with political power shaped how they applied a passage to their lives, our experiences will shape how we read. Hopefully we will never again say "This is just a plain reading of the text!" when it comes to faith and politics.

This is not a reason for despair: while we are shaped by our political contexts, theological commitments, and personal histories, we can expect God to speak to us in the midst of them. This is, however, reason for humility and caution in our interpretations.

The book of Jeremiah itself testifies to the difficulty we have interpreting Scripture for our political participation. More than the other prophetic books, Jeremiah is a book about conflict—not just military conflict but theological conflict as well. Jeremiah is not the only prophet in the book; there are false prophets who try to convince the people of God that Babylon won't capture them, that God wouldn't punish them so severely, that this exile won't last. The drama of the book is a conflict over the nature of judgment, the meaning of the exile, and ultimately the word of God.[53] Who hears God correctly? Who is correctly interpreting the "signs of the times"? Who understands what God demands of us in this moment in time, in this place in the world? What is God's plan for his people?

Jeremiah was desperately concerned that the people of God would hear *and* do God's word. He knew that failure to hear and do God's words would lead the people of God into destruction. This was not a meaningless squabble or merely a hermeneutical dispute. This was a matter of life and death.[54]

In the aftermath of two contentious elections in 2016 and 2020, Christians may have been tempted to turn away from political activity altogether. We may look at our own recent history and decide that political power is too corrupting, navigating policy issues is too divisive, or making decisions between poor candidate choices is too exhausting. There is something appealing about reading Jeremiah's instructions to the exiles as an excuse for withdrawal from the messy political world. We focus on building faithful families and homes, pray for our leaders, and leave it at that. But regardless of our political context or theological commitments, Jeremiah's words find their place within a larger story of Scripture in which God's people are always oriented *outward*.

From Abraham's call in Genesis 12:3 that "all peoples on earth will be blessed through you," to Jeremiah's command to "seek the peace and prosperity of the city," to the eschatological image of a redeemed city, God's concern has always been for all of creation. His people are given instructions toward that end, not toward self-preservation *or* isolation from the world. We should strive to build flourishing families and churches, but not at the expense of the commission God gave at the beginning and never rescinded: to care for all of creation (Gen. 1:27–28).

Conclusion

The Promise and Peril
of Biblical References in Politics

At the 2020 Republican National Convention, Vice President Mike Pence gave a typical election-year speech. Accepting the Republican Party's nomination, Pence waxed poetic about President Trump's leadership over the prior four years: he endured "unrelenting attacks" but got up every day to "fight to keep the promises that he made to the American people."[1]

He praised Trump for "rebuilding" the military, appointing judges who make pro-life and pro–Second Amendment decisions, creating a strong economy, and getting a COVID-19 vaccine to the American people. He decried the "violence and chaos" on American streets, proclaimed the administration's support for law enforcement, and criticized then-candidate Biden for describing America as systemically racist. He described the "time of testing" the country was facing, and the "time of choosing" in front of them: between Trump's path of "freedom and opportunity" and Biden's path of "socialism and decline."

Pence ended by encouraging the gathering to "run the race marked out for us" and to "fix our eyes on Old Glory and all she represents. Let's fix our eyes on this land of heroes and let their courage inspire." Pence drew on the language of Hebrews 12:1–3:

175

"Therefore, since we are surrounded by such a great cloud of witnesses, let us throw off everything that hinders and the sin that so easily entangles. And let us run with perseverance the race marked out for us, fixing our eyes on Jesus, the pioneer and perfecter of faith. For the joy set before him he endured the cross, scorning its shame, and sat down at the right hand of the throne of God. Consider him who endured such opposition from sinners, so that you will not grow weary and lose heart."

Pence replaced "Jesus, the pioneer and perfecter of faith" with "Old Glory" and "this land of heroes." He drew on familiar language for purposes entirely foreign to the biblical text. In a speech during election season at the Republican National Convention, this was no accident or slip. It was intentional wording—for what purpose? Why use biblical language without quoting it directly or correctly? In the past, politicians and preachers and regular people often used biblical language in casual, imprecise ways—often as a function of living in a world so full of the Bible that the words just naturally worked their way into everyday language. Today, we're more likely to draw on biblical language intentionally in order to lend moral weight or religious authority to our speech.

A Bible-Haunted Nation

One difficulty with examining biblical arguments in American political life is the blurry line between direct reference and vague invocation of popular biblical language. Throughout American history, politicians, spiritual leaders, and government officials at all levels have seamlessly woven biblical language into their speeches and press releases. They don't have to quote a verse to invoke a kind of transcendence, divine authority, or shared religious experience. Speaking of the "kingdom of God," attributing our freedom or liberty to a "gift from God," or responding to a critic with a line about "turning the other cheek" can all access the *power* of biblical references without submitting to their *content*.

This is the promise and peril of the Bible in political life. The language of Scripture has been watered down to the degree of political talking point, but its constant use also highlights a deep desire in people for transcendence, a universal moral order, and a part to play in a cosmic story. By quoting just part of the verse from Hebrews, Pence could evoke divine authority without actually relying on Scripture to shape his political activity. He could *use* Scripture rather than submit to its authority.

So many politicians—Democrats and Republicans alike—draw on biblical language not only for the purpose of accessing shared, historic, communal language but also as an attempt to meet a felt need among people for a political and social life shaped by something *more* than the fights and fleeting concerns of the moment. People want the political decisions of the moment to find a place within a larger story outside themselves. They are looking for a firm foundation for the weighty moral questions of the day.

We are a Bible-haunted nation. How we respond is of crucial importance: Will we champion the unique power, authority, and distinctive narrative of Scripture to motivate political work, or will we continue to halfheartedly cheer when a politician gives the Bible a PR boost? Hopefully these chapters have given you a sense of the hermeneutical questions, moral quandaries, and spiritual formation problems that impact our reading and use of Scripture in political arguments. Hopefully these chapters have given you tangible examples you can wrestle with, in community with people who are different from you and disagree with you. Hopefully these chapters can help shape better, more productive, and more faithful conversations among Christians about what we're doing when we cite the Bible in our political disputes.

Regardless of what role we play in this conversation—pastor leading a congregation, family member navigating politics at the dinner table, or Bible study member hashing out a difficult passage—we can learn from one crucial figure in Scripture to guide our work.

Hearing the Word against Us

In 2 Kings 22, Josiah becomes king at the ripe age of eight. He rules for eighteen good and faithful years, the Bible tells us, and in the eighteenth year of his reign the Book of the Law is discovered in the neglected temple of the Lord. The high priest Hilkiah gives the book to Shaphan, the secretary, who reports to the king that the book has been found and reads it for him. Josiah tears his robes as he hears the laws that have been broken and the destruction that is surely coming for God's wayward people. He commands the high priest to go inquire of the Lord about the book, and Hilkiah goes to the prophet Huldah for guidance.

Huldah tells Hilkiah words no high priest or king wants to hear: "This is what the Lord says: I am going to bring disaster on this place and its people, according to everything written in the book the king of Judah has read. Because they have forsaken me and burned incense to other gods and aroused my anger by all the idols their hands have made, my anger will burn against this place and will not be quenched" (2 Kings 22:16–17).

What does any of this have to do with interpreting the Bible for politics? We throw the word "prophetic" around a lot these days—to describe angry social media posts, criticisms of both political parties, or "speaking truth to power." We find in Huldah's example a prophetic witness we can adopt in our own contexts. She is not a powerful person: biblical scholar Ellen Davis says that Huldah is "connected" to the main power of the kingdom but does not serve within the palace as an official court prophet, likely because of her gender.[2] But Huldah receives God's word, accepts it as authoritative for the people of God, and recognizes how it speaks to the political and social moment she is in. She is not afraid to tell the king and the high priest about God's coming judgment, and she knows it is coming because she can interpret God's law *and* the people's failing.

Huldah faithfully interprets God's words, and she *remembers* what God has said when others have forgotten it. The drama of the story is rooted in forgetfulness: the people have not only lost the law but have forgotten their own history with their faithful God. This is the perennial problem of the people of God—forgetting what God has promised. Huldah is a preserver of shared cultural memory, a faithful receiver of God's word who passes it on to the next generation. She fulfills a crucial role described in 2 Timothy 1:14: "Guard the good deposit that was entrusted to you."[3]

We also find in Josiah's response an important example for us: Josiah is one of the very few examples in Scripture of a powerful person hearing God's word *against them*. It is in Josiah's interest as king to believe that God will allow Judah to flourish and prosper in spite of their sin. He wants to hear that even if they have broken the law, God will not punish them. It is incredibly rare—in biblical history and in our own history—to be able to hear the word of the Lord as a word against our own interests.[4] Dietrich Bonhoeffer, the German pastor and anti-Nazi dissident who helped found the Confessing Church, said something similar. In a 1932 speech, he challenged the church, "Has it not become terribly clear, again and again, in all that we have discussed with one another here, that we are no longer obedient to the Bible?" But more than giving a pious scolding, Bonhoeffer described the perennial problem for the church's relationship to political power: "We prefer our own thoughts to those of the Bible. We no longer read the Bible seriously. We read it no longer *against* ourselves but only *for* ourselves."[5]

This is the goal for us today: that we would rightly receive and interpret the Bible, hearing it even when it speaks *against* us. We need prophetic Christians today—not people who enjoy feeling brash or bold or who joyfully enter into conflict, but people who can carefully and courageously read God's *Word* and God's *world*. We need people who will "guard the good deposit" of Scripture *and* help us remember our own immediate history—the good and the bad. We need people who can understand the text well *and* understand their context well. We need people who can think well about ethics and politics *and* who have been spiritually formed in such a way that they can read the Word against their own interests.

And we need Christians who can model Josiah's faithful response of hearing the word of the Lord against themselves. It is no accident that many of the examples of faithful biblical interpretation in this book are examples from the history of the Black church. White Christians in America have historically failed at hearing the word of the Lord against ourselves, especially when spoken by our Black brothers and sisters, as well as other believers of color.

The Bible is itself the product of diversity and unity: one redemptive story given by God, but given to us through the various perspectives of a diverse cast of characters. It is also a book written very often from the perspective of the oppressed and marginalized—God's people suffering under Pharaoh or Babylon or Rome. Our interpretation of Scripture must be done in a way that models this diversity and recognizes this perspective. Many of us have learned that reading in community is better. We learn more about God when we gather together and listen to each other's questions and insights. But we also read better in the communion of the *saints*: drawing on the diverse perspectives of Christians throughout time and across geography, focusing especially on those voices that have gone unnoticed or ignored.

This task is no small one, and our efforts will be inevitably feeble and fallen, as we are. But one beautiful thing about learning our history—the global history of the church and the history of our own little place in it—is that we are reminded that Christ is faithful to his church even in her failures, and he works in unexpected places while our earthly kingdoms crumble.

This history of the Bible in American public life risks leaving us in a place of despair. We can feel defeated by reading about the endless times that Christians failed to hear the word of the Lord against themselves, about the ways that expediency and political power shaped interpretations more than faithfulness to God did. Surely we can't overcome these pressures; surely we will succumb to our predecessors' failures. In a certain sense, this sense of defeat might be just what we need. We need to have our certainty and confidence deflated a little bit. But we are not without hope or help in our interpretive attempts. The Holy Spirit has not abandoned Christ's church, even when we are tempted to. Just as these chapters contained examples of great faithfulness and great failure, we will see the same in our own churches—and in ourselves. Perhaps the most hopeful message for us today is the reminder that we will falter and fail in our interpretations, but God will not falter or fail us.

Earlier in his 1932 speech, Bonhoeffer recounted a man telling him matter-of-factly, "The church is dead." Bonhoeffer's response was unexpected. The "faithless world" that is nevertheless "full of pious illusion" says the church is not dead but only weak and promises to serve it with vigor until it rises in power again. But the believer, he says, knows: "The church lives in the midst of dying, solely because God calls it forth out of death into life, because God does the impossible against us and through us."[6]

Rather than throwing up our hands and abandoning the church or throwing ourselves into reviving the institution at any cost, we can share Bonhoeffer's faithful posture. We can withstand hearing the word against us because we know that our witness does not stand or fall on our own strength—instead it relies on the mighty hand and outstretched arm of God.

The church lives in the midst of dying, because God is faithful to his people.

ACKNOWLEDGMENTS

This book is the product of time spent with people and in communities where I learned to love the Bible enough to spend my life trying to figure out how to read it faithfully. There are too many Awana leaders, youth pastors, and Sunday school teachers to thank, but they each shaped my love for the Bible. I am especially indebted to my seminary professors, the women who showed up to study Jeremiah with me for six months in Dallas, Texas, and the bewildered youth volunteers who tried to answer all my questions in high school.

The Durham and Duke Divinity communities have been the exact right places to write this book, and I am thankful for many professors, friends, and church members not named here. I must thank especially Kat Burgett for being my truly unfailing summer writing companion and talking me down from many an existential cliff, as well as the slightly less unfailing Justin Rasmussen. Kendall Vanderslice has been my dearest friend in Durham and the best person to process book writing (and everything else in life) with. I wouldn't have made it through this without her. I will forever be thankful for the ways Sharon Miller has supported and encouraged me, especially since she can now do this over breakfast. Sarah Neff and Rhody Mastin have made Duke a home for me, and I'm immeasurably grateful for their welcome and friendship. My church family in Durham welcomed a strange new member with some church baggage with open arms, and I love them dearly for it. Finally, Luke Bretherton got more than he was bargaining for when he took on a student who would write a book in her first year of the program, and he has been generous with his time and wisdom from the beginning.

I am also eternally grateful for many other people who read early drafts of this book and offered their insight and expertise: Malcolm Foley, Jennifer Powell McNutt, Heather Joy Zimmerman, Joey Cochran, Andrea Humphries, Kendra Sharrard, and my mom, Debbie Schiess, who has been subjected to my drafts for nearly all my life.

Don Gates guided this book from the earliest stages to completion, and I am immensely grateful for his wisdom, guidance, and support. Katelyn Beaty has a 100 percent success rate for asking me if I want to write a book, and I am deeply grateful for her work in making this one better.

I am also thankful for a family that has loved me my whole life long, taught me the Bible with their words and their lives, and does not disown me even when I talk about religion and politics in public. Momma, Daddy, and Kendra Woo especially.

This book was written because of the people who taught me to love the Bible, but it was also written because our loving and gracious God did not abandon me when his people thought I was more of a liability than a gift. This is my meager act of praise in response to his overwhelming faithfulness to me.

NOTES

Introduction

1. Brad East, *The Church's Book: Theology of Scripture in Ecclesial Context* (Grand Rapids: Eerdmans, 2022), 285.

Chapter 1 A City on a Hill

1. Michael Parker, *John Winthrop: Founding the City upon a Hill* (New York: Routledge, 2013), 4.

2. Daniel T. Rodgers, *As a City on a Hill: The Story of America's Most Famous Lay Sermon* (Princeton: Princeton University Press, 2018), 1, 25.

3. Richard Gamble, *In Search of the City on a Hill: The Making and Unmaking of an American Myth* (New York: Bloomsbury, 2012), 7.

4. Parker, *John Winthrop*, 39.

5. Parker, *John Winthrop*, 40.

6. John Winthrop, "A Modell of Christian Charity (1630)," Collections of the Massachusetts Historical Society, accessed February 10, 2023, https://history.hanover.edu/texts/winthmod.html. Spellings have been modified for ease of reading.

7. Jon Butler, "Religion in Colonial America," in *Religion in American Life: A Short History*, by Jon Butler, Grant Wacker, and Randall Balmer (New York: Oxford University Press, 2011), 52.

8. Winthrop, "A Modell of Christian Charity."

9. Abram C. Van Engen, *City on a Hill: A History of American Exceptionalism* (New Haven: Yale University Press, 2020), 7.

10. Rodgers, *As a City on a Hill*, 125.

11. Rodgers, *As a City on a Hill*, 235; John Vile, *The Bible in American Law and Politics* (Lanham, MD: Rowman & Littlefield, 2020), 104.

12. John F. Kennedy, "Address of President-Elect John F. Kennedy Delivered to a Joint Convention of the General Court of the Commonwealth of Massachusetts,"

The State House, Boston, January 9, 1961, John F. Kennedy Presidential Library and Museum, accessed January 28, 2023, https://www.jfklibrary.org/archives/other-resources/john-f-kennedy-speeches/massachusetts-general-court-19610109.

13. Gamble, *In Search of the City on a Hill*, 1.

14. Ronald Reagan, "Farewell Address to the Nation," January 11, 1989, Ronald Reagan Presidential Library and Museum, accessed January 28, 2023, https://www.reaganlibrary.gov/archives/speech/farewell-address-nation.

15. Rodgers, *As a City on a Hill*, 239–40; John Fea, *Believe Me: The Evangelical Road to Donald Trump* (Grand Rapids: Eerdmans, 2018), 45.

16. Gamble, *In Search of the City on a Hill*, 143.

17. The film, titled "John Winthrop and the Founding of America," is available on YouTube at https://www.youtube.com/watch?v=-CaLshwQrTM.

18. Daniel White, "Read Hillary Clinton's Speech Touting 'American Exceptionalism," *Time*, September 1, 2016, https://time.com/4474619/read-hillary-clinton-american-legion-speech/.

19. Rodgers, *As a City on a Hill*, 8.

20. Inspired by the "Y'all Version" of the Bible created by theologian John Dyer, available at https://yallversion.com/.

21. Gamble, *In Search of the City on a Hill*, 4.

22. See Anna Case-Winters, *Matthew: A Theological Commentary on the Bible* (Louisville: Westminster John Knox, 2015), 79; Craig Blomberg, *Matthew* (Nashville: Broadman & Holman, 1992), 103; and David P. Gushee and Glen H. Stassen, *Kingdom Ethics: Following Jesus in Contemporary Context*, 2nd ed. (Grand Rapids: Eerdmans, 2016), 199.

23. John Chrysostom, *The Gospel of Matthew*, Homily 15.6, in *Matthew 1–13*, ed. Manlio Simonetti, Ancient Christian Commentary on Scripture, New Testament 1a (Downers Grove, IL: IVP Academic, 2011), 92.

24. David Garland, *Reading Matthew: A Literary and Theological Commentary* (Macon, GA: Smyth & Helwys, 2001), 60.

25. Jonathan T. Pennington, *The Sermon on the Mount and Human Flourishing* (Grand Rapids: Baker Academic, 2017), 168.

26. Eric Nelson, *The Hebrew Republic: Jewish Sources and the Transformation of European Political Thought* (Cambridge, MA: Harvard University Press, 2010). See also Eran Shalev, *American Zion: The Old Testament as a Political Text from the Revolution to the Civil War* (New Haven: Yale University Press, 2013), 23.

27. Parker, *John Winthrop*, 27.

28. Mark Noll, *America's God: From Jonathan Edwards to Abraham Lincoln* (Oxford: Oxford University Press, 2002), 39.

29. Francis J. Bremer, *John Winthrop: America's Founding Father* (Oxford: Oxford University Press, 2003), 181.

30. Butler, "Religion in Colonial America," 51.

31. Butler, "Religion in Colonial America," 58.

32. The history of jeremiads in America is varied and includes an entire tradition of African American jeremiads. Also see Butler, "Religion in Colonial America," 62.

33. Parker, *John Winthrop*, 30.

34. Butler, "Religion in Colonial America," 62.

35. Walter Brueggemann, *Theology of the Old Testament*: *Testimony, Dispute, Advocacy* (Minneapolis: Fortress, 2005), 503.

36. Matthew Rowley, "Reverse-Engineering the Covenant: Moses, Massachusetts Bay and the Construction of a City on a Hill," *Journal of the Bible and Its Reception* 8, no. 2 (2021): 210.

37. Winthrop, "A Modell of Christian Charity."

38. Butler, "Religion in Colonial America," 54.

39. Rodgers, *As a City on a Hill*, 48.

40. We have reason to think that Winthrop may have quoted some of the passages in "A Model of Christian Charity" from memory, as the language is not precise to any known available translation. See Gamble, *In Search of the City on a Hill*, 30.

41. Richard Bauckham, *The Bible in Politics: How to Read the Bible Politically* (Louisville: Westminster John Knox, 2011), 1.

42. Oliver O'Donovan, *Desire of the Nations: Rediscovering the Roots of Political Theology* (Cambridge: Cambridge University Press, 1999), 45.

43. O'Donovan, *Desire of the Nations*, 2.

44. John Webster, *Holy Scripture: A Dogmatic Sketch* (New York: Cambridge University Press, 2003), 6.

45. Gamble, *In Search of the City on a Hill*, 13–14.

Chapter 2 Submission and Revolution

1. Jerry Markon, Fenit Nirappil, and Wesley Lowery, "Sharp Emotions, Further Protests Deepen Nation's Divide over Race and Policing," *Washington Post*, July 10, 2016, https://www.washingtonpost.com/politics/police-arrest-black-lives-matter-activist-deray-mckesson-200-other-protesters/2016/07/10/f79a12ac-46d0-11e6-bdb9-701687974517_story.html.

2. Lincoln Mullen, "The Fight to Define Romans 13," *The Atlantic*, June 15, 2018, https://www.theatlantic.com/ideas/archive/2018/06/romans-13/562916/.

3. Harry S. Stout, "Religion, Communications, and the Ideological Origins of the American Revolution," *The William and Mary Quarterly* 34, no. 4 (Oct 1977): 521, and Mark Noll, *In the Beginning Was the Word: The Bible in American Public Life, 1492–1783* (New York: Oxford University Press, 2016), 289.

4. Daniel L. Dreisbach, *Reading the Bible with the Founding Fathers* (New York: Oxford University Press, 2017), 26, 73; Mark Noll, *Christians in the American Revolution* (Washington, DC: Christian University Press, 1977), 41, 45, 47.

5. Dreisbach, *Reading the Bible*, 76.

6. Eran Shalev, "Evil Counselors, Corrupt Traitors, and Bad Kings: The Hebrew Bible and Political Critique in Revolutionary America and Beyond," in *Resistance to Tyrants, Obedience to God: Reason, Religion, and Republicanism at the American Founding*, ed. Dustin Gish and Daniel Klinghard (New York: Lexington Books, 2013), 105.

7. Donald Barr Chidsey, *The Loyalists: The Story of Those Americans Who Fought against Independence* (New York: Crown, 1973), 84. See also Alice M.

Baldwin, *The New England Clergy and the American Revolution* (New York: Ungar, 1958), 3.

8. James P. Byrd, *Sacred Scripture, Sacred War: The Bible and the American Revolution* (New York: Oxford University Press, 2013), 16.

9. Noll, *Christians in the American Revolution*, 103.

10. There were obviously varied political theories and theological arguments from Loyalist clergy, so this is a generalization. For more, see John E. Ferling, *The Loyalist Mind: Joseph Galloway and the American Revolution* (University Park: Pennsylvania State University Press, 1977).

11. Charles Inglis, "The Duty of Honouring the King," New York, January 30, 1780. The full sermon is available at http://anglicanhistory.org/charles/inglis.html.

12. Noll, *Christians in the American Revolution*, 25.

13. While few saw the irony of their appealing to the exodus in support of their own political project but not on behalf of actually enslaved people, some did. One example was a 1775 sermon on Amos 5:21, when Samuel Andrews preached that true repentance meant "a flight from personal evils," including slavery. See Noll, *In the Beginning*, 281.

14. Shalev, "Evil Counselors," 110.

15. Noll, *In the Beginning*, 280.

16. Eran Shalev, *American Zion: The Old Testament as a Political Text from the Revolution to the Civil War* (New Haven: Yale University Press, 2013), 30–31.

17. Noll, *In the Beginning*, 280.

18. For one example of this approach, see Samuel West's sermon titled "On the Right to Rebel against Governors," which was given at the request of the Massachusetts governing body in Boston in 1776. The full sermon is available online at http://www.edchange.org/multicultural/speeches/samuel_west_rebel.html.

19. Gregg L. Frazer, *God against the Revolution: The Loyalist Clergy's Case against the American Revolution* (Lawrence: University Press of Kansas, 2018), 46. Frazer is critical of the Patriots' interpretation.

20. Dreisbach, *Reading the Bible*, 133.

21. Gary L. Steward, *Justifying Revolution: The Early American Clergy and Political Resistance* (New York: Oxford University Press, 2021), 9.

22. Jonathan Mayhew, *A Discourse Concerning Unlimited Submission and Non-Resistance to the Higher Powers* (Boston: Fowle, 1750), 24.

23. Mayhew, *Discourse Concerning Unlimited Submission*, 29.

24. Noll, *In the Beginning*, 304–5.

25. Jonathan Boucher, "On Civil Liberty," in *View of the Causes and Consequences* (London: Robinson, 1797), 504–5.

26. Noll, *In the Beginning*, 281.

27. Noll, *In the Beginning*, 303.

28. For examples of these writings, see Boucher, "A Farewell Sermon," in *View of the Causes and Consequences*, 591; Boucher, "On Civil Liberty," 499; Charles Inglis, S.P.G. MSS. Vol. B. 2, No. 74, in *Life and Letters of Charles Inglis*, ed. John Wolfe Lydekker (New York: Macmillan, 1936), 208.

29. Douglas J. Moo, *The Epistle to the Romans*, New International Commentary on the New Testament (Grand Rapids: Eerdmans, 1996), 808.

30. Witherington gives a few reasons for the 57 CE date: Paul wrote Romans shortly before taking the collection to Jerusalem (Rom. 15:23–28), which means it was written after the Corinthian epistles. Romans 16:1 indicates it was likely written from Corinth: Phoebe carried the letter, and the Gaius mentioned in 16:23 is likely the same one mentioned in 1 Corinthians 1:14. Ben Witherington III, *Paul's Letter to the Romans: A Socio-rhetorical Commentary* (Grand Rapids: Eerdmans, 2004), 7.

31. Robert Jewett, *Romans: A Commentary* (Minneapolis: Fortress, 2007), 785–86.

32. Craig S. Keener, *Romans*, New Covenant Commentary (Eugene, OR: Cascade Books, 2009), 156.

33. C. E. B. Cranfield, *Romans 9–16* (London: Black, 2004), 652; Jewett, *Romans*, 784.

34. James D. G. Dunn, *Romans 1–8*, Word Biblical Commentary 38A (Dallas: Word, 1988), 759.

35. The Greek word *hypakouō* (obedience) is used only in relationship to God and the gospel. Michael Gorman, *Romans: A Theological and Pastoral Commentary* (Grand Rapids: Eerdmans, 2022), 254.

36. Jewett, *Romans*, 789.

37. N. T. Wright, "Paul's Gospel and Caesar's Empire," in *Paul and Politics: Ekklesia, Israel, Imperium, Interpretation*, ed. Richard A. Horsley (Harrisburg, PA: Trinity Press International, 2000), 172.

38. Gorman, *Romans*, 254.

39. Neil Elliott, "Romans 13:1–7 in the Context of Imperial Propaganda," in *Paul and Empire: Religion and Power in Roman Imperial Society*, ed. Richard A. Horsley (Harrisburg, PA: Trinity Press International, 1997), 196.

40. Cranfield, *Romans 9–16*, 664.

41. Victor Paul Furnish, *The Moral Teaching of Paul: Selected Issues* (Nashville: Abingdon, 1979), 155–56; Bruce W. Winter, *Seek the Welfare of the City: Christians as Benefactors and Citizens* (Grand Rapids: Eerdmans, 1994), 33, 35–36.

42. Cranfield, *Romans 9–16*, 666.

43. Cranfield, *Romans 9–16*, 668; Dunn, *Romans 1–8*, 765.

44. Oliver O'Donovan, *Self, World and Time: Ethics as Theology* (Grand Rapids: Eerdmans, 2013), 1:79–82.

45. Noll, *In the Beginning*, 296–97.

46. Kristina Benham, "British Exodus, American Empire: Evangelical Preachers and the Biblicisms of Revolution," in *Every Leaf, Line, and Letter: Evangelicals and the Bible from the 1730s to the Present*, ed. Timothy Larsen (Downers Grove, IL: IVP Academic, 2021), 17.

Chapter 3 "The Bible through Slave-Holding Spectacles"

1. Mark Noll, *The Civil War as Theological Crisis* (Chapel Hill: University of North Carolina Press, 2006).

2. Robert J. Miller, *Both Prayed to the Same God: Religion and Faith in the American Civil War* (Lanham, MD: Lexington Books, 2007), 43. See also Noll, *Civil War as Theological Crisis*, 17. Noll argues that "reasoning about the war

reflected long-standing habits of mind. For more than a century before 1860, American theologians had been uniting historical perspectives with specific aspects of American intellectual experience."

3. Elizabeth Fox-Genovese and Eugene D. Genovese, *The Mind of the Master Class: History and Faith in the Southern Slaveholders' Worldview* (New York: Cambridge University Press, 2005), 493.

4. Mark Noll, *God and Race in American Politics: A Short History* (Princeton: Princeton University Press, 2008), 35.

5. See David Brion Davis, *The Problem of Slavery in the Age of Revolution, 1770–1823* (Ithaca, NY: Cornell University Press, 1975), 525.

6. Jamie L. Brummitt, "'How *Dare* Men Mix Up the Bible So with Their Own *Bad* Passions': When the Good Book Became the Bad Book in the American Civil War," *Material Religion* 18, no. 2 (2022): 138–37.

7. Brummitt, "How *Dare* Men Mix Up the Bible," 145.

8. Noll, *Civil War as Theological Crisis*, 32–33.

9. James P. Byrd, *A Holy Baptism of Fire and Blood: The Bible and the American Civil War* (New York: Oxford University Press, 2021), 15.

10. Albert Harrill, "The Use of the New Testament in the American Slave Controversy: A Case History in the Hermetical Tension between Biblical Criticism and Christian Moral Debate," *Religion and American Culture* 10, no. 2 (2000): 163; John Patrick Daly, *When Slavery Was Called Freedom: Evangelicalism, Proslavery, and the Causes of the Civil War* (Lexington: University Press of Kentucky, 2002), 65.

11. Harrill, "Use of the New Testament," 151.

12. John R. McKivigan, *The War against Proslavery Religion: Abolitionism and the Northern Churches, 1830–1865* (Ithaca, NY: Cornell University Press, 1984), 30.

13. Leonard Bacon, *Slavery Discussed in Occasional Essays, from 1833 to 1846* (New York: Baker and Scribner, 1846), 180.

14. John Coffey, *Exodus and Liberation: Deliverance Politics from John Calvin to Martin Luther King Jr.* (New York: Oxford University Press, 2014), 84.

15. Paul Harvey, *Bounds of Their Habitation: Race and Religion in American History* (New York: Rowman & Littlefield, 2017), 76.

16. Stephen R. Haynes, *Noah's Curse: The Biblical Justification of American Slavery* (New York: Oxford University Press, 2002), 5, 9.

17. Thomas Virgil Peterson, *Ham and Japheth: The Mythic Word of Whites in the Antebellum South* (Metuchen, NJ: Scarecrow, 1978), 117.

18. David M. Whitford, *The Curse of Ham in the Early Modern Era: The Bible and the Justifications for Slavery* (New York: Routledge, 2017), 172. Whitford also details the larger history of the curse of Ham and colonialist exploitation.

19. Coffey, *Exodus and Liberation*, 82–84.

20. Molly Oshatz, *Slavery and Sin: The Fight against Slavery and the Rise of Liberal Protestantism* (New York: Oxford University Press, 2012), 17.

21. The Jubilee was particularly important: the abolitionist publication *The Liberator* had 150 references to "Exodus" but over 550 to "Jubilee." It was not only a liberationist text but also an eschatological one, and it could be more directly

connected with Jesus's sermon in Luke 4, a sermon that displayed Christ as the "Great Reformer" and centered the "liberationist orthopraxy" of Christianity. See Coffey, *Exodus and Liberation*, 125–26.

22. Harrill, "Use of the New Testament," 153.

23. Oshatz, *Slavery and Sin*, 62. They argued that the Canaanites were not synonymous with later African populations, that the curse expired when Israel lost the land to Canaan, and that slavery would be justified only if it was exactly this (one preacher proclaimed that if someone could prove himself an Israelite, find Canaanites for slaves, and take them and himself to Canaan, then that was fine). See Davis, *Problem of Slavery*, 554.

24. Harrill, "Use of the New Testament," 152.

25. McKivigan, *War against Proslavery Religion*, 30–31.

26. See Harrill, "Use of the New Testament," 152, 159.

27. Oshatz, *Slavery and Sin*, 71.

28. Turner, "Confessions," as quoted in Herbert Aptheker, *Nat Turner's Slave Rebellion* (New York: Humanities Press, 1966), 138.

29. Harrill, "Use of the New Testament," 161–62.

30. Frederick Douglass, *My Bondage and My Freedom* (New York: Miller, Orton and Mulligan, 1855), 144.

31. Albert J. Raboteau, *The Black Experience in American Evangelicalism* (New York: Routledge, 1996), 104.

32. Coffey, *Exodus and Liberation*, 4, 147. Origen, Augustine, and other early Christians talked about the exodus as prefiguring the spiritual redemption Christ brought his people. Eusebius, in his *Ecclesiastical History*, compares the battle of the Milvian Bridge in 312 to the exodus.

33. Allen Dwight Callahan, *The Talking Book: African Americans and the Bible* (New Haven: Yale University Press, 2006), xi.

34. Callahan, *Talking Book*, xiii.

35. Callahan, *Talking Book*, 11.

36. Noll, *Civil War as Theological Crisis*, 49.

37. James Cone, "Content and Method of Black Theology," *Journal of Religious Thought* 32, no. 2 (1975): 94.

38. James Cone, *God of the Oppressed* (New York: Seabury, 1975), 60; Cone, "Content and Method," 97.

39. See discussion of Walker's work in Lisa Bowens, *African American Readings of Paul* (Grand Rapids: Eerdmans, 2020), 98.

40. Peter P. Hinks, ed., *David Walker's Appeal to the Coloured Citizens of the World* (University Park: Pennsylvania State University Press, 2000), 6, 14.

41. Hinks, *David Walker's Appeal*, 40.

42. For more description of the myriad biblical allusions in Stewart and analysis of gender dynamics in her writing, see Valerie C. Cooper, *Word, Like Fire: Maria Stewart, the Bible, and the Rights of African Americans* (Charlottesville: University of Virginia Press, 2011).

43. Maria Stewart, "Religion and the Pure Principles of Morality," in Cooper, *Word, Like Fire*, 43, 48.

44. Stewart, "Religion and the Pure Principles of Morality," 45.

45. Stewart, "Religion and the Pure Principles of Morality," 81.

46. Stewart, "Religion and the Pure Principles of Morality," 61, 80, 68.

47. For some examples, see Oshatz, *Slavery and Sin,* 57–59; Harrill, "Use of the New Testament," 149.

48. Donald G. Mathews, *Religion in the Old South* (Chicago: University of Chicago Press, 1977), 157.

49. Mathews, *Religion in the Old South,* 175.

50. Callahan, *Talking Book,* xi, xiii.

51. Jonathan Blanchard, *A Debate on Slavery: Held in the City of Cincinnati, on the First, Second, Third, and Sixth Days of October, 1845, upon the Question: Is Slave-holding in Itself Sinful, and the Relation between Master and Slave a Sinful Relation? Affirmative: Rev. J. Blanchard, Negative: N. L. Rice, D.D.* (Cincinnati, OH: W.H. Moore, 1846), 359–60.

52. Byrd, *Holy Baptism of Fire and Blood,* 9.

53. Jordan T. Watkins, *Slavery and Sacred Texts: The Bible, the Constitution, and Historical Consciousness in Antebellum America* (New York: Cambridge University Press, 2021).

54. Byrd, *Holy Baptism of Fire and Blood,* 53.

55. Noll, *Civil War as Theological Crisis,* 19.

56. Coffey, *Exodus and Liberation,* 131.

57. See discussion of Wilson's words in Byrd, *Holy Baptism of Fire and Blood,* 48.

Chapter 4 Your Kingdom Come

1. Walter Rauschenbusch, *A Theology for the Social Gospel* (New York: Macmillan, 1917), 24.

2. This definition originally appeared in Shailer Mathews and Gerald Birney Smith, *A Dictionary of Religon and Ethics* (New York: Macmillan, 1921), 415. Cited in Christopher H. Evans, *The Social Gospel in American Religion* (New York: New York University Press, 2017), 2.

3. Evans, *Social Gospel in American Religion,* 1.

4. Ronald C. White Jr. and C. Howard Hopkins, *The Social Gospel: Religion and Reform in Changing America* (Philadelphia: Temple University Press, 1976), xi.

5. Charles Howard Hopkins, *The Rise of the Social Gospel in American Protestantism, 1865–1915* (New Haven: Yale University Press, 1940), 56–57, 125.

6. Timothy L. Smith, *Revivalism and Social Reform: American Protestantism on the Eve of the Civil War* (Gloucester, MA: Abingdon, 1976), 148.

7. Gary Dorrien, "Social Salvation: The Social Gospel as Theology and Economics," in *The Social Gospel Today,* ed. Christopher H. Evans (Louisville: Westminster John Knox, 2001), 101.

8. Smith, *Revivalism and Social Reform,* 152.

9. Smith, *Revivalism and Social Reform,* 162.

10. Smith, *Revivalism and Social Reform,* 151. Smith calls it the "evangelical origins of social Christianity" (148).

11. Dorrien, "Social Salvation," 107.

12. Evans, *Social Gospel in American Religion,* 9.

13. Jacob Henry Dorn, *Washington Gladden: Prophet of the Social Gospel* (Columbus: Ohio State University Press, 1966), 141. Gladden "gradually" rejected Calvinism and accepted modern biblical criticism, moving from a more conservative theological tradition to "full-blown liberalism."

14. Richard D. Knudten, *The Systematic Thought of Washington Gladden* (New York: Humanities Press, 1968), 91–93.

15. Knudten, *Systematic Thought*, 90–91; Dorn, *Washington Gladden*, 158–68. Gladden argued that revelation itself is infallible (on account of the doctrine of God) but the written record of it is fallible, with a fairly wide gap between the two.

16. Dorn, *Washington Gladden*, 160.

17. Dorn, *Washington Gladden*, 158–68.

18. For more on the context of Gladden's congregation in Ohio, see Hopkins, *Rise of the Social Gospel*, 81–97.

19. Washington Gladden, *Tools and the Man: Property and Industry under the Christian Law* (New York: Houghton, Mifflin, 1893), 1–2.

20. Washington Gladden, *The Nation and the Kingdom: Annual Sermon before the American Board of Commissioners for Foreign Missions* (Boston: The Board, 1909).

21. Gladden, *The Nation and the Kingdom*, 3, 9, 11.

22. Gladden, *The Nation and the Kingdom*, 4, 22.

23. Gladden, *The Nation and the Kingdom*, 7.

24. Gladden, *The Nation and the Kingdom*, 9, 14, 16, 18.

25. Gladden, *The Nation and the Kingdom*, 24.

26. Evans, *Social Gospel in American Religion*, 136–37.

27. Evans, *Social Gospel in American Religion*, 161.

28. White and Hopkins, *Social Gospel*, xi; Gary Dorrien, *Social Ethics in the Making: Interpreting an American Tradition* (Malden, MA: Wiley-Blackwell, 2009), 60; Harry Antonides, *Stones for Bread: The Social Gospel and Its Contemporary Legacy* (Jordan Station, ON: Paideia, 1985); Rosemary Skinner Keller, "Women Creating Communities—and Community—in the Name of the Social Gospel," in Evans, *Social Gospel Today*, 69–70.

29. Reinhold Niebuhr, *Moral Man and Immoral Society* (New York: Scribner's Sons, 1932).

30. Reinhold Niebuhr, *The Children of Light and the Children of Darkness* (New York: Scribner, 1960).

31. See discussion of Montgomery's words in David Moberg, *The Great Reversal: Evangelism versus Social Concern* (New York: Holman, 1972), 34–35.

32. Andrew L. Whitehead and Samuel L. Perry, *Taking Back America for God: Christian Nationalism in the United States* (New York: Oxford University Press, 2020), 10.

33. Dorrien, *Social Ethics in the Making*, 60.

34. Timothy Tseng and Janet Furness, "The Reawakening of the Evangelical Social Consciousness," in Evans, *Social Gospel Today*, 114.

35. Timothy L. Smith coins the phrase "great reversal" in his book *Revivalism and Social Reform* (New York: Abingdon, 1957). David Moberg describes this shift across many denominations in *Great Reversal*, 30–43.

36. Moberg, *Great Reversal*, 34.
37. Moberg, *Great Reversal*, 35.

Chapter 5 A Stick of Dynamite

1, King's speech deserves to be listened to as well as read. The transcript and an audio recording can be found at "Read Martin Luther King Jr.'s 'I Have a Dream' Speech in its Entirety," NPR, January 16, 2023, https://www.npr.org/2010/01/18/122701268/i-have-a-dream-speech-in-its-entirety.

2. David L. Chappell, *A Stone of Hope: Prophetic Religion and the Death of Jim Crow* (Chapel Hill: University of North Carolina Press, 2004), 87.

3. Esau McCaulley, *Reading While Black: African American Biblical Interpretation as an Exercise in Hope* (Downers Grove, IL: IVP Academic, 2020), 49.

4. Johnny E. Williams, *African American Religion and the Civil Rights Movement in Arkansas* (Jackson: University Press of Mississippi, 2003), 114. Also, even if it is sometimes said that many churches shrank from engaging in the conflict, it was out of real fear. Churches were burned, bombed, and so on, regardless of the political activity of the congregants. Paul Harvey, *Freedom's Coming: Religious Culture and the Shaping of the South from the Civil War through the Civil Rights Era* (Chapel Hill: University of North Carolina Press, 2012), 194.

5. These examples are from Williams, *African American Religion*, 112–13, 118–19.

6. Harvey, *Freedom's Coming*, 199.

7. See discussion of Mays's speech in Davis W. Houck and David E. Dixon, eds., *Rhetoric, Religion and the Civil Rights Movement: 1954–1965* (Waco: Baylor University Press, 2006), 56–64.

8. Harvey, *Freedom's Coming*, 192.

9. See discussion of Hamer in Harvey, *Freedom's Coming*, 197–98.

10. Marion A. Boggs, "The Crucial Test of Christian Citizenship," in Houck and Dixon, *Rhetoric, Religion and the Civil Rights Movement*, 271–77.

11. Everett Tilson, *Segregation and the Bible: A Searching Analysis of the Biblical Evidence* (New York: Abingdon, 1958).

12. Harvey, *Freedom's Coming*, 47.

13. Paul Harvey, "Religion, Race, and the Right in the South, 1945–1990," in *Politics and Religion in the White South*, ed. Glenn Feldman (Lexington: University Press of Kentucky, 2005), 103.

14. Harvey, *Freedom's Coming*, 39.

15. John Dittmer, *Local People: The Struggle for Civil Rights in Mississippi* (Champaign: University of Illinois Press, 1995), 63.

16. Harvey, "Religion, Race, and the Right," 104–5.

17. J. Russell Hawkins, *The Bible Told Them So: How Southern Evangelicals Fought to Preserve White Supremacy* (New York: Oxford University Press, 2021), 49, 51–52.

18. Harvey, "Religion, Race, and the Right," 107.

19. Harvey, "Religion, Race, and the Right," 107.

20. Harvey, "Religion, Race, and the Right," 105.

21. Jemar Tisby, *The Color of Compromise: The Truth about the American Church's Complicity in Racism* (Grand Rapids: Zondervan, 2019), 148.

22. Jacquelyn Dowd Hall, "The Long Civil Rights Movement and the Political Uses of the Past," *Journal of American History* 91, no. 4 (March 2005): 1234.

23. Richard Lischer, *The Preacher King: Martin Luther King, Jr. and the Word That Moved America*, rev. ed. (New York: Oxford University Press, 2020), 32.

24. Lischer, *The Preacher King*, 44.

25. Clayborne Carson, ed., *The Autobiography of Martin Luther King, Jr.* (New York: Warner Books, 1993), 18.

26. Lischer, *Preacher King*, 225.

27. Lewis V. Baldwin, *The Voice of Conscience: The Church in the Mind of Martin Luther King, Jr.* (New York: Oxford University Press, 2010), 105.

28. Martin Luther King Jr., "A Realistic Look at Race Relations," unpublished paper, delivered at the Second Anniversary of the NAACP Legal Defense and Educational Fund, Waldorf Astoria Hotel, New York City, May 17, 1956.

29. Martin Luther King Jr., *Stride toward Freedom: The Montgomery Story* (New York: Harper, 1958), 84.

30. Lischer, *Preacher King*, 211.

31. Benjamin E. Mays, "Eulogy for Martin Luther King Jr., Morehouse College, Atlanta, Georgia, April 9, 1968," American Public Media, accessed February 10, 2023, http://americanradioworks.publicradio.org/features/blackspeech/bmays.html.

32. Martin Luther King Jr., "The Significant Contributions of Jeremiah to Religious Thought," in *The Papers of Martin Luther King, Jr.*, vol. 1, *Called to Serve, January 1929–June 1951*, ed. Clayborne Carson, Ralph Luker, and Penny A. Russell (Berkeley: University of California Press, 1992).

33. Tisby, *Color of Compromise*, 151.

34. Paul Harvey, *Martin Luther King: A Religious Life* (Lanham, MD: Rowman & Littlefield, 2021), 123.

35. Harvey, *Martin Luther King*, 123.

36. "Martin Luther King Jr.'s 'I Have a Dream' Speech." Quotations from this speech in this section are taken from this transcript.

37. Clarence B. Jones and Stuart Connelly, *Behind the Dream: The Making of the Speech That Transformed the Nation* (New York: Palgrave Macmillan, 2011), 112.

38. This language of weaving the biblical and contemporary stories and struggles is how theologian James Cone describes Black theology. See James Cone, "Content and Method of Black Theology," *Journal of Religious Thought* 32, no. 2 (1975): 96.

39. James Cone, *Speaking the Truth: Ecumenism, Liberation, and Black Theology* (Grand Rapids: Eerdmans, 1986), 24.

40. Lischer, *Preacher King*, xxxii.

41. Lischer, *Preacher King*, 217.

42. John Webster, *Holy Scripture: A Dogmatic Sketch* (New York: Cambridge University Press, 2003), 6.

43. This is a development: earlier in his public career, King appealed to shared biblical and patriotic values, but later in his career, as the majority of the country opposed him, he began to more fully embrace the prophetic voice as a voice of condemnation from God to God's people. Lischer, *Preacher King*, 182.

44. Lischer, *Preacher King*, 183.

45. Emerson B. Powery and Rodney S. Sadler Jr., *The Genesis of Liberation: Biblical Interpretation in the Antebellum Narratives of the Enslaved* (Louisville: Westminster John Knox, 2016), 163.

46. Lischer, *Preacher King*, 224.

47. Albert Raboteau, *Slave Religion: The Invisible Institution in the Antebellum South* (New York: Oxford University Press, 2004), 208–9.

48. George Shulman, *American Prophecy: Race and Redemption in American Political Culture* (Minneapolis: University of Minnesota Press, 2008), 106.

49. Chappell, *Stone of Hope*, 83.

50. Chappell, *Stone of Hope*, 85.

51. Shulman, *American Prophecy*, 102.

52. Baldwin, *Voice of Conscience*, 157.

53. For more on thinking through King as a public figure and sinful person, see McCaulley, *Reading While Black*, 49.

54. Lischer, *Preacher King*, 184.

Chapter 6 Magic of the Market

1. Politicians like Mike Pence and Sarah Palin have quoted it, attributing it to characters as various as Thomas Jefferson, John Locke, and Henry David Thoreau, though its origin is probably a US magazine from the 1830s. Eugene Volokh, "Who First Said, 'The Best Government Is That Which Governs Least'? Not Thoreau," *Washington Post*, September 6, 2017, https://www.washingtonpost.com/news/volokh-conspiracy/wp/2017/09/06/who-first-said-the-best-government-is-that-which-governs-least-not-thoreau/.

2. Eric R. Crouse, *The Cross and Reaganomics: Conservative Christians Defending Ronald Reagan* (New York: Lexington Books, 2013), 1.

3. Kim Phillips-Fein, *Invisible Hands: The Making of the Conservative Movement from the New Deal to Reagan* (New York: Norton, 2009), x.

4. This movement also has a much longer and more complicated story behind it. See Phillips-Fein, *Invisible Hands*, especially 70–72.

5. Pat Robertson, "A Christian Action Plan for the 1980s," originally published in *Bible Economics Today* 2, no. 6 (December/January 1980), available online at *Gary North's Specific Answers*, December 7, 2014, https://www.garynorth.com/public/14577.cfm.

6. Robertson, "A Christian Action Plan for the 1980s."

7. Phillips-Fein, *Invisible Hands*, 227.

8. "America Threatened by Creeping Bureaucracy: Freedom's Greatest Threat," *The Thomas Road Family Journal-Champion* 1, no. 4 (1978): 36.

9. Daniel K. Williams, *God's Own Party: The Making of the Christian Right* (New York: Oxford University Press, 2010), 163–65.

10. Arthur Schlesinger, "Forgetting Reinhold Niebuhr," *The New York Times*, September 18, 2005, https://www.nytimes.com/2005/09/18/books/review/forgetting-reinhold-niebuhr.html.

11. Crouse, *Cross and Reaganomics*, 98.

12. Crouse, *Cross and Reaganomics*, 67.

13. Ronald Reagan, "A Time for Choosing Speech, October 27, 1964," Reagan Presidential Library and Museum, accessed February 10, 2023, https://www.reaganlibrary.gov/reagans/ronald-reagan/time-choosing-speech-october-27-1964.

14. David Domke and Kevin Coe, *The God Strategy: How Religion Became a Political Weapon in America* (New York: Oxford University Press, 2004), 3–4; Bill Scher, "When Reagan Dared to Say 'God Bless America,'" *Politico*, July 17, 2015, https://www.politico.com/magazine/story/2015/07/reagan-god-bless-america-120286/.

15. Phillips-Fein, *Invisible Hands*, 257.

16. Ronald Reagan, "National Affairs Campaign Address on Religious Liberty," Dallas, Texas, August 22, 1980, quoted in Brian T. Kaylor, *Presidential Campaign Rhetoric in an Age of Confessional Politics* (New York: Lexington Books, 2011), 47–48.

17. "Obscure to some, this verse was familiar to Sunbelt evangelicals: it was the verse Jerry Falwell cited while traveling the country speaking on Reagan's behalf, that Washington for Jesus organizers singled out to summarize their event, pastors like W. A. Criswell paraphrased to fuel their jeremiads, and countless Christian citizens heard repeated in their pulpits, pews, and home Bible study. The fact that Reagan had seen fit to quote it was, in their minds, a sign that their country was now in good hands." Darren Dochuk, *From Bible Belt to Sunbelt: Plain-Folk Religion, Grassroots Politics, and the Rise of Evangelical Conservatism* (New York: Norton, 2010), 396.

18. Ronald Reagan, "President Reagan's Remarks at the National Religious Broadcasters Convention, January 30, 1984," Ronald Reagan Presidential Library and Museum, accessed February 10, 2023, https://www.reaganlibrary.gov/archives/speech/president-reagans-remarks-national-religious-broadcasters-convention.

19. Ronald Reagan, "President Reagan's Remarks at the Annual Conservative Political Action Conference Dinner, March 2, 1984," Ronald Reagan Presidential Library and Museum, accessed February 10, 2023, https://www.reaganlibrary.gov/archives/speech/remarks-annual-conservative-political-action-conference-dinner-0.

20. Ronald Reagan, "Proclamations, February 3, 1983: Year of the Bible," Ronald Reagan Presidential Library and Museum, accessed February 10, 2023, https://www.reaganlibrary.gov/archives/speech/proclamations-february-3-1983.

21. Meg Kunde, "Making the Free Market Moral: Ronald Reagan's Covenantal Economy," *Rhetoric and Public Affairs* 22, no. 2 (2019): 217, 237.

22. "Reaganomics" is not a very precise term. It can refer to supply-side economics, cutting taxes, capping government spending, balancing the budget, or reducing federal regulations. See Crouse, *Cross and Reaganomics*, 2–3.

23. Some other examples of the theological defenses of capitalism in this period include Wayne Grudem and Barry Asmus, *The Poverty of Nations: A Sustainable*

Solution (Wheaton: Crossway, 2013); Wayne Grudem, *Business for the Glory of God: The Bible's Teaching on the Moral Goodness of Business* (Wheaton: Crossway, 2003); Marvin Olasky, *Compassionate Conservatism: What It Is, What It Does, and How It Can Transform America* (New York: Free Press, 2000); Brian Griffiths, *The Creation of Wealth: A Christian's Case for Capitalism* (Downers Grove, IL: InterVarsity, 1984); George Weigel, *Catholicism and the Renewal of American Democracy* (Mahwah, NJ: Paulist Press, 1989); Richard John Neuhaus, *The Naked Public Square* (Grand Rapids: Eerdmans, 1984).

24. Crouse, *Cross and Reaganomics*, 2, 9.

25. Ronald H. Nash, *Poverty and Wealth: The Christian Debate over Capitalism* (Westchester, IL: Crossway, 1986), 9.

26. Nash, *Poverty and Wealth*, 12, 18.

27. Nash, *Poverty and Wealth*, 60, 61.

28. Nash, *Poverty and Wealth*, 167.

29. Nash, *Poverty and Wealth*, 164.

30. Nash, *Poverty and Wealth*, 167.

31. Kenneth J. Collins, *Power, Politics and the Fragmentation of Evangelicalism: From the Scopes Trial to the Obama Administration* (Downers Grove, IL: IVP Academic, 2012), 175.

32. Ronald Sider, *Rich Christians in an Age of Hunger: A Biblical Study* (Downers Grove, IL: InterVarsity Press, 1978), 114, 88, 90, 171.

33. David Chilton, *Productive Christians in an Age of Guilt-Manipulators: A Biblical Response to Ronald J. Sider* (Tyler, TX: Institute for Christian Economics, 1981). For more on Christian reconstructionism, see Crawford Gribben, *Survival and Resistance in Evangelical America: Christian Reconstruction in the Pacific Northwest* (New York: Oxford University Press, 2021).

34. Chilton, *Productive Christians*, 2, 8, 9, 20–23.

35. Chilton, *Productive Christians*, 33, 34, 43.

36. Chilton, *Productive Christians*, 43.

37. The phrases he quotes from Scripture are from Prov. 10:2–4 and 13:4–11. Chilton, *Productive Christians*, 36, 40.

38. John Jefferson Davis, *Your Wealth in God's World: Does the Bible Support the Free Market?* (Phillipsburg, NJ: Presbyterian and Reformed, 1984), 77.

39. Brian Griffiths, *The Creation of Wealth: A Christian's Case for Capitalism* (Downers Grove, IL: InterVarsity, 1984), 60.

40. Nash, *Poverty and Wealth*, 169.

41. Davis, *Your Wealth in God's World*, 83.

42. Some examples include the following: condemnations of violence (Joel 3:2–3, 5–6; Amos 1:11–12; 2:1–3; Hab. 2:12–13; Jer. 49:16; 51:35, 49; Ezek. 25:15), rebellion against YHWH's rule (Nah. 1:9–15), oppression of the poor (Mal. 3:4; Isa. 10:20; 19:20), gloating in others' destruction (Ezek. 25:3), taking advantage of others' destruction (Ezek. 26:2), and slavery (Ezek. 29:7).

43. Chilton, *Productive Christians*, 43; Davis, *Your Wealth in God's World*, 52

44. Nash, *Poverty and Wealth*, 80; Chilton, *Productive Christians*, 41.

45. Nash, *Poverty and Wealth*, 168; Davis, *Your Wealth in God's World*, 51.

46. David L. Baker, *Tight Fists or Open Hands? Wealth and Poverty in Old Testament Law* (Grand Rapids: Eerdmans, 2009), 307.

47. Ronald Nash, "Socialism, Capitalism, and the Bible," *Imprimis* 14, no. 7 (July 1985): https://imprimis.hillsdale.edu/socialism-capitalism-and-the-bible/.

48. Crouse, *Cross and Reaganomics*, 51.

49. Nash, *Poverty and Wealth*, 59.

50. Julie Nelson, *Economics for Humans*, 2nd ed. (Chicago: University of Chicago Press, 2018), 1–50.

51. Jim Wallis, "A Wolf in Sheep's Clothing," *Sojourners* 15, no. 5 (May 1986): 20.

52. Chilton, *Productive Christians*, 10.

Chapter 7 Late Great United States

1. Hal Lindsey and C. C. Carlson, *The Late Great Planet Earth* (Grand Rapids: Zondervan, 1970), 89.

2. Matthew Avery Sutton, *American Apocalypse: A History of Modern Evangelicalism* (Cambridge, MA: Harvard University Press, 2014), 325.

3. Axel R. Schäfer, *Evangelicals and Empire: White Conservative Protestants in US Cold War Politics and Society* (Grand Rapids: Eerdmans, 2018), 378.

4. For more background on the conflict, a good brief summary can be found in Angela M. Lahr, *Millennial Dreams and Apocalyptic Nightmares: The Cold War Origins of Political Evangelicalism* (New York: Oxford University Press, 2007), 3–4.

5. Daniel Wojcik, *The End of the World As We Know It: Faith, Fatalism, and Apocalypse in America* (New York: New York University Press, 1997), 32.

6. Paul S. Boyer, *When Time Shall Be No More: Prophecy Belief in Modern American Culture* (Cambridge, MA: Belknap, 1992), 127.

7. Lahr, *Millennial Dreams*, 14, 16.

8. See discussion of Eisenhower's quote in Axel R. Schäfer, *Piety and Public Funding: Evangelicals and the State in Modern America* (Philadelphia: University of Pennsylvania Press, 2012), 26.

9. See discussion of Graham's words in Marshall Frady, *Billy Graham: A Parable of American Righteousness* (New York: Simon & Schuster, 2006), 198.

10. Crawford Gribben, *Writing the Rapture: Prophecy Fiction in Evangelical America* (New York: Oxford University Press, 2009), 16.

11. Timothy P. Weber, *On the Road to Armageddon: How Evangelicals Became Israel's Best Friend* (Grand Rapids: Baker, 2004), 199.

12. Weber, *On the Road to Armageddon*, 200.

13. Robert Jewett, *Mission and Menace: Four Centuries of American Religious Zeal* (Minneapolis: Fortress, 2008), 263.

14. Historian Crawford Gribben notes that dispensationalists (and conservatives more generally) were moving away from too much focus on prophecy and "literal" interpretation, but then many "found the establishment of Israel too good an opportunity to resist." Lots of books were written or rewritten. Gribben, *Writing the Rapture*, 8.

15. Schäfer, *Evangelicals and Empire*, 385.

16. Wojcik, *End of the World*, 37–38.

17. Jewett, *Mission and Menace*, 260.

18. One scholar notes that many rapture novelists of the '70s "noticeably tightened up" the prophetic scenarios in their fiction in order to conform more closely with Lindsey's account—a sign of both Lindsey's popularity and the complicated relationship between prophetic fiction and nonfiction during this period. Gribben, *Writing the Rapture*, 126.

19. Stephen D. O'Leary, *Arguing the Apocalypse: A Theory of Millennial Rhetoric* (New York: Oxford University Press, 1994), 136.

20. Amy Johnson Frykholm, *Rapture Culture: Left Behind in Evangelical America* (New York: Oxford University Press, 2004), 15. For a description of the problem of defining dispensationalism, see Craig A. Blaising, "Dispensationalism: The Search for Definition," in *Dispensationalism, Israel and the Church: The Search for Definition*, ed. Craig A. Blaising and Darrell L. Bock (Grand Rapids: Zondervan, 1992), 13–34.

21. For an example of how this is described in contemporary dispensationalism, see the Dallas Theological Seminary doctrinal statement: "We believe that different administrative responsibilities of this character are manifest in the biblical record, that they span the entire history of mankind, and that each ends in the failure of man under the respective test and in an ensuing judgment from God. We believe that three of these dispensations or rules of life are the subject of extended revelation in the Scriptures, viz., the dispensation of the Mosaic Law, the present dispensation of grace, and the future dispensation of the millennial kingdom."

22. Weber, *On the Road to Armageddon*, 36–37.

23. Frykholm, *Rapture Culture*, 18.

24. O'Leary, *Arguing the Apocalypse*, 164.

25. Lindsey, introduction to *The Late Great Planet Earth*.

26. Lindsey, *Late Great Planet Earth*, 31.

27. See discussion of Lindsey's words in O'Leary, *Arguing the Apocalypse*, 170.

28. Lindsey, *Late Great Planet Earth*, 83, 73.

29. Mark Hitchcock and Thomas Ice, *The Truth Behind Left Behind: A Biblical View of the End Times* (Colorado Springs: Multnomah, 2004), 163, 67.

30. See Craig A. Carter, *Interpreting Scripture with the Great Tradition: Recovering the Genius of Premodern Exegesis* (Grand Rapids: Baker Academic, 2018), 4–15. For an example of this in a central figure in the development of Western theology, see Augustine, *De doctrina Christiana*, book 2.

31. David C. Steinmetz, "The Superiority of Pre-Critical Exegesis," *Theology Today* 37, no. 1 (1980): 27–38.

32. Some of them were more theologically motivated in these decisions. As my friend and Old Testament scholar Heather Zimmerman points out, the dispensational distinctive of emphasizing the contrast between the church and Israel leads to literal interpretations of promises made to Israel in the Old Testament. This is another difference between dispensational theologians (then and now) and the popularizers of dispensational theology: the former make these connections between the larger theology and hermeneutical decisions, the latter do not.

33. Lindsey, *Late Great Planet Earth*, 62.

34. See discussion of Graham's words in Lahr, *Millennial Dreams*, 20.

35. Lindsey, *Late Great Planet Earth*, 181.

36. See discussion of Lindsey's ideas in Jewett, *Mission and Menace*, 260–61.

37. Such as the Camp David Accords signed by Israel and Egypt in 1978. See Weber, *On the Road to Armageddon*, 197.

38. See discussion of Lindsey's ideas in Weber, *On the Road to Armageddon*, 198.

39. Hal Lindsey, *The 1980s: Countdown to Armageddon* (New York: Bantam Books, 1980), 132–33, 149.

40. Lindsey, *The 1980s*, 175, 76.

41. For more on this, see Crawford Gribben, "After *Left Behind* and the Paradox of Evangelical Pessimism," in *Expecting the End: Millennialism in Social and Historical Context*, ed. Kenneth G. Newport and Crawford Gribben (Waco: Baylor University Press, 2006), 121.

42. Schäfer, *Evangelicals and Empire*, 381.

43. Frykholm, *Rapture Culture*, 107.

44. Lahr, *Millennial Dreams*, 19.

45. Jennie Chapman, *Plotting Apocalypse: Reading, Agency, and Identity in the Left Behind Series* (Jackson: University Press of Mississippi, 2013), 138.

46. Andrew Pierce, "Millennialism, Ecumenism, and Fundamentalism," in Newport and Gribben, *Expecting the End*, 87.

47. Michael J. Gorman, *Reading Revelation Responsibly: Uncivil Worship and Witness* (Eugene, OR: Cascade Books, 2011), 23, 53.

48. See discussion of Winstanley's ideas in Andrew Bradstock, "Sowing in Hope: The Relevance of Theology to Gerrard Winstanley's Political Programme," *The Seventeenth Century* 6, no. 2 (Fall 1991): 189.

49. Allan A. Boesak, *Comfort and Protest: Reflections on the Apocalypse of John of Patmos* (Philadelphia: Westminster, 1987), 19.

50. Boyer, *When Time Shall Be No More*, 94.

51. John Collins, "Introduction: Towards the Morphology of a Genre," *Semeia* 14 (1979): 9.

52. Frykholm, *Rapture Culture*, 110, 114.

53. Eugene Peterson, *Reversed Thunder: The Revelation of John and the Praying Imagination* (New York: HarperCollins, 2011), 44–45.

54. Gorman, *Reading Revelation Responsibly*, 37, 47.

55. Richard Bauckham, *The Theology of the Book of Revelation* (New York: Cambridge University Press, 1993), 159.

56. Elizabeth Dwoskin, "On Social Media, Vaccine Misinformation Mixes with Extreme Faith," *Washington Post*, February 16, 2021, https://www.washington post.com/technology/2021/02/16/covid-vaccine-misinformation-evangelical-mark -beast/.

Chapter 8 Prayer, Politics, and Personal Faith

1. We don't have the space to address the fascinating and complicated history of the National Prayer Breakfast (originally the Presidential Prayer Breakfast) and its relationship to International Christian Leadership (or "The Fellowship"

or "The Family"). For more on that, see Kevin Kruse, *One Nation Under God: How Corporate America Invented Christian America* (New York: Basic Books, 2015), and Jeff Sharlet, *The Family: The Secret Fundamentalism at the Heart of American Power* (New York: HarperCollins, 2008).

2. Berton Dulce and Edward J. Richter, *Religion and the Presidency: A Recurring American Problem* (New York: Macmillan, 1962), v–vi.

3. David Weiss, "Civil Religion or Mere Religion? The Debate over Presidential Religious Rhetoric," in *The Rhetoric of American Civil Religion: Symbols, Sinners, and Saints,* ed. Jason A. Edwards and Joseph M. Valenzano III (New York: Lexington Books, 2016), 134. Weiss is describing Robert Bellah's "Civil Religion in America," *Daedalus: Journal of the American Academy of Arts and Sciences* 96, no. 1 (Winter 1967): 1–21.

4. Kevin Coe, David Domke, and Penelope Sheets, "Barack Obama and the Expansion of American Civil Religion," in Edwards and Valenzano, *Rhetoric of American Civil Religion,* 184–85.

5. Brian T. Kaylor, *Presidential Campaign Rhetoric in an Age of Confessional Politics* (New York: Lexington Books, 2011), 127.

6. Kenneth J. Collins, *Power, Politics and the Fragmentation of Evangelicalism: From the Scopes Trial to the Obama Administration* (Downers Grove, IL: IVP Academic, 2012), 97.

7. Guy Lawson, "George W.'s Personal Jesus," *GQ,* December 31, 2004, https://www.gq.com/story/george-bush-jesus-adviser-beliefs.

8. Mark J. Rozell, "Introduction: Religion and the Bush Presidency," in *Religion and the Bush Presidency,* ed. Mark J. Rozell and Gleaves Whitney (New York: Palgrave Macmillan, 2007), 1.

9. George W. Bush, *A Charge to Keep: My Journey to the White House* (New York: HarperCollins, 2001), 136.

10. David L. Holmes, *The Faiths of the Postwar Presidents: From Truman to Obama* (Athens: University of Georgia Press, 2012), 252–54.

11. Lawson, "George W.'s Personal Jesus."

12. At a November 4, 2000, campaign rally in Memphis, Tennessee, Gore followed up the 2 Thessalonians and Galatians references with: "Some people are tired of prosperity. Some people are tired of the 22 million jobs. They look back to a period eight years ago and they say we were better off then than we are now. I don't agree." As quoted in Kaylor, *Presidential Campaign Rhetoric,* 93–94.

13. Kaylor, *Presidential Campaign Rhetoric,* 96.

14. Kaylor, *Presidential Campaign Rhetoric,* 96–97.

15. See discussion of Land's words in Todd Starnes, "Bush Inauguration, Speech Filled with Prayers, Spiritual References," *Baptist Press,* January 22, 2001, https://www.baptistpress.com/resource-library/news/bush-inauguration-speech-filled-with-prayers-spiritual-references/.

16. See Collins, *Power, Politics, and the Fragmentation of Evangelicalism,* 40–45. He traces evangelical cultural engagement and identity throughout American history, describing in particular how the Scopes Monkey Trial shaped conservative Christians' sense of embattlement and embarrassment.

17. "'Missed you at Bible study' were quite literally the very first words I heard spoken in the Bush White House," David Frum wrote in his memoir titled *The Right Man: The Surprise Presidency of George W. Bush* (New York: Random House, 2003), 3–4.

18. George W. Bush, remarks at the White House Conference on Faith-Based and Community Initiatives in Philadelphia, Pennsylvania, *New York Times*, December 12, 2002, https://www.nytimes.com/2002/12/12/politics/text-of-remarks -by-bush-in-philadelphia.html.

19. Carin Robinson and Clyde Wilcox, "The Faith of George W. Bush: The Personal, Practical, and Political," in *Religion and the American Presidency*, ed. Mark J. Rozell and Gleaves Whitney (New York: Palgrave, 2007), 218–19.

20. Robinson and Wilcox, "Faith of George W. Bush," 220.

21. See discussion of Bartlett's statements in Lawson, "George W.'s Personal Jesus."

22. See discussion of Wead's and Land's statements in Lawson, "George W.'s Personal Jesus."

23. Michael Wear, *Reclaiming Hope: Lessons Learned in the Obama White House about the Future of Faith in America* (Nashville: Nelson, 2017), 58.

24. Transcripts of presidential prayer breakfast speeches can be found online at The American Presidency Project, https://www.presidency.ucsb.edu/documents.

25. Kaylor, *Presidential Campaign Rhetoric*, 91.

26. Kaylor, *Presidential Campaign Rhetoric*, 112.

27. Five months before the 2008 election, a national survey showed that 10 percent of Americans believed Obama to be a Muslim. By August 2010, Pew Research found that almost double that amount (18 percent) believed him to be a Muslim. A 2015 poll found that 29 percent of Americans thought this. Holmes, *Faiths of the Postwar Presidents*, 312–13. Sarah Pulliam Bailey, "A Startling Number of Americans Still Believe President Obama Is a Muslim," *Washington Post*, September 14, 2015, https://www.washingtonpost.com/news/acts-of-faith/wp/2015/09 /14/a-startling-number-of-americans-still-believe-president-obama-is-a-muslim/.

28. Barack Obama, in an interview with Ted Olsen and Sarah Pulliam Bailey, "Q&A: Barack Obama," *Christianity Today,* January 23, 2008, https://www .christianitytoday.com/ct/2008/januaryweb-only/104-32.0.html.

29. Clarence E. Walker and Gregory D. Smithers, *The Preacher and the Politician: Jeremiah Wright, Barack Obama, and Race in America* (Charlottesville: University of Virginia Press, 2012), 16–17.

30. Holmes, *Faiths of the Postwar Presidents*, 284–85.

31. Barack Obama, "Remarks at the Selma Voting Rights March Commemoration in Selma, Alabama, March 4, 2007," The American Presidency Project, accessed February 10, 2023, presidency.ucsb.edu/documents/remarks-the-selma -voting-rights-march-commemoration-selma-alabama.

32. For more analysis on this, see Kaylor, *Presidential Campaign Rhetoric*, 113.

33. Lisa Miller, "Q&A: What Barack Obama Prays For," *Newsweek*, July 11, 2008, https://www.newsweek.com/qa-what-barack-obama-prays-92685.

34. Barack Obama, keynote address at the Democratic National Convention, July 27, 2004.

35. Holmes, *Faiths of the Postwar Presidents*, 279.

36. David Nakamura and Michelle Boorstein, "At Prayer Breakfast and with Birth-Control Decision, Obama Riles Religious Conservatives," *Washington Post*, February 2, 2012, https://www.washingtonpost.com/local/at-prayer-breakfast -and-with-birth-control-decision-obama-riles-religious-conservatives/2012/02 /02/gIQAgy1blQ_story.html.

37. Peter Wehner, "Barack Obama's Divisive Theology," *Commentary*, February 3, 2012, https://www.commentary.org/peter-wehner/barack-obama-theology -taxes/.

38. Ralph Reed, quoted in David Nakamura and Michelle Boorstein, "At Prayer Breakfast, Obama Says Christian Faith Guides His Policies," *Washington Post*, February 2, 2012, https://www.washingtonpost.com/politics/at-prayer-breakfast -obama-says-christian-faith-guides-his-policies/2012/02/02/gIQAzNyakQ_story .html?tid=usw_passupdatepg.

39. Peter Wehner, "Barack Obama's Divisive Theology."

40. Obama said this in the "Call to Renewal" speech delivered at the Building a Covenant for a New America conference in Washington, DC, in 2006. The transcript is available at "Obama's 2006 Speech on Faith and Politics," *New York Times*, June 28, 2006, https://www.nytimes.com/2006/06/28/us/politics /2006obamaspeech.html. Political theorist Denis Lacorne describes the same dynamic of "epiphany" versus "choice": Denis Lacorne, *Religion in America: A Political History*, trans. George Holoch (New York: Columbia University Press, 2011), 162.

41. See Max Perry Mueller, "Religion (and Race) Problems on the Way to the White House: Mitt Romney and Barack Obama's 'Faith' Speeches," in *Religion in the Age of Obama*, ed. Juan M. Floyd-Thomas and Anthony B. Pinn (New York: Bloomsbury, 2018), 19–35.

42. Collins, *Power, Politics, and the Fragmentation of Evangelicalism*, 210.

43. Obama, "Call to Renewal."

Chapter 9 "Give unto Caesar What Is Caesar's"

1. Anugrah Kumar, "Donald Trump Compares Himself to Billy Graham; Says 'My Favorite Book Is the Bible,'" *Christian Post*, August 21, 2015, https://www .christianpost.com/news/donald-trump-compares-himself-to-billy-graham-says -my-favorite-book-is-the-bible-143450/.

2. Hunter Walker, "Donald Trump Just Dodged Two Questions about the Bible," *Insider*, August 26, 2015, https://www.businessinsider.com/donald-trump -refused-to-name-favorite-bible-verse-2015-8.

3. "President Trump's Rose Garden Speech on Protests," CNN, June 1, 2020, https://www.cnn.com/2020/06/01/politics/read-trumps-rose-garden-remarks /index.html.

4. Katie Rogers, "Protesters Dispersed with Tear Gas So Trump Could Pose at Church," *New York Times*, June 1, 2020, https://www.nytimes.com/2020/06 /01/us/politics/trump-st-johns-church-bible.html.

5. "President Trump Walks across Lafayette Park to St. John's Church," You-Tube, accessed February 10, 2023, posted by C-SPAN, https://www.youtube.com /watch?v=5ShnqmiKLE8.

6. Elizabeth Bruenig, "The Last Temptation of Trump," *New York Times*, June 2, 2020, https://www.nytimes.com/2020/06/02/opinion/trump-bible-speech -st-johns-church.html.

7. Julia Duin, "The Christian Prophets Who Say Trump Is Coming Again," *Politico*, February 18, 2021, https://www.politico.com/news/magazine/2021/02 /18/how-christian-prophets-give-credence-to-trumps-election-fantasies-469598.

8. Sarah Pulliam Bailey, "'It's Just Like God to Use a Young Jewish Couple to Help Christians': Trump's Evangelical Advisers Defend Kushner," *Washington Post*, July 25, 2017, https://www.washingtonpost.com/news/acts-of-faith/wp /2017/07/25/jared-kushner-has-an-unusual-group-singing-his-praises-evangelical -leaders/.

9. Gregory E. Sterling, "Capitol Rioters Made a Mockery of Christian Values," CNN, January 14, 2021, https://edition.cnn.com/2021/01/14/opinions/capitol-rio ters-made-mockery-of-christianity-sterling/index.html.

10. See discussion of Jeffress's words in Bob Allen, "'Evangelical Elite' Just Doesn't Get It, Claims Pastor and Trump Supporter," Baptist News Global, March 16, 2016, https://baptistnews.com/article/evangelical-elite-just-doesnt-get -it-claims-pastor-and-trump-supporter/.

11. See discussion of Jeffress's words in Alan Bean, "Jesus and John Wayne: Must We Choose?," Baptist News Global, October 31, 2016, https://baptistnews .com/article/jesus-and-john-wayne-must-we-choose/.

12. Sarah Pulliam Bailey and Jenna Johnson, "Why So Many Evangelicals Have Faith in Donald Trump," *Washington Post*, January 18, 2016, https://www .washingtonpost.com/politics/why-so-many-evangelicals-have-faith-in-donald -trump/2016/01/18/636ce386-bdfd-11e5-83d4-42e3bceea902_story.html.

13. Jerry Falwell Sr., "Ministers and Marches," Thomas Road Baptist Church, March 21, 1965, accessed via Jerry Falwell Library.

14. "He knew 'one big thing,' and that big thing was the Bible." Michael Sean Winters, *God's Right Hand: How Jerry Falwell Made God a Republican and Baptized the American Right* (New York: HarperCollins, 2012), 5.

15. Winters, *God's Right Hand*, 5.

16. Winters, *God's Right Hand*, 113.

17. Jerry Falwell, "The Maligned Moral Majority," *Newsweek*, September 21, 1981, 17.

18. See discussion of Falwell Sr.'s words in William J. Petersen and Stephen Board, "Where Is Jerry Falwell Going?," *Eternity*, July–August 1980, 19.

19. Karen Swallow Prior, "The Fake 'Holy War' over Donald Trump's 'Get Even' Advice," *Christianity Today*, October 3, 2012, https://www.christianitytoday .com/ct/2012/october-web-only/donald-trump-at-liberty-get-even.html.

20. Jerry Falwell Jr., as quoted in Jose A. DelReal, "Trump Received a Glowing Welcome from Falwell at Liberty University – But Not Everyone Was Convinced," *Washington Post*, January 18, 2016, https://www.washingtonpost.com/news/post

-politics/wp/2016/01/18/trump-received-a-glowing-welcome-at-liberty-university
-but-not-everyone-was-convinced/.

21. Jerry Falwell Jr., "Trump Is the Churchillian Leader We Need," *Washington Post*, August 19, 2016, https://www.washingtonpost.com/opinions/jerry
-falwell-jr-trump-is-the-churchillian-leader-we-need/2016/08/19/b1ff79e0-64b1
-11e6-be4e-23fc4d4d12b4.

22. Falwell, "Trump Is the Churchillian Leader We Need."

23. Jerry Falwell, "Here's the Backstory of Why I Endorsed Donald Trump," *Washington Post*, January 27, 2016, https://www.washingtonpost.com/news/acts
-of-faith/wp/2016/01/27/jerry-falwell-jr-heres-the-backstory-of-why-i-endorsed
-donald-trump/.

24. Jerry Falwell Jr. (@JerryFalwellJr), "Jesus said love our neighbors as ourselves but never told Caesar how to run Rome—he never said Roman soldiers should turn the other cheek in battle or that Caesar should allow all the barbarians to be Roman citizens or that Caesar should tax the rich to help [the] poor. That's our job." January 25, 2018, 7:15 p.m., https://twitter.com/jerryfalwelljr
/status/956682026714845184.

25. The hypocrisy is evident according to this *Vox* article: "Falwell Jr. and his evangelical allies have done nothing but make the promulgation of 'Biblical values' a cornerstone of their political lobbying. In that context, Falwell's tweet is all the more egregious." Tara Isabella Burton, "Evangelical Jerry Falwell Jr. Defends Trump: Jesus 'Never Told Caesar How to Run Rome,'" *Vox*, January 26, 2018, https://www.vox.com/2018/1/26/16936010/evangelicals-jerry-falwell-trump
-caesar-rome.

26. Joe Heim interview with Jerry Falwell Jr., "Jerry Falwell Jr. Can't Imagine Trump 'Doing Anything That's Not Good for the Country,'" *Washington Post*, January 1, 2019, https://www.washingtonpost.com/lifestyle/magazine/jerry-falwell
-jr-cant-imagine-trump-doing-anything-thats-not-good-for-the-country/2018/12
/21/6affc4c4-f19e-11e8-80d0-f7e1948d55f4_story.html.

27. Michael Massing, "How Martin Luther Paved the Way for Donald Trump," *The Nation*, April 19, 2018, https://www.thenation.com/article/archive/how-martin
-luther-paved-the-way-for-donald-trump/.

28. Alec Ryrie, "Martin Luther Was the Donald Trump of 1517," *Foreign Policy*, May 23, 2017, https://foreignpolicy.com/2017/05/23/martin-luther-was-the
-donald-trump-of-1517/, and Alexander M. Santora, "Did Martin Luther Spawn Donald Trump?," northjersey.com, October 23, 2017, https://www.northjersey
.com/story/opinion/contributors/2017/10/23/opinion-did-martin-luther-spawn
-donald-trump/790333001/.

29. William Henry Lazareth, *Christians in Society: Luther, the Bible, and Social Ethics* (Minneapolis: Fortress, 2001), 10–12, 26.

30. Lyman Stone, "Two Kingdom Theology in the Trump Era," *First Things*, April 26, 2018, https://www.firstthings.com/web-exclusives/2018/04/two-kingdom
-theology-in-the-trump-era.

31. For more on Luther's political theology, see Robert C. Crouse, *Two Kingdoms and Two Cities: Mapping Theological Traditions of Church, Culture, and Civil Order* (Minneapolis: Fortress, 2017); Heinrich Bornkamm, *Luther's Doctrine*

of the Two Kingdoms in the Context of his Theology, trans. Karl H. Hertz (Minneapolis: Fortress, 1966); James Martin Estes, *Peace, Order and the Glory of God: Secular Authority and the Church in the Thought of Luther and Melanchthon, 1518–1559* (Leiden: Brill, 2005).

32. Anna Case-Winters, *Matthew*, Belief: A Theological Commentary on the Bible (Louisville: Westminster John Knox, 2015), 257.

33. Kim Huat Tan, *Mark*, New Covenant Commentary (Eugene, OR: Cascade Books, 2015), 164.

34. Michael Card, *Matthew: The Gospel of Identity*, Biblical Imagination Series (Downers Grove, IL: InterVarsity, 2013), 199.

35. Warren Carter, *Matthew and the Margins: A Sociopolitical and Religious Reading* (Maryknoll, NY: Orbis Books, 2000), 440.

36. Tan, *Mark*, 165.

37. Diane G. Chen, *Luke*, New Covenant Commentary (Eugene, OR: Cascade Books, 2017), 264–65.

38. Case-Winters, *Matthew*, 258.

39. Tertullian, "De Fuga in Persecutione," quoted in D. H. Williams, ed., *Matthew: Interpreted by Early Christian Commentators* (Grand Rapids: Eerdmans, 2018), on Matt. 22:15–22.

40. Augustine, "Homily on John 40.9," in *Homilies on the Gospel of John, 1–40*, ed. Alan Fitzgerald, trans. Edmund Hill (New York: New City Press, 2009), 603.

41. Card, *Matthew*, 199.

42. Eugene Boring, *Mark: A Commentary*, New Testament Library (Louisville: Westminster John Knox, 2006), 336. For a description of the range of positions, see Craig Blomberg, *Matthew*, New American Commentary (Nashville: Broadman & Holman, 1992), 331.

43. Chen, *Luke*, 265.

44. Ambrose, *Letters, 1–91*, trans. Mary Melchior Beyenka (Washington, DC: Catholic University of America Press, 1954), 371.

45. Boring, *Mark*, 334.

46. John T. Carroll, *Luke: A Commentary*, New Testament Library (Louisville: Westminster John Knox, 2012), 398.

47. Boring, *Mark*, 336.

48. Stephanie A. Martin, *Decoding the Digital Church: Evangelical Storytelling and the Election of Donald J. Trump* (Tuscaloosa: University of Alabama Press, 2021), 111.

49. Martin, *Decoding the Digital Church*, 82.

Chapter 10 Seek the Peace and Prosperity of the City

1. For example, C. A. Strine, "Embracing Asylum Seekers and Refugees: Jeremiah 29 as Foundation for a Christian Theology of Migration and Integration," *Political Theology* 19, no. 6 (2018): 478–96.

2. Tim Keller, "City: The World That Is," YouTube, Gospel in Life Series, accessed February 10, 2023, https://www.youtube.com/watch?v=vSqfs030cn4.

3. Just a few examples: Richard Bourne, *Seek the Peace of the City: Christian Political Criticism as Public, Realist, and Transformative* (Eugene, OR: Cascade Books, 2009); Bruce W. Winter, *Seek the Welfare of the City: Christians as Benefactors and Citizens* (Grand Rapids: Eerdmans, 1994); Eldin Villafañe, *Seek the Peace of the City: Reflections on Urban Ministry* (Grand Rapids: Eerdmans, 1995); Duane K. Friesen, *Artists, Citizens, Philosophers: Seeking the Peace of the City; An Anabaptist Theology of Culture* (Independence, MO: Herald, 2000).

4. See Sirach, Tobit, Baruch, 2 Maccabees, and exilic imagery in the Dead Sea Scrolls. John Hill, "'Your Exile Will Be Long': The Book of Jeremiah and the Unended Exile," in *Reading the Book of Jeremiah: A Search for Coherence*, ed. Martin Kessler (Winona Lake, IN: Eisenbrauns, 2004), 149.

5. Marien A. Halvorson-Taylor, *Enduring Exile: The Metaphorization of Exile in the Hebrew Bible* (Leiden: Brill, 2011), 1.

6. Winter, *Seek the Welfare of the City*, 1, 17.

7. Kari Kloos, "Sustaining Hope in Times of Crisis," in *Augustine and Apocalyptic*, ed. John Doody, Kari Kloos, and Kim Paffenroth (Lanham, MD: Rowman & Littlefield, 2014), 118.

8. J. Kevin Coyle, "Augustine and Apocalyptic: Thoughts on the Fall of Rome, the Book of Revelation, and the End of the World," *Florilegium* 9 (1987): 1.

9. Augustine, "Sermon: The Sacking of the City of Rome," in *Augustine: Political Writings*, ed. E. M. Atkins and R. J. Dodaro (New York: Cambridge University Press, 2001), 9.

10. For more on this, from a variety of perspectives, see R. A. Markus, *Saeculum: History and Society in the Theology of St Augustine* (New York: Cambridge University Press, 1970); Charles T. Mathewes, *The Republic of Grace: Augustinian Thoughts for Dark Times* (Grand Rapids: Eerdmans, 2010); Eric Gregory, *Politics and the Order of Love: An Augustinian Ethic of Democratic Citizenship* (Chicago: University of Chicago Press, 2008).

11. Augustine, *City of God* 19.17, trans. Henry Bettenson (New York, Penguin Books: 2003).

12. Augustine, *City of God* 19.17.

13. Kate Shellnutt, "Biden Invokes Augustine in Call for American Unity," *Christianity Today*, January 20, 2021, https://www.christianitytoday.com/news/2021/january/president-biden-inauguration-augustine-psalm-30-catholic.html.

14. Augustine, *City of God* 19.24.

15. Oliver O'Donovan, *Desire of the Nations: Rediscovering the Roots of Political Theology* (Cambridge: Cambridge University Press, 1999), 83.

16. Justo L. González, *The Mestizo Augustine: A Theologian between Two Cultures* (Downers Grove, IL: IVP Academic, 2016), 81–98.

17. Augustine, *City of God* 17.4.

18. Michael Sweeney, "Books 17 & 18: Prophecy as Proof in Augustine's City of God," in *The Cambridge Companion to Augustine's City of God* (New York: Cambridge University Press, 2021), 211, 219.

19. Sweeney, "Books 17 & 18," 220–21.

20. Augustine, *Contra Faustus* 12.36, in *The Works of Saint Augustine*, ed. Boniface Ramsey (Hyde Park, New York: New City Press, 1990), 148–49.

21. Augustine, *Sermons on Selected Lessons of the New Testament*, sermon 1.14, in *A Select Library of the Nicene and Post-Nicene Fathers of the Christian Church*, Series 1, ed. Philip Schaff (Grand Rapids: Eerdmans, 1978), 6:250.

22. Joan O'Donovan and Oliver O'Donovan, *Bonds of Imperfection: Christian Politics, Past and Present* (Grand Rapids: Eerdmans, 2004), 56.

23. He also preached many sermons on Jeremiah, but today we have only twenty-five out of approximately three hundred. Jean Calvin, *Sermons on Jeremiah*, ed. Blair Reynolds (New York: Mellen, 1990), iii.

24. John Calvin, *Jeremiah and Lamentations*, ed. Alister McGrath and J. I. Packer (Wheaton: Crossway, 2000), ix.

25. John Calvin, preface, in *Calvin's Commentaries*, trans. John Owen (Grand Rapids: Eerdmans, 1950), 17:28.

26. Heiko A. Oberman, *John Calvin and the Reformation of the Refugees* (Geneva: Librairie Droz, 2009), 187. Barbara Pitkin notes that there is disagreement about some of the history here, but contemporary refugee experience certainly made an impact on Calvin and thus on his preaching and interpretation. See Barbara Pitkin, *Calvin, the Bible, and History* (New York: Oxford University Press, 2020), 122, 138. For more on the Geneva Bible and exile, see Jennifer Powell McNutt, "The Bible for Refugees in Calvin's Geneva," in *Global Migration and Christian Faith: Implications for Identity and Mission*, ed. M. Daniel Carroll R. and Vincent E. Bacote (Eugene, OR: Wipf and Stock, 2021), 18–33.

27. William R. Stevenson, "Calvin and Political Issues," in *The Cambridge Companion to John Calvin*, ed. Donald K. McKim (Cambridge: Cambridge University Press, 2004), 173–74.

28. Marta García-Alonso, "Biblical Law as the Source of Morality in Calvin," *History of Political Thought* 32, no. 1 (Spring 2011): 548.

29. García-Alonso, "Biblical Law," 548; David VanDrunen, *Natural Law and the Two Kingdoms: A Study in the Development of Reformed Social Thought* (Grand Rapids: Eerdmans, 2010), 73.

30. Calvin, *Institutes* 3.19.15, ed. John T. McNeill, trans. Ford Lewis Battles (Philadelphia, PA: Westminster Press, 1960).

31. García-Alonso, "Biblical Law," 545–48.

32. Calvin, *Institutes* 3.19.15.

33. Calvin, *Institutes* 3.19.15.

34. Philip Benedict, *Christ's Churches Purely Reformed: A Social History of Calvinism* (New Haven: Yale University Press, 2002), 89.

35. Benedict, *Christ's Churches Purely Reformed*, 89, 105.

36. Pitkin, *Calvin, the Bible, and History*, 2.

37. Pitkin, *Calvin, the Bible, and History*, 131.

38. Pete Wilcox, "Calvin as Commentator on the Prophets," in *Calvin and the Bible*, ed. Donald K. McKim (New York: Cambridge University Press, 2006), 124.

39. John Calvin, "On Civil Government," in *Luther and Calvin on Secular Authority*, ed. Harro Höpfl (New York: Cambridge University Press, 1991), 78–79.

40. Jean Calvin, *Jeremiah and Lamentations*, trans. John Owen, Calvin's Commentaries 19 (Grand Rapids: Eerdmans, 1950), 412.

41. Calvin, *Jeremiah and Lamentations*, 413.

42. Calvin, *Jeremiah and Lamentations*, 423.

43. For an example of articulating this theological movement, see Daniel L. Smith-Christopher, *A Biblical Theology of Exile* (Minneapolis: Fortress, 2002), 6. There is one key figure in this tradition we will name only once: Mennonite theologian John Howard Yoder. While Yoder's work on Jeremiah 29 was an important part of this tradition, Yoder was a long-term serial sexual abuser and used his theology to justify his abuse. For more on Yoder and the implications of his abuse on his theology, see Brad East, *The Church's Book: Theology of Scripture in Ecclesial Context* (Grand Rapids: Eerdmans, 2022), 177–94.

44. Walter Brueggemann, *The Theology of the Book of Jeremiah* (New York: Cambridge University Press, 2007), 5–6.

45. Niels Peter Lemche, *Ancient Israel: A New History of Israelite Society* (Sheffield: JSOT Press, 1988), 180.

46. Walter Brueggemann, *Preaching Jeremiah: Announcing God's Restorative Passion* (Minneapolis: Fortress, 2020), xvii.

47. Walter Brueggemann, *Cadences of Home: Preaching among Exiles* (Louisville: Westminster John Knox, 1997), 11.

48. Walter Brueggemann, *To Build, to Plant: A Commentary on Jeremiah 26–52* (Grand Rapids: Eerdmans, 1991), 30.

49. For an alternative use of Jeremiah 29 that recognizes these dynamics and articulates the significance of Jeremiah's letter for community organizing and other political work, see Luke Bretherton, *Christianity and Contemporary Politics: The Conditions and Possibilities of Faithful Witness* (Malden, MA: Wiley-Blackwell, 2010), 4–6.

50. Postcolonial theology—theology that criticizes dominant Western forms of theology as inherently shaped by European colonialism—also draws on Jeremian themes of home, migration, and deportation. See Steed Vernyl Davidson, *Empire and Exile: Postcolonial Readings of the Book of Jeremiah* (New York: T&T Clark, 2011), 130–71, and especially Robert P. Carroll, "Exile! What Exile? Deportation and Discourses of Diaspora," in *Leading Captivity Captive: "The Exile" as History and Ideology*, ed. Lester L. Grabbe (Sheffield: Sheffield Academic Press, 1998), 64.

51. Brueggemann, *Theology of the Book of Jeremiah*, 66.

52. David Fitch, "The Benedict Option's False Dichotomy," *Christianity Today*, March 2, 2017, https://www.christianitytoday.com/ct/2017/february-web-only/benedict-options-false-dichotomy.html.

53. Christopher R. Seitz, *Theology in Conflict: Reactions to the Exile in the Book of Jeremiah* (New York: de Gruyter, 1989), 5.

54. Stephen E. Fowl and L. Gregory Jones, *Reading in Communion: Scripture and Ethics in Christian Life* (Grand Rapids: Eerdmans, 1991), 91.

Conclusion

1. Mike Pence, "Full Transcript: Mike Pence's R.N.C. Speech," *New York Times*, August 26, 2020, https://www.nytimes.com/2020/08/26/us/politics/mike-pence-rnc-speech.html. Quotations from Pence in this section are drawn from this transcript.

2. Ellen F. Davis, *Biblical Prophecy: Perspectives for Christian Theology, Discipleship, and Ministry* (Louisville: Westminster John Knox, 2014), 5.

3. Thank you, Jessica Hooten Wilson, for highlighting for me the role that collective memory and history plays in this passage.

4. Davis, *Biblical Prophecy*, 5.

5. Dietrich Bonhoeffer, "2/17 Address in Gland," in *Dietrich Bonhoeffer Works* (Minneapolis: Fortress, 1996), 11:378 (emphasis added).

6. Bonhoeffer, "2/17 Address in Gland," 11:375–76.

Kaitlyn Schiess (ThM, Dallas Theological Seminary) is a writer, speaker, and theologian. She is the author of *The Liturgy of Politics: Spiritual Formation for the Sake of Our Neighbor* and is a regular cohost on the *Holy Post* podcast with Skye Jethani and Phil Vischer. Her writing has appeared in the *New York Times*, *Christianity Today*, *Christ and Pop Culture*, *Relevant*, and *Sojourners*. Schiess is currently a doctoral student in political theology at Duke Divinity School. She lives in Durham, North Carolina.